Land, Labour & Rights

10 Daniel Thorner Memorial Lectures

Edited by Alice Thorner

10 Daniel Thorner Memorial Lectures

Land, Labour & Rights

Edited by Alice Thorner

Anthem Press
London

Anthem Press is an imprint of
Wimbledon Publishing Company
PO Box 9779
London SW19 7QA

This edition first published by Wimbledon Publishing Company 2002

First published by Tulika, India (hardback) 2001

British Library Cataloguing in Publication Data
Data available

ISBN
1 84331 070 8 (hbk)
1 84331 071 6 (pbk)

1 3 5 7 9 10 8 6 4 2

Printed by Newton Printing Ltd, London, UK. www.newtonprinting.com

Contents

Preface

As a student, Daniel Thorner did not set out to become a specialist on India, on agrarian structure or on economic development. Nor did he ever consider himself an economist. Paradoxically, this is how he is remembered in India. Our friends Ashok Desai and Jasodhara Bagchi have each referred to him affectionately as 'an Indian economist'. In fact, most of his publications in the 1950s and 60s could be so interpreted as to class him in this category. He is best known for studies on the financing and construction of the railway network; on the long-term trend of national income from the colonial period onward; on the characterization of land-holding and landless rural classes (his *malik–kisan–mazdur* model which has passed into current vocabulary); on the ground-level effects of state-by-state land reforms; on the strengths as well as the weaknesses of data provided by the decennial Census, the National Sample Survey, the large-scale Agricultural Labour and Rural Credit Enquiries, the state-wise and central food production estimates, for purposes of analysis and planning; on shares of benefit from canal irrigation; on schemes for dividing the Indian peninsula into ecological and agrarian regions; on the 'green revolution'; on the prospects for rural cooperatives; on the rise of a new category in the countryside of educated, risk-taking cultivators, whom he called 'gentlemen farmers'.

In Daniel's own view, his intellectual career was that of a historian and followed a logical, ever-widening path. From an initial interest in trade with the enemy during the American revolution he moved on to British constitutional questions, and from there to the lively public controversy in Victorian Britain as to whether the empire was a source of profit or a millstone. The exclusion from this debate of any prospect of giving up England's most precious colony, the 'jewel in the crown', gave Daniel the idea of studying British economic and political relations with India. For his Columbia University doctoral thesis he picked the topic of the campaign waged by London merchants and Manchester mill-owners for the building of the Indian railways.

Daniel began his research on India in standard historical fashion by working his way systematically through the relevant parliamentary debates during the first half of the nineteenth century. In 1939–40, a fellowship enabled him to delve into the India Office archives in Whitehall, then the administrative hub of the empire. It was in London that he and I came to know P.N. Haksar, K.T. Chandy and other Indian students, all firmly dedicated to freeing their country from imperial rule. Inspired by socialist ideals, they envisioned an independent India, economically modern, with justice for all. Sharing similar goals, we rapidly developed fast friendships and a deep commitment to the cause of Indian nationalism. We read whatever we could find about India, and drank in everything our new friends told us about their own lives, their families, their communities. From then onward Daniel's interest in India ceased to be purely academic. He viewed his scholarly work as a contribution to the struggle for building a new India.

Soon after our return to the US in 1940, Daniel was called to Washington to join a new agency, the Office of Strategic Studies, which had been set up hastily to fill in glaring gaps in the US government's knowledge about everywhere in the world with the exception of Western Europe and Latin America. He later shifted to the Board of Economic Warfare, where his work on the origins of the Great Indian Peninsular and the Bombay, Baroda and Central India served as a qualification for expertise on contemporary rail transport.

As a member of a committee which met to consider what action, if any, should be taken in view of the Bengal famine, he failed to convince his senior colleagues that ships should be diverted to carry rice to Calcutta. After a brief stint in the war-time merchant-marine, he was despatched to India to serve in the US Lend-Lease Mission, the function of which was to strengthen the Indian infrastructure in order to meet the needs of the Allied war effort.

Daniel's arrival in Delhi opened a new phase. He was able to tour extensively, visiting monuments in Mathura, Gwalior, Agra, Ellora and Ajanta, as well as railway workshops.

Contacts with his British and Indian counterparts, experienced officers seconded to government from the ranks of business enterprise, enlarged his grasp of the Indian economy as a whole. Common interests brought him together with Scindia Shipping's perspicacious H.M. Trivedi. Among the families of our London friends, who welcomed him into their homes, he established particularly close ties with P.N.'s uncle, the redoubtable Panditji, proprietor of the well-stocked Pandit Brothers household linen emporia in Chandni Chowk and Connaught Place, a paragon of culture, a great gourmet and a distinguished connoisseur of Indian classical music. Characteristically, Daniel also found occasion to frequent a canal-side village on the Meerut road, where he came to be accepted by the inhabitants as a regular visitor.

Again in the US after the war, Daniel finally defended his thesis and obtained the coveted Ph.D. It appeared in 1950 under the title: 'Investment in Empire: British Railway and Steam Shipping Enterprises in India, 1825–1849'. As a participant in Owen Lattimore's Sinkiang seminar in the Johns Hopkins University, he prepared a paper (which eventually became a chapter in O. Lattimore, ed., *Sinkiang, Pivot of Asia*, 1950) on Anglo–Russian rivalry in Inner Asia.

Recruited for the pioneering South Asia Regional Studies programme in the University of Pennsylvania by Professor W. Norman Brown, Daniel taught courses on India's history, geography, economy, society and culture. Both of us took advantage of the possibility of studying Sanskrit with Professor Brown, who combined a mastery of India's ancient languages and civilization with a lively interest in the current political situation. We also listened attentively to the fascinating lectures on Indian art by Stella Kramrisch. Under the guidance of Simon Kuznets, who was later invited to advise the government of independent India on setting up a statistical system, Daniel began his investigations of the bases of national income estimates. In quite another field, he produced a study on Sir Henry Maine and the codification of British–Indian law.

Breaking new ground, Daniel arranged for Dr Chen Han-seng, a Chinese historian whom he had come to know in Delhi, to undertake a study of agrarian differentiation in South Asia. Chen's exhaustively researched text, identifying twenty-one ecological and economic regions in India and Pakistan, eventually became the core of a volume containing illustrative maps and land-use statistics as of 1930, published by Oxford University Press, Karachi, in 1996.

When he returned to India on sabbatical leave in 1952, Daniel intended to compare the recently inaugurated community projects with the well-publicized 'village uplift' efforts of the colonial period. He quickly discovered that while the older philanthropic enterprises had faded away, the new ones had barely started. On behalf of the Social Science Division of UNESCO, he set up a series of immigration studies in India, Ceylon, Thailand, Indonesia and East Pakistan.

He had already begun to follow the progress of land reform laws through the state legislatures, checking the definitions adopted for terms such as cultivator, occupancy tenant, crop-sharer and their equivalents in local languages, when we came to Kashmir for the hot season in 1953. Throughout the previous winter he had gone into villages and interrogated peasants on several occasions. It was in the rural areas surrounding Srinagar that he perfected his field-work technique. A colleague in the University of Kashmir assigned a graduate student named Banerjee Mishra to accompany Daniel and interpret for him. Together they reached the villages on foot, located the headman or a senior resident, and devoted hours to conversations, often seated on the floor in a stuffy loft with a dozen or more peasants. From these interlocutors Daniel learned who had owned the land before the reform, who had gained from the new laws, who remained poor, what further changes might be expected or would in their opinion prove beneficial. The fruit of this research was published by Sachin Choudhuri in the *Economic Weekly* dated 12 September 1953. Years later, after Daniel's death, grey-haired scholars come up to me and introduce themselves, saying, I went to the villages with Dr Thorner after the History Conference in one place or another.

In effect, Daniel had many more occasions to talk with landholders and labourers in their homes and in the fields. Because he had worked with Owen Lattimore, who was accused by a US Senate Committee of losing China to the communists, and since he was not ready to provide names of fellow academics who could in their turn be charged with un-American beliefs or activities, Daniel lost not only his passport but all chance of pursuing a university career in his own country. Our stalwart Bombay friends, Harubhai and Jyoti Trivedi, together with Suresh and Usha Desai, persuaded us to stay on in India until the storm of intolerance at home blew over. Usha's father, Motabhai Setalvad, helped Daniel to obtain the privilege of remaining in India without a valid passport.

The wait extended for seven years, during which Daniel carried on a succession of studies, notably on the Sarda canal for the National

Council for Applied Economic Research, on census working force data for the Indian Statistical Institute, and on agricultutral production co-operatives for the Indian Cooperative Union. A number of articles based on this work appeared in the *Economic Weekly* and other journals, Although never a faculty member in an Indian university, Daniel gave lectures, participated in seminars and attended conferences. He was frequently consulted by Indian students and also by foreigners coming from the US, Britain or the Commonwealth to do research in India. He liked to think that his advice and example had some influence in the subsequent appearance of a new generation of Indian economic and social historians capable of bringing to bear on India's past and present the powerful searchlight of sophisticated, modern social science methods.

Through cordial exchanges with leading Indian scholars and public figures (e.g., Professor P.C. Mahalanobis; economists K.N. Raj, K.S. Krishnaswami, Khaliq Naqvi, Ashok Mitra, P.C. Joshi, Amartya Sen; anthopologist Iravati Karve; sociologist A.R. Desai; historians Nurul Hasan, Satish Chandra, Bipan Chandra, Tapan Raychaudhuri; Census Comissioners Asok Mitra, B.A. Kulkarni; communist leader P.C. Joshi; sculptor Sankho Choudhuri; musician Vilayat Khan), through acquaintance with administrators and journalists, and through involvement in everyday urban and rural existence, Daniel continued to widen his comprehension of India's social, economic and political complexity.

In 1960 we flew off to Paris. Thanks to the intervention of the economist Charles Bettelheim and historian Clemens Heller, Daniel was invited as a visiting professor to the Ecole des Hautes Etudes. No offer could have delighted him more. He considered himself a follower of the Annales school of history which insisted on taking into account long-term geographic, economic and demographic perspectives. Fernand Braudel, founder of this influential intellectual current, reigned as President of the Sixth Section (social sciences) of the Ecole. With the active support of the ethnologist Louis Dumont, Daniel was soon elected to a chair in the Ecole, where he remained until his death in 1974.

During his Paris years, Daniel made frequent trips to India and kept up his field tours. He edited a volume of writings by one of his revered mentors, Dr H.H. Mann, an English chemist who went out to work for the Bengal tea planters before the end of the nineteenth century. He stayed on to set up India's first Agricultural College (in Poona) and also conducted valuable socio-economic surveys in Maharashtrian villages. In collaboration with Jacques Bertin, director of the cartographic laboratory of the Ecole, Daniel devised a programme of district-wise data collection and processing to provide tables, maps and graphs for the agrarian regions which had been delineated by Chen Han-seng.

Constantly Daniel reflected upon the nature and the place in history of the social class constituted by the peasantry in Europe as well as in India and elsewhere in Asia. Together with Basile Kerblay, his colleague in the Ecole, and with the British historian of Russia, R.E.F. Smith, he recovered the original Russian text and arranged for the publication in an English translation of the seminal monograph, *The Theory of Peasant Economy*, by A.V. Chayanov (D. Thorner, B. Kerblay, R.E.F. Smith, eds, Homewood, Illinois, 1966). The appearance of this book, which included an introduction by Daniel placing Chayanov's work in the intellectual context of the inter-war years, called forth a spate of discussions and publications by anthropologists, sociologists and historians in many countries, some as far away as South America. In the same vein Daniel contributed to the ongoing international reconsideration of Karl Marx's modes of production. Had there ever been an Asiatic mode of production? Did modern India emerge from a feudal past? How useful is it to describe the present economic phase, particularly with regard to the rural areas, as semi-feudal? Could the concept of peasant economy serve as an additional mode of production? Might it be considered as a persistent feature underlying major historical changes? Articles by Daniel in the 1960s dealing these knotty questions on a theoretical level alternated with analyses of recent developments in Indian agriculture and industry.

Although the emergence of Bangladesh is signalled in Daniel's bibliography by a single brief note written for the second edition of a French post-war world history, to which Daniel and I had contributed the chapter on India and Pakistan, his presence in Dhaka in January–April 1972 is vividly remembered by Bangladeshi friends and admirers.

He came with a research plan to compare agrarian structure and agricultural production on the two sides of the border separating West and East Bengal. Visiting villages, as was his wont, in the districts surrounding Dhaka and Comilla, he felt himself transported backward in time to rural India of the early 1950s. He did not encounter in the

Brahmaputra delta the transformations which he had recorded in many parts of India and ascribed to larger national processes of industrialization and overall economic development. Crucial political events very soon put an end to any thought of academic studies. Daniel remained in Dhaka through the initial months of the military crackdown. He managed to keep the Institute of Development Studies open, to organize the payment of salaries to the clerical staff, and to help spirit economists and their families out across the borders.

A couple of months before Daniel died of cancer, our good friend for over thirty-five years, P.N., came through Paris and called upon him. Enlivened by this unexpected boon, Daniel felt strong enough to walk P.N. the short distance from our house to the metro station. As I recall, this was his last outdoor venture.

Later, in Delhi, Haksar and I talked about organizing a memorial for Daniel. We decided upon a series of lectures. Since Daniel had been associated with Professor Mahalanobis and had worked for the Indian Statistical Institute, of which Permeshwar had become the chairman, the ISI was the logical choice for a sponsor. To reflect the breadth of Daniel's own range, we agreed that topics in all social science disciplines and also in the fields of public policy and human rights might be chosen. In order to make attendance possible for people in different parts of the country, we hit upon the idea that the venue might move from town to town, taking into account on each occasion the convenience of the lecturer.

So long as Permeshwar lived the two of us, with occasional advice from friends, selected the successive speakers. We tried to identify relatively young persons who showed signs of promise in their respective fields. Looking back today over the earlier names in the list, I feel that our expectations have been largely justified.

The very first lecturer was Utsa Patnaik. As a student of economics in Cambridge, she had taken advice from Daniel with regard to her studies on agrarian structure and capitalist development. Utsa kindly agreed to my request to prepare an Introduction bringing out the import of the ten lectures so far delivered. The names and topics of the nine following speakers appear in the table of contents. Since P.N. himself is no longer alive, N. Krishnaji, K.S. Krishnaswami, Krishnaraj, Ashok Mitra, K. Saradamoni and Chandan Mukherjee have participated in the selection process. I am happy to announce here that Dr Madhura Swaminathan has undertaken to prepare the eleventh lecture to be delivered in Calcutta in early 2002 on a topic related to problems of food security.

While making plans for this volume with our publisher, Indu Chandrasekhar, I came upon a copy of a paper which Daniel had written in his student days on Disraeli's brilliant symbolic stroke of bestowing upon Queen Victoria the title 'Empress of India'. It seemed appropriate to us to reproduce this essay since it represents an apparently precocious sally of Daniel's into a domain of historical writing which has now become quite fashionable.

I thank the ten lecturers who prepared the chapters collected in this volume, and who responded promptly to our enquiry as to whether they would like to add a few words at the beginning or end to bring the piece up to date. I should also like to thank the chairmen of the successive sessions—in Delhi: Dr P.C. Joshi, the late Ravinder Kumar; in Bombay: Dr Jyotiben Trivedi, Professor Kirit Parikh; in Hyderabad: K.T. Chandy, Professor Hanumantha Rao; in Calcutta: A.K. Bagchi; in Madras: A. Vaidyanathan; in Bangalore: K.T. Chandy, K.S. Krishnaswami; in Trivandrum: Professor K.N. Raj. I also express my warm appreciation to a considerable number of others who assisted us in making local arrangements. I cannot refrain from mentioning the names of P.N.'s secretary, P.K. Unnikrishnan, of Dr T.S. Arthanari in Bangalore, of Dr S. B. Rao in Calcutta, of Dr Bimal Jalan, Sandip Ghose in Mumbai.

July 2001 ALICE THORNER

Introduction

Utsa Patnaik

The lectures in memory of Daniel Thorner comprising this volume were delivered in various cities in India over a period of sixteen years, between April 1985 and April 2001. This is a period which began with some degree of trade liberalization, while from 1991 the adoption of the neo-liberal economic policy regime marked a decisive shift away from the strategy of state-directed development; the period ends in the first year of a new millennium. At the threshold of the new century and a new millennium it seems appropriate to cast one's mind back and discuss briefly the agrarian question in general, and to locate the agrarian question for India in particular, within the changing conjuncture inherent in the increasing dominance of the neo-liberal regime.

Agrarian Questions Old and New: The Last Century and the Present

The century which has ended has been a most momentous one with respect to the agrarian question. At the beginning of the century, the colonized and subordinated countries in Asia and Latin America were characterized by feudal or semi-feudal production relations and a predominant share of agriculture in national output. The underdeveloped periphery of Europe, namely, Eastern Europe and Russia, still carried at that time strong remnants of serfdom in their agrarian relations despite its earlier formal abolition; even in the advanced capitalist countries of the time, agriculture had a much larger part to play than it has today. The most remarkable development in the first half of the last century was the emergence of a wave of peasant movements which swept across the entire colonized, exploited world as well as the peripheral capitalist world; and the linking up of the workers' political movements inspired by the philosophy of praxis, with these peasant movements whose entire character and content was changed as a consequence from more or less radical peasant movements, to revolutionary democratic peasant movements.[1]

The major architects of this linkage of the workers' parties and agrarian movements were also therefore the successful leaders of socialist revolution, namely, V.I. Lenin and Mao Zedong. The 1905 Revolution in Russia following Russia's humiliating defeat by Japan in the Russo–Japanese war, saw widespread peasant uprising for the seizure of landlords' estates. Exactly the same happened in the months before the Bolshevik Revolution. The lessons of the experience of the 1905 uprisings were quickly learnt and integrated by Lenin into a crucial change of the RSDLP's agrarian programme, from the nationalization of land which it had advocated up to that time, to the seizure and redistribution of land to the revolutionary peasantry, thus forming the basis for the *smytchka* or worker–peasant alliance which carried the Bolshevik Revolution to victory in 1917.[2] In China the ultra-left programmatic understanding of Li Li San had led to the Communists being massacred in the premature Canton uprising. Not until Mao Zedong first theoretically recognized the importance of the peasant movements in Hunan in 1926, seeing them as the expression of a powerful revolutionary force;[3] and integrated this understanding into a programme of anti-feudal agrarian reform in the base areas, could the workers' party in China expand its influence, live amongst and draw upon the peasant masses in its guerrilla struggle against Japanese imperialism and in the civil war, achieving victory at last in 1946.[4] Thus, within a span of a mere thirty years, from 1917 to 1947, that is, well within the working life-span of an individual, an increasingly vast area and population in Europe and Asia had embarked upon socialist transformation. The old relations of property were smashed forever, and while the capitalist world reeled under the Great Depression, the Soviet Union industrialized at a pace unprecedented for any country in history, reducing the proportion of population dependent on agriculture from 60 to 16 percent in a single generation.[5] In Vietnam the 'military art of people's war', as Vo Nguyen Giap was to describe the guerrilla struggle of the Vietnamese people led by the Communist Party against domination by a succession of western imperialist powers,[6] similarly developed further the strategy of anti-feudal agrarian reform as the basis for the enlistment of mass support for the liberation struggle, culminating in the May 1975 victory and unification of the country—the last great revolutionary victory of the twentieth century. Within fifteen years of this, from 1990, the Soviet Union disintegrated in a process which had started as economic and political reform within the collective system, but quickly degenerated into the private appropriation of collective property overseen by Northern economic experts and international lending institutions advocating 'shock therapy' to usher in capitalism—a process which has plunged Russia and Ukraine in particular into massive economic and demographic crisis, halving their national income by 1996 and sharply raising the death rate of their able-bodied population—a degree of collapse far greater than that inflicted by Nazi invasion and war.[7]

In India the colonial period had seen a large number of localized, intense anti-feudal agrarian struggles, many of which fused with the anti-imperialist national movement. The Communist Party played a major role in mobilizing the peasantry in the two most important and widespread of these movements, namely, Telengana and Tebhaga. But there was no generalization of the agrarian movement under the leadership of the workers' party into a pan-Indian revolutionary movement, in the way that had been witnessed in Russia or in East Asia. Many objective difficulties existed in India, which were relatively less important elsewhere: for one, the strength and efficiency, honed over two centuries, of the repressive apparatus of the unitary British colonial state, as compared to moribund tsarism in Russia or the internal bickerings of rival imperialist powers in semi-colonial China. For another, the relative strength of the English-educated Indian bourgeoisie which seized the leadership of the national movement particularly after Gandhiji's return from South Africa and his brilliant political innovation—the *satyagraha*, which perfectly suited the requirements of a movement which wished to stave off revolution while taking over the legacy of power.

The agrarian question in the colonial period in India essentially revolved around two main issues: the monopoly control over land by rentiers who were the agents for the extraction of surplus, which then went in substantial part to the state via cash taxes; and the vulnerability of the peasantry to the vagaries of the world market in the completely open, liberalized, export-oriented economy of British India, which was kept forcibly so in the interests of the colonizing power. The objective of libralized trade was to transfer a part of the internal revenues to Britain in the very useful form of unpaid direct imports, or appropriation of the foreign exchange earnings from India's export surplus to other countries.[8] These features in turn led to the indebtedness of the peasantry to extortionate moneylenders and traders in order to grow export crops to meet the cash demands on them.[9] The agrarian movements of the peasantry and their demands therefore developed in the main around these two issues.

A distinction has to be drawn between British India and the princely states, and between the exploitation and problems faced by the settled plough-cultivators as opposed to those faced by tribal communities still dependent to some extent on forest resources. The first issue, namely, the anti-feudal struggle, dominated in the backward princely states which had oppressive *jagirdari* systems but where peasant production was generally less commercialized and less oriented to the world market. In British India, on the other hand, the agrarian relations had long been changed to facilitate not only higher surplus extraction but specifically to promote tax-financed export production, thus giving rise to a higher degree of pauperization and landlessness, which was greatly accelerated as the world agricultural recession beginning from the mid-twenties and deepening into the Depression of the thirties meant plunging prices and pushed more farmers to the edge of starvation. The world market impacted more directly and severely in British India and its effects were devastating in the inter-war period, owing to the maintenance of record levels of sterling transfer to Britain taking the usual form of large export surplus of non-food crops to the extent of politically imposed liabilities, even as prices fell drastically.[10] Per capita food availability in British India fell by 29 per cent in the inter-war period and conditions of famine vulnerability were created, with outbreak of actual famine in Bengal from 1943.[11] The tribes-predominant areas which existed in both the princely states and British India on the other hand saw struggles directed against the appropriation of tribal land and resources by plains outsiders, which made the tribal struggles relatively inward-looking, although on many issues such as rent reduction and re-occupation or forcible harvesting of illegally alienated land, there was also integration with the struggle of the non-tribal peasantry.

This feature of substantially differing agrarian relations, differing levels of integration into the world market, and the specific nature of exploitation faced by the tribals, all made for a degree of complexity of the agrarian question which defied a simple unitary understanding but required a correspondingly complex adjustment of the parameters of the programme of struggle in accordance with varying conditions. This posed a difficult challenge for the left movement. In the princely states the militant anti-feudal peoples' struggles in Telengana, where feudal land monopoly under a *jagirdari* system prevailed, cleared the way, it appears, for top-down legal reforms once the struggle was militarily suppressed by the new Indian state. The subsequent enactment of laws of *jagirdari* abolition and tenancy reform led to a large spate of evictions of tenants by landlords by 1955 in the Marathwada and Karnataka areas of the re-organized state, as evaluation studies show. It was only in Telengana, owing to the high level of consciousness generated by the earlier militant struggle, that tenants resisted and only a few were evicted, while a much higher proportion bought ownership rights than was the case in other areas with no history of struggle.[12]

Independence and the *Dirigiste* Strategy

At Independence, the nature of the principal contradiction in the agrarian economy was fairly clear. The principal contradiction was that between the mass of the working peasantry and labourers on the one hand, and the minority of landlords, traders and moneylenders who monopolized control over land and money capital, thereby exploiting the peasantry through rent, interest and exorbitant traders' margins. The principal contradiction was no longer as earlier, that between the Indian people as a whole, and imperialism and its local allies. While imperialism was by no means dead, it was on the retreat in the context of the post-war shambles that was the advanced world, while de-colonization allowed space for third world countries like India to try to de-link from the earlier international division of labour under which they had been completely open and liberalized economies geared to metropolitan growth, not national growth. They could now protect their economies and undertake state intervention in the interests of national development—in which they were helped by the existence and aid of the socialist camp. The old liberalizers were silenced; the new liberalizers had not yet appeared.

From Independence up to the mid-eighties the Indian state followed a policy of state-directed or *dirigiste* industrial development with substantial recourse to protection of domestic agriculture and industry through tariffs and quantitative restrictions. With such insulation against the volatility of the global market, domestic agriculture-manufacturing terms of trade show an improvement for agriculture at varying rates over different sub-periods, compared to very large fluctuations in the international terms of trade for primary producers. This strategy of *dirigisme* ran into aggregate demand constraints quite early, by the sixties, owing to the basic failure to undertake comprehensive redistributive land reforms, which resulted in very slow growth of the mass rural market for manufactures—an argument explored to some extent in my first Daniel Thorner Memorial Lecture delivered in 1985.

The non-left political forces, economists and planners in India have consistently underestimated the role of effective re-distributive land reforms for breaking the economic and social power of the rural landed minority, thereby widening the social base of rural investment, and raising the rate of growth of both retained and commoditized output. They underestimated its importance as a precondition for measures of mass poverty reduction and for providing an expanding market for industry, and its importance for reducing the old class, caste and gender-based forms of inequalities which express themselves in high levels of illiteracy, declining sex ratios, atrocities against *dalits* and the persistence of child labour. Only in some states where the left movement has been influential were substantive measures of land reform undertaken, with a very positive impact despite their relatively limited nature—viz. not destroying the monopoly of landed property but stabilizing the livelihoods of the poor through owner-like security of tenure, and revival of local government.

The neo-liberal argument that export pessimism and controls were the problems underlying industrial stagnation is incorrect. India's exports in fact grew faster on average under the regime of controls up to 1990, than they have grown under the trade-liberalized regime from 1991 to date. Industrial growth was similarly faster, and predictably so, in the eighties when the state's fiscal stance was expansionary, than it has been in the nineties when more deflationary policies were followed. The *dirigiste* strategy had some major achievements—a diversified range of industries including capacities in heavy industries was built up, a privileging of wage goods production led to foodgrains output trebling by the early eighties, and this formed the basis for a public grain procurement and distribution system which through buffer stock operations moderated price fluctuations for both producers and consumers. But widespread underemployment, a high incidence of rural poverty spilling over into proliferating urban slums, poor coverage of villages with respect to primary education and health care, and an occupational structure which was much the same as in 1950, continued to characterize the economy up to the early eighties.

For a brief period, however, the Seventh Plan period spanning 1985 to 1990, it did appear that there was a new dynamism in the agrarian economy imparted by the new phenomenon of large-scale state expenditures on rural infrastructure and employment generation programmes, which were expanded especially sharply during the 1987 drought. Compared to a planned expenditure of 7.8 per cent of GDP on these areas over the period, the actual expenditure averaged as high as 13.2 per cent of GDP, and this had its strong multiplier effects on employment and incomes, given the high marginal propensity to consume in a low-income population. The rural occupational structure shifted towards non-farm employment (which accounted for 29 per cent of males employed by 1990 compared to 25 per cent in 1980), in turn associated with higher real earnings, and with resulting labour market tightness the real wages of labour in crop production also rose substantially. At the same time, a number of state governments responsive to local popular demands extended the coverage of the public distribution system to villages in the course of the eighties, and many gave additional subsidy out of state budgets over and above the central subsidy, to keep basic staples affordable for the poor. Consequently, we find that measured rural poverty in many states in India shows a marked trend decline up to 1990–91, and at an all-India level too the incidence of rural poverty declined from 45 per cent in 1978 to 35 per cent by 1990–91. While there are many problems both with the definition and hence with the measurement of income poverty, as long as one consistent methodology is used, the trends can be established: there is no doubt that as a trend the incidence of income poverty did decline in the eighties quite significantly.[13] The independently measured trends in public expenditure, employment and real wages are consistent with this conclusion.

These positive developments were, however, short-lived and quickly reversed as India entered a new economic policy regime of loan-conditional, deflationary structural adjustment combined with trade liberalization from 1991 under the guidance of the Bretton Woods Institutions, initiating important changes which accelerated after subordination to the WTO discipline from 1995. Within a single decade, 1991 to date, these policies have induced a crisis of livelihoods in agriculture and led to a new conjuncture, such that, we would argue below, the principal contradiction in the agrarian sphere may be said to be changing once more towards that between imperialist globalization and the Indian peasantry.

The New Agrarian Question arising from Structural Adjustment and Trade Liberalization in the Nineties

Policies of macroeconomic deflation and contraction, combined with removal of barriers to international trade and capital flows, form the core of neo-liberal reforms. The driving force behind the neo-liberal agenda of deflation and liberalization are the interests of global finance capital, which has come to dominate over all other types of capital from the last quarter of the last century.[14] The main instrument for the initiation of the policy regime suiting its interests in developing countries, has been international debt arising from balance of payments problems, carrying strict conditionalities whose implementation is monitored through the supra-national lending institutions, the IMF and the World Bank, otherwise known as the Bretton Woods institutions, to which the World Trade Organization has been added from 1995 for monitoring and enforcing the trade and other agreements including the Agreement on Agriculture in GATT 1994.[15]

There is irony in the fact that India's rulers abandoned *dirigiste* planning-for-development, and entered an export-promotion regime located within domestic deflationary efforts, precisely at the worst possible time: when the preceding nearly two decades of neo-liberal deflationary policies across the capitalist world had already slowed down expansion of advanced country markets, and when an important subset of India's trading partners (the erstwhile Soviet Union) was seeing a process of total economic collapse, followed from 1997 by financial crisis and rapid deflation in the Southeast Asian economies. Whatever little benefits of export growth might have accrued with trade liberalization, have evaporated under these circumstances, while, on the other hand, the costs of such liberalization to the Indian economy have proved to be extremely high. The most important costs have been de-industrialization, a serious threat to food security for the masses, and greatly increased vulnerability of the peasantry to the volatility of global prices combined with exposure to unfair trade. All these processes taken together have, apart from their other effects, precipitated the present ongoing crisis of livelihoods in the agrarian sector, which is reminiscent of the deep crisis of the inter-war years.

The threat to food security emanates from several related sets of policies followed in the nineties. First, a general macroeconomic contraction involving a sharp cut-back in rural development and employment-generating expenditures : from over 13 per cent of GDP during the Seventh Plan it has reduced to less than 9 per cent of GDP during the next Plan, and in many ensuing years has fallen below 5 per cent. Through the adverse multiplier effects of this cut-back of expenditures rural incomes have contracted, the proportion of rural workers in non-farm employment which had risen up to 1990 has reverted back to the level of the early eighties. Despite a succession of thirteen years of good monsoons since the 1987 drought, income deflation has markedly reduced purchasing power with the majority, and has raised the share of property incomes in total incomes generated within agriculture. A so-called 'Fiscal Responsibility Bill' is currently before Parliament which seeks to put a statutory cap on the fiscal deficit and thereby make any possible expansionary policy impossible, while there is of course no conceptual, leave alone statutory, cap on rural unemployment and poverty. In a number of states under the pressure of corporate agro-business interests land reform measures are being rolled back: legislation has been already passed or is on the anvil seeking to facilitate lease and purchase of farmland by companies, by relaxing land ceiling levels and other measures.

Second, the central food subsidy has been sought to be cut by repeatedly raising the issue prices of foodgrains from the public distribution system to a greater extent than procurement prices paid to farmers were raised. This simply priced out the poor from the PDS, leading to decline in sales and the build-up of food stocks with the Food Corporation of India far in excess of buffer norms, while the subsidy bill was not in fact reduced either but went increasingly to meet the costs of stock-holding. There have been two major episodes of excess stocks build-up while many more people go hungry: the first episode, up to 1995–96, saw a near-doubling of the issue price and rise in rural income poverty combined with food stocks of over 30 million tonnes, which at that time the government could manage to reduce through exports, as world cereal prices were then ruling high.[16] The second episode is from late 1998 as, in another misconceived attempt to cut the food subsidy, issue prices were again nearly doubled in the succeeding eighteen months, sales again predictably fell, which, combined with record procurement, has led to a build-up of stocks with the FCI in excess of 40 million tonnes by mid-2000 and in excess of 50 million tonnes by mid-2001, three times the buffer needs. At the same time, there is widespread agrarian distress owing to lack of purchasing power and a rise in rural income poverty.[17] Further, National Sample Survey data show that the rural per capita consumption of cereals in kilograms has been falling in every state in India except two—Kerala and West Bengal.[18]

The irrationality of this outcome is compounded by government's renewed attempts to sell abroad, but now by subsidizing heavily, as the world price now is less than half that prevailing during 1996. The rational solution of using food stocks for large-scale employment generation and asset creation programmes, as had been done during the 1987 drought, eludes the present state which is now the prisoner of incorrect ideas, viz. the belief that the fiscal deficit will rise with such a programme, and rigid adherence to curbing the fiscal deficit and pleasing the BWI, even at the expense of growing mass hunger.

While the popular press talks of 'record harvests' and a glut of foodgrains, the reality is that the rate of foodgrains growth has sharply decelerated, in fact halved, to 1.7 per cent (compound annual) during 1990–91 to 2000–01 compared to 3.4 per cent during the preceding decade.[19] The population growth rate too has decelerated but to a much smaller extent, to 1.9 per cent during the nineties, so that per capita foodgrain output has been falling during the reforms decade. I had predicted at the very inception of the new policies that with trade liberalization and primary export thrust, we in India too could expect a decline in per head food output, as the powerful magnet of the advanced countries' effective demand with its own specific commodity structure starts to restructure our own cropping patterns away from the foodgrains our population needs and towards exports demanded by them, just as it had done in the trade-liberalized regime of colonial times.[20] A labourer in Madhya Pradesh with a wage less than a dollar a day cannot compete to retain land under *jowar* and *ragi*, his staple food, against the competition of the advanced country consumer with sixty dollars a day who wants cheap meat; and as long as there is unfettered operation of the market (which responds only to effective demand, never to human needs), it will always achieve conversion of that land to soyabean production for cheap livestock feed exports.

The main element in the decline in per head food crops has been large shifts of sown area away from foodgrains towards export crops and exported agro-based goods (raw cotton, cotton yarn, soyabean processed into soyameal for livestock feed with nine-tenths being exported, vegetables and fruit, prawn culture): by 1996 as much as 7 million hectares had been diverted away from foodgrains (mainly the coarse grains and pulses) to these export crops. As export growth sharply fell after that owing to recession in advanced country markets, there was some reversal to the staples up to 1998–99, but once again with the picking up of export growth in the last two years, the decade ends in 2001 with a 4 per cent decline in sown area under the food staples compared to 1990–91, and with a halving of the trend foodgrains growth rate.

The impact of a decade of income-deflating policies overseen by the BWI in India, in eroding purchasing power and hence the effective demand of the poorer majority of the population, thus becomes starkly clear when we see the build-up of unprecedented, enormous stocks of grain over a period when grain supply growth has halved and per head output has actually fallen. Although the problem of excess stocks has been created in the first place by neo-liberal policies promoting unemployment and poverty, it is now being used as an excuse to urge for winding up mandatory procurement by the FCI, while the working of the PDS has been substantially curtailed already with targeting from 1997, adversely affecting the poorest consumers.

But mass income deflation and undermining of food security are only part of the adverse impact. The present full-blown agrarian crisis manifests itself in the enmeshing of large segments of the farmers, especially those producing export crops, in escalating and unrepayable debt, leading to loss of assets including land, to suicides, sales of bodily vital organs,[21] distress sales of children and prostitution of women. In a single state, Andhra Pradesh alone, over one thousand farmers, mainly growing cotton, have committed suicide by ingesting pesticides since 1997–98, and the contagion has spread to hitherto prosperous regions as well, such as Punjab. The unprecedented agrarian crisis is the direct result of the increasing exposure of Indian farmers to the volatility of global prices since 1990–91, to which unfair trade from heavily subsidized foreign goods has been added more recently as quantitative restrictions on imports have been progressively removed from 1998–99 onwards, being replaced by a low 35 per cent tariff across the board from mid-2000 (even though higher tariffs were permissible even under the WTO discipline). By April 2001 the last tranche of quantitative restrictions had been abolished.

The unfair nature of trade faced by Indian farmers in this new unprotected environment arises from the very high subsidies and transfers which advanced countries make to their farmers and agro-business corporations. The objective of high subsidies is to dominate the global market for cereals and dairy products despite their much higher unit costs of production compared to costs in most developing countries. Taking the OECD countries together, about one-third of their total coarse grains output and one-fifth of total wheat output was exported in the mid-nineties. Advanced country subsidies were not always as astronomical as they are today: in 1980, producer subsidy equivalent (PSE) payments annually as percentage of annual value of agricultural production was only 9 per cent in the USA, 15 per cent in Canada, 25 per cent average in ten countries of the EU, and 5 per cent in Australia.

Between 1980 and 1986, however, in response to a decline in world prices, there was very rapid increase in PSE payments, raising its proportion to farm output value in 1986 to the astronomical levels of 45 per cent in the US, 54 per cent in Canada, 66 per cent in the same ten EU countries, and 19 per cent in Australia.[22] A downward trend in global cereal prices (as occurred during this period) always leads to more farm support in advanced countries under the pressure of their agro-business and farmer lobbies, which in the long run further compounds their problem of excess supply and sparks an aggressive attempt to penetrate developing country markets. Since agriculture itself accounted for a relatively small share of GDP in these industrialized countries (usually below 10 per cent and in some below 5 per cent), it was possible for them to make transfers accounting for such a large share of agriculture's contribution to GDP as half to two-thirds. It is obvious that neither India nor any other developing country could possibly allocate even a much lower fraction, leave alone half to two-thirds of agricultural output value as PSEs; it would amount in India's case to a quarter to one-third of the entire GDP of the country!

The highly inflated mid-eighties' levels of subsidy in advanced countries were deliberately made the base (more precisely, the base level is the average for 1984–86), from which a mere one-fifth reduction commitment was then made by the advanced countries in the Agreement on Agriculture of GATT 1994, compared to 13 per cent reduction to be undertaken by eligible developing countries. The US had already satisfied its reduction commitment by 1996, with $75 billion as total transfers. Over the two years ending in 1999, however, it has again raised transfers to a record $96 billion, to compensate for falling cereals prices which are at a historic low.[23]

While adverse movement of primary products prices has been a secular trend since the eighties, a brief period of high prices in the early nineties—which induced expansion of cash crops in India on the basis of loans by producers—has been followed by crashing prices over a range of commodities. Cotton producers have been the worst affected because both yield as well as price expectations have not been realized, plunging many lakhs of farmers into unviable debt. The reduction of priority-sector lending under the reforms and the resulting squeeze on bank credit to farmers have led to a higher proportion of debt being incurred from private creditors at high interest. The more than one thousand cases of suicides by farmers are only the tip of the iceberg: the colonial agrarian problem of consumption debt, asset loss and destitution has been resurrected on a large scale in a mere decade of exposure to global price fluctuations combined with withdrawal of support measures from the state.

Contrary to the World Bank's own 1993 price projections, which had predicted firm or rising cereal prices but falling prices of other primary exports, even world cereal prices have been in an unusual trough since 1997, suggesting that the market-distorting effects of prolonged, very high farm subsidies in advanced countries are manifesting themselves in over-production and excess stocks. Moreover, this is occurring against the backdrop of two decades of deflationary policies across the globe, which has reduced purchasing power and capacity to import by those who most need to eat: the forty-six countries of Sub-Saharan Africa, for example, saw a 10 per cent fall in GDP per head during the decade of the eighties and stagnation in the nineties; while under 'shock therapy' Russia and Ukraine have seen a more than 45 per cent fall in GDP per head in the nineties. The present Indian scenario of more hunger with higher food stocks, produced by income-deflating policies in the nineties, is but a replication of the situation at the global level. Having removed protection completely at this juncture, the Indian government is importing low world prices with their ruinous effects on foodgrain producers, into the economy. Thus the crisis is being generalized from export-crop producers to the far larger numbers of foodgrains producers as well.

The conjuncture today is strongly reminiscent of the years presaging the Great Depression. World stocks of primary products had built up from 1925 onwards, leading to falling export prices. Rigid adherence to ideas of 'sound finance' and balanced budgets in every country led to deflationary measures being followed (including in India) as state revenues from customs dropped, reducing in turn the capacity of the country to import, and inducing income decline for export producers in trading partner countries. What started as recession deepened into depression from 1930, as every country deflated,[24] with all Keynes's warnings, based on his revolutionary theory of income determination, going unheeded. Similarly, we find that not only developing countries' primary export prices, but from 1996 world prices even of cereals, where advanced countries dominate, have been moving downwards, while the neo-liberal policies—which are essentially the same as the pre-Keynesian policies of the twenties—of income deflation, wage restraint, caps on fiscal deficit, etc., exercise a contractory effect on mass incomes everywhere (except the last remaining large area of economic sovereignty, China). It is difficult to identify new sources of world capitalist expansion since the largest market, the US, as well as the EU, remain substantially protectionist,[25] nor is there a net inflow of capital into developing countries to buoy up their growth.

The trends outlined above lead to the conclusion that the principal contradiction within the agrarian economy of India is moving decisively, once more, towards that between farmers as a whole and imperialist globalization under the dominance of the economic agenda of finance capital.[26] The present agrarian crisis is likely to deepen, not ameliorate, as long as the macroeconomic policies remain what they have been in the nineties.

Notes

[1] Radical peasant movements not influenced by working-class ideology have been very important in the history of China and in Latin America, but less so in India.

[2] V.I. Lenin (1972).

[3] Mao Zedong (1967).

[4] William Hinton's classic *Fanshen* (1969) still remains the best first-hand account of agrarian reform in a Chinese village. See also his *Shenfan* (1984) for the cultural revolution period.

[5] Isaac Deutscher (1967).

[6] Vo Nguyen Giap, *The Military Art of People's War*, Foreign Languages Publishing House, Hanoi.

[7] The mechanisms underlying the collapse have been well analysed in a series of articles by Russian economists in a special issue of *Social Scientist,* Vol. 28 Nos 7–8, July–August 2000.

[8] Indian producers of export surplus to Britain were paid out of internal tax revenues and had no claim either on sterling from sale of their goods in Britain, or on foreign exchange earned from export surplus to third countries. For a diagrammatic exposition of the links between the budget and transfer through trade see U. Patnaik (1984).

[9] The mechanisms involved have been described by a number of historians; an attempt at analytical synthesis may be found in U. Patnaik (1976).

[10] For example, the second highest transfer of Home Charges of 28.8 million pounds sterling was in 1933–34, nearly three-tenths of the budget expenditures. See *Cambridge Economic History of India*, Vol. 2.

[11] G. Blyn (1966); U. Patnaik (1991).

[12] See A.M. Khusro (1958).

[13] Earlier statistical analysis such as Ahluwalia (1974) and Ravallion and Datt (1996), had shown that the incidence of poverty varies directly with the price of food, and inversely with per capita foodgrains output. With the inclusion of public expenditure in rural areas as the third variable in the model, a better fit is obtained to the trends in the eighties. See A. Sen (1996), A. Sen and U. Patnaik (1997).

[14] For the implications of finance capital's dominance over policy see P. Patnaik (1999).

[15] Agriculture was included for the first time in the history of GATT, during the Uruguay Round culminating in GATT 1994, as also were agreements related to intellectual property and investment.

[16] See U. Patnaik (1997a).

[17] See U. Patnaik (1997b) and J. Ghosh (2000) for a discussion of food stocks build-up.

[18] A comparison of the NSS Rounds on consumption gives this trend over 1973 to 1993.

[19] Growth rates are from official annual *Economic Survey*, various years.

[20] See U. Patnaik (1993).

[21] Indebted farmers are taken by agents offering Rs 40,000 per kidney, to

unknown places in big cities for the organ-removal operation. Evidence from concerned farmers at Seed Tribunal organized on September 2000 at Bangalore by Kisan Sabhas, NGOs and the Research Foundation for Science, Technology and Development, Delhi.

[22] K.A. Ingersen, A.J. Rayner and R.C. Hine (eds) (1994).

[23] PSE and total transfer data are given in the annual OECD reports. Figures quoted from OECD (2000).

[24] For the agricultural depression and deflationary policies see C.P. Kindelberger (1986).

[25] Between the signing of GATT 1994 to date, developing countries have reduced average protection by twice the extent that developed countries have done. The Multi-Fibre Agreement which restricts entry of textile exports from developing countries into advanced countries remains in force, and non-trade barriers are extensively used by advanced countries.

[26] As recession continues in advanced countries, as it is bound to do as long as the interests of finance capital with its contractionary agenda dominate, there is greater pressure on developing countries to competitively deflate and devalue, and open up their markets, in order to export more non-grain primary products and simple manufactures at falling unit prices, and to absorb the grains, dairy products and manufactures that are in excess supply in low-growth advanced countries.

References

Blyn, G. (1966). *Agricultural Trends in India 1891–1949: Output, Area and Productivity,* University of Philadelphia Press, Philadelphia PA.

Deutscher, I. (1967). *The Unfinished Revolution: Russia 1917–67,* Oxford University Press, Oxford.

Ghosh, J. (2000). 'Agriculture', in *The Indian Economy 1999–2000: An Alternative Survey,* Delhi Science Forum, Delhi.

Hinton, W. (1969). *Fanshen,* Random House, New York.

——— (1984). *Shenfan,* Pan Books in association with Martin, Secker and Warburg, London.

Ingersen, K.A., A.J. Rayner and R.C. Hine (eds) (1994). *Agriculture in the Uruguay Round,* St Martin's Press, London.

Kindelberger, C.P. (1986). *The World in Depression 1929–39,* University of California Press; also Penguin Books, 1987.

Khusro, A.M. (1958). *Economic and Social Effects of Jagirdari Abolition and Land Reforms in Hyderabad,* Osmania University, Hyderabad.

Lenin, V.I. (1972). 'The Agrarian Programme of Social Democracy in the First Russian Revolution', *Collected Works,* Vol. 13, Progress Publishers, Moscow.

Mao Zedong (1967). 'Report of an Investigation of the Peasant Movement in Hunan, March 1927', *Selected Works,* Vol. 1, Foreign Languages Publishing House, Beijing.

Patnaik, P. (1999). 'Capitalism in Asia at the end of the Millennium', *Monthly Review,* Vol. 51, No. 3, July–August.

Patnaik, U. (1976). 'The Process of Commercialization under Colonial Conditions',

Working Paper, Centre for Economic Studies and Planning, Jawaharlal Nehru University, Delhi; included in U. Patnaik (1999).

———— (1984). 'Tribute Transfer and the Balance of Payments in the *Cambridge Economic History of India*', *Social Scientist*, Vol. 12, No. 12; included in U. Patnaik (1999).

———— (1991). 'Food Availability and Famine: A Longer View', *Journal of Peasant Studies*, Vol. 19, No. 1; included in U. Patnaik (1999).

———— (1993). 'The Likely Impact of Economic Liberalization and Structural Adjustment on Food Security in India', ILO and National Commission for Women, January.

———— (1996). 'Export-Oriented Agriculture and Food Security in Developing Countries and in India', *Economic and Political Weekly*, Vol. XXXI, Nos. 35–37 (Special Number).

———— (1997a). 'The Political Economy of State Intervention in the Food Economy', *Economic and Political Weekly*, Budget Issue, April.

———— (1997b). 'Agriculture and Rural Development', in *Alternative Economic Survey*, Delhi Science Forum, Delhi.

———— (1998). 'Alternative Strategies of Agrarian Change in relation to Resources for Development in China and India', in D. Nayyar (ed.), *Economics as Ideology and Experience: Essays presented to Ashok Mitra*, Cass, London.

———— (1999). *The Long Transition: Essays on Political Economy*, Tulika, Delhi.

Ravallion, M. and G. Datt (1995). 'Growth and Poverty in Rural India', Background Paper to the 1995 *World Development Report*, WPS1405, World Bank, Washington DC.

Sen, A. (1996). 'Economic Reforms, Employment and Poverty: Trends and Options', *Economic and Political Weekly*, Vol. 31, Nos 35–37 (Special Number).

Sen, A. and U. Patnaik (1997). 'Poverty in India', paper under DSA Programme, Centre for Economic Studies and Planning, Jawaharlal Nehru University, December.

Sivasubramonian, S. (1965). 'National Income of India, 1900–01 to 1946–47', mimeo., Delhi School of Economics, University of Delhi.

Social Scientist, Special Issue on Russia, Vol. 28, Nos. 7–8, July–August 2000.

Vo Nguyen Giap, *The Military Art of People's War*, Foreign Languages Publishing House, Hanoi.

The Royal Titles Bill of 1876

Daniel Thorner

The Historical Background of the Royal Titles Bill

After the Indian Rebellion of 1857–58, the government of India was taken out of the hands of the East India Company and was placed under the direct supervision of the Crown as the representative of the nation. Although considered at the time by both the Palmerston Government and its successor, the Derby–Disraeli Ministry, it was deemed inadvisable to present the Queen with the title of 'Empress of India' in the Government of India Bill of 1858. At a time when British swords 'were reeking with carnage', Disraeli hinted, it would have been most unwise to have added to the titles of the Queen.[1]

Although there was little outward sign of disturbance in India from 1858 to 1876, it was nevertheless seen fit to maintain a large standing army there. During this period the country was being transformed by extensive economic developments. Millions of pounds of British capital were invested in the construction of railroads, which opened hitherto inaccessible markets and expanded the older ones, permitting a constant increase in the importation of goods from England and in the exportation of Indian raw materials and goods.[2]

Throughout the nineteenth century there was a continual expansion of the Russian Empire in Asia. In the decade before 1876 Russia conquered the remnants of the old Tartar kingdoms in Central Asia, and advanced her frontiers southward until the Russian outposts

This is an unpublished essay by Daniel Thorner, written in 1937. The author's note to the title of the essay reads as follows: 'This investigation of the addition of the title, "Empress of India", to Queen Victoria's formal style, was undertaken for a seminar paper at the suggestion of Professor Carlton J.H. Hayes in the winter of 1936–1937.'

were 'only a few days march from those of Her Majesty's dominions in India'.[3] This expansion caused deep misgivings in England, especially since it was known that the Indian masses were aware of the conquest of their former masters, the Tartars, by 'the Great Prince' from the distant north 'who has brought about so wonderful a revolution'.[4] In this context, the assumption of the title, 'Empress of India', by Queen Victoria was intended to show Russia that England had absolutely no idea of permitting any foreign power to make the slightest encroachment in India, and also to counteract the prestige of the great Emperor from the north with the Indian masses, among whom existed a long tradition of great conquerors from the north.

This double development, the advance of Russia and the internal changes within India, combined to make the British intensely concerned for the future of British control in India. The introduction of capitalist modes of production and distribution, and the resulting expansion of economic life, led to the disintegration of the rigid caste system and its psychology, and of the narrow village economy of the Indian populace. A slow, but ever-increasing transformation of Indian life began to take place in this period as a result; a turning-over and readjustment of social relationships leading to insecurity and instability in the position of the individual within society. The older symbols of authority and the corresponding 'Weltanschauung' lost their basis and consequently their appeal in this changing social process. It was felt that a new stabilizing symbol or concept was necessary, one which would link up India's glorious imperial past with her present position in the British Empire.[5]

Aside from Russia and India, there were factors within Great Britain itself which made possible the passage of the Royal Titles Bill in 1876. The decade of the sixties witnessed a vigorous economic expansion, leading to the necessity for new markets in which to sell goods, and for colonial areas in which accumulated capital might be invested more profitably than at home.[6]

Along with these economic developments went changes in the British attitudes toward imperial affairs. As instances of the great interest in the Empire, the wide sale in the late sixties of Dilke's book, *Greater Britain*, and the founding of the Royal Colonial Society in 1868 may be cited. The Abyssinian War, the forthright stand in favour of imperialism taken by Disraeli and the Conservative Party in 1872, the interest in the Suez Canal, the writings and activities of Froude, Seeley,

Bury and many others, all served to build up a strong current of imperialist feeling in Great Britain.[7]

India was the most important member of the British Empire, and it was fully realized that the continued possession of India was essential to the well-being of Great Britain. The growing imperialist feeling in England, combined with the knowledge of Russian designs and activities and of the internal situation in India, led to a feeling of insecurity about the continued possession of India, and concurrently, to a desire to strengthen and externalize the ties which bound India to Britain.

These factors created a situation in which Great Britain had to be empire-conscious, alert to every threat of danger and to every opportunity for strengthening the Empire. But there is one other factor whose importance should not be neglected—the personal role and influence of Queen Victoria. There is no doubt that the Queen wanted to become Empress of India; indeed, there is good evidence to believe that she had tried unsuccessfully at least twice before 1876 to have Parliament authorize her to assume this title.[8] The tour of India by the Prince of Wales in 1875, and the hearty welcome which he received there, seem to have convinced the Queen that the time was ripe for her to take the title of Empress of India. She secured the rather unwilling consent of Disraeli, who felt that it would be better to wait for a somewhat later time, but who finally agreed to introduce the Bill when he realized that sentiment in Parliament was in favour of passing it. Thus the stage was set for the introduction of the Royal Titles Bill in the 1876 session of Parliament.[9]

The Royal Titles Bill in Parliament

For the first time in several years, the Queen opened Parliament in person. This created much excitement in Great Britain, even affecting the dignified members of Parliament, some of whom were battered about in the mad rush to secure a glimpse of Victoria. The Queen's Address, which was read by the Lord Chancellor, gave notice of the Royal Titles Bill in the following terms:

> I am deeply thankful for the uninterrupted health which my dear Son, the Prince of Wales, has enjoyed during his journey through India. The hearty affection with which he has been received by my Indian subjects of all classes and races assures me that they are happy

> under my rule, and loyal to my throne. At the time that the direct Government of my Indian Empire was transferred to the Crown, no formal addition was made to the style and titles of the Sovereign. I have deemed the present and fitting opportunity for supplying this omission, and a Bill upon the subject will be presented to you.[10]

It is significant to note that there was a marked difference apparent in the reception given to this part of the Queen's Address by Liberals and Conservatives. Referring to this passage, Earl Granville, Liberal leader in the House of Lords, stated, 'My Lords, I venture to say that, in regard to the dignity of Her Majesty herself, no name can appeal to the imagination so forcibly as that of Victoria, Queen of Great Britain and Ireland.'[11] On the other hand, Mr Mulholland, in seconding the address of the Commons in reply to Her Majesty's Speech, declared:

> The time, therefore, seems to have been happily chosen for Her Majesty to crown this great Empire that we have built up in the East, by assuming a title long foreshadowed by events. That Her Majesty should now become Empress of India, in fact as she has long been in name, will be accepted as a graceful symbol of the more intimate connection that we hope may follow the visit of Her Royal son. It is possible to underrate the influence of imagination in national affairs —with an Oriental people it may be difficult to overrate it; and I can conceive nothing more likely to kindle and preserve a national sentiment of loyalty among our fellow-subjects in India than this direct connection with the August Head of our ancient Monarchy by a yet more splendid title.[12]

Before describing the principal arguments for and against the Bill, it may be helpful to trace in summary fashion its passage through Parliament. The Royal Titles Bill was introduced in the House of Commons and read for the first time on 17 February 1876; read for the second time on 9 March; considered in Committee on 16, 20 and 23 March; and read for the third time on 23 March, thus passing from the House of Commons to the House of Lords. The Government defeated the most important amendment offered by the Opposition, by a vote of 305 to 200. In the House of Lords the Bill was read first on 24 March; for the second time on 30 March; considered in Committee on 3 April; and read for the third time, and therefore passed, on 7 April. In the

Lords, the Government defeated the most important resolution of the Opposition, introduced by Shaftesbury, by 137 to 91.

Before proceeding to an analysis of the major arguments for and against the Bill, it may be advisable to explain briefly just what the disputants conceived to be the nature of the question under discussion. They all agreed that it was a quarrel over words, but over very important words. Indeed, the entire complex of symbols representing authority, loyalty and empire, one might almost say the propaganda of empire, was thoroughly examined. It cannot be emphasized too strongly that at no time was there any objection to the cold fact of empire, to the existing relations of domination and subordination. The real issues, as they were conceived in Parliament, were such questions as: Would the title 'Empress of India' be acceptable to the traditional modes of thinking about and externalizing authority in both England and India, so that it could serve as a symbol of unity and stability for both? On this particular question, no less a statesman than W.R. Forster could say that "'Empress'. . . is a word not very suited to English ideas, and the Imperial [i.e. despotic] idea of government is not one very pleasing to English feelings. I would prefer the old phrase of King or Queen.'[13] The members of Parliament were fully aware of the necessity for examining the historical development and traditions of Great Britain, India and the colonies, to ascertain whether the proposed title would evoke the desired reactions or would give rise to antagonistic feelings and sentiments. There were long and detailed analyses of the difference in the meanings of the symbols 'Emperor' and 'King', and the differing social responses to each. It must not be presumed that quarrels over words are unimportant. Political discussions frequently do centre about the meanings, context and use of a word. Disraeli was fully aware of the fact that the meanings of symbols and the reactions they called forth constituted the key problems of the whole discussion, and stated clearly the general importance to the statesman of the problem of political symbolism when he said, 'It is only by the amplification of titles that you can often touch and satisfy the imaginations of nations; and that is an element which Governments must not despise.'[14]

There were eight major arguments offered in support of the Bill giving the Queen permission to assume the title of Empress of India. (1) It would simply recognize an accomplished fact, an already existent state of affairs. (2) It would show British determination to maintain the Empire, and would repudiate the doctrines of the Little

Englanders. (3) It would manifest deeper interest in India on the part of Great Britain. (4) It would attach the Indian people directly to the Crown. (5) It would unite India with the Empire symbolically. (6) The Indian people and princes wanted the Queen to assume the new title. (7) It would serve as a warning to all world powers that Great Britain would never stand for encroachments in India. (8) It would counteract the influence of the Russian Empire symbolically and politically.

The tacit assumption underlying almost every argument in favour of the Bill was that it simply recognized the relations of power already existing between the Crown and the Indian people and princes, and it was thought that the reactions in India would be favourable to it for that reason. This is shown clearly in the speech of the Duke of Richmond and Gordon, which was the introductory address on the Bill in the House of Lords: '. . . when you are dealing with such people and Princes as those of India, there is a great deal in a name, and the name of Empress does convey to their minds the position which Her Majesty justly and legitimately holds more than any other title she could assume.'[15] That this general argument was accepted by the Opposition also, but to prove a different point, is shown in Samuelson's denial of the necessity to complete or recognize 'the transfer of the dominion of India from the East India Company to the Crown'.[16]

The second argument advanced in favour of the new title was that it would show the British determination to maintain the Empire and repudiate the doctrines of the Little Englanders. Disraeli spoke very clearly on this point:

> I cannot myself doubt that it [the title] is one also that will be agreeable to the people of the United Kingdom; because they must feel that such a step gives a seal, as it were, to that sentiment which has long existed, and the strength of which has been increased by time, and that it is the unanimous determination of the people of this country to retain our connection with the British Empire. And it will be an answer to those mere economists and those foreign diplomatists who announce to us that India is to us only a burden or a danger. By passing this Bill, then, and enabling Her Majesty to take this step, the House will show, in a manner that is unmistakable, that they look upon India as one of the most precious possessions of the Crown, and their pride that it is a part of Her Empire and governed by Her Imperial Throne.[17]

The third argument in favour of the Bill was more gentle and sentimental in tone. Sir George Bowyer, for example, asserted that the Bill would give great satisfaction in India, for it would spread the feeling there that England took pride in India, that England was beginning to have a deeper interest in the welfare of India, and that 'we are anxious that our rule there should be one of strict justice. . . .'[18] Disraeli stated that the Bill would show 'that there is a sympathetic chord between us and them. . .'.[19] Even that 'enfant terrible' of the House, John A. Roebuck, agreed that the Bill was an opportunity for 'the people of England to express kindness and good feeling toward the people of India'.[20]

The fourth argument maintained that the new title would attach the Indian people and princes directly to the Crown, and thus clarify the exact nature of the relations between the political power in India and that in Great Britain. This aspect of the Bill was obvious to everyone who participated in the discussion and only one or two variants of the argument will be given here. Sir George Campbell, acknowledged as a leading authority on India, asserted that he desired a title that would mark the imperial character of British rule, and show the Queen to be 'superior to all other power in India'.[21] Sir George Bowyer emphasized another aspect of this argument when he stated that the Bill would convince the Indian people that the British desired to continue long 'to possess her [India] to be an honour and a glory to the Imperial Crown'.[22] Lord Elcho stated on this point that '. . . he hoped that the effect of the assumption of the new title would be to strengthen and consolidate our paramount power in the East, and that it would draw still closer the ties which united the Empire of India to the United Kingdom.'[23]

Argument five maintained that the new title would act as a symbol of unity and stability between England and India. Disraeli almost reached lyrical heights in speaking of the term 'Empress' as a symbol of stability in India:

> The population of India is not the population it was when we carried the Bill of 1858. There has been a great change in the habits of the people. That which the Press could not do, that which our influence had failed in doing, the introduction of railroads has done, and the people of India move about in a manner which never could have been anticipated, and are influenced by ideas and knowledge which

> before never reached or touched them. . . . The nations and populations that can pronounce the word Emperor, and that habitually use it, will not be slow to accept the title of Empress. That is the word which will be adopted by the nations and population of India, and in announcing, as Her Majesty will do, by her Proclamation, that she adopts that title, confidence will be given to her Empire in that part of the world, and it will be spoken in language that cannot be mistaken that the Parliament of England have resolved to uphold the Empire of India.[24]

Lord Napier and Ettrick, referring to the title as a stabilizing factor, stated that, 'He believed that the assumption of the proposed title by the Queen would have a salutary and confirmatory effect in persuading our Indian fellow-subjects that their lot was cast in for ever with the fortunes of England. . . .'[25]

The sixth argument, one which was vigorously debated, revolved around statements that the people and princes of India quite definitely wanted the new title. Although no evidence was ever offered to prove this assertion—reasons of public policy, it was said, forbade citation of the evidence—almost every important speaker in favour of the Bill maintained that the people and princes of India wanted the new title—Disraeli, Northcote, Bowyer, the Duke of Richmond and Gordon, Lord Napier and Ettrick, the Marquis of Salisbury and the Lord Chancellor, all emphasized this point. For example, Disraeli flatly stated, 'It is desired in India. It is anxiously expected. . . . They know in India what this Bill means, and they know that what it means is what they wish.'[26] Lord Northcote, in answer to a question whether the Indians had been consulted, replied that the Indians wanted it.[27]

The seventh argument is linked very closely with the second and the last, since it asserted that the Bill would warn all powers that Great Britain never would stand for encroachments on her power in India. Lord Napier and Ettrick expressed this when he

> . . . ventured to say that both in foreign countries and in India the impression had been gaining of late years that this country was not prepared to resume those risks and to make those sacrifices which it had done in the past to preserve the dignity of the Crown and the entirety of the Empire.

He thought the assumption of a new title would be a good warning to

Europe and India that Britain was resolved to possess India forever.[28] Disraeli asked the House not '. . . to let Europe suppose for a moment that there are any in this House who are not deeply conscious of the importance of our Indian Empire. . . . I will not believe that any Member of this House seriously contemplates the loss of our Indian Empire.'[29] And, finally, Northcote urged the Members, '. . . let us show tonight that we have no fear that we shall lose our Indian Empire, or ever be compelled to retrace the step we are now adopting.'[30]

The last major argument in favour of the Bill asserted that it would counteract the influence of the Russian Empire in India, both symbolically and politically, and serve as a warning to the Tsar. The discussion in Parliament on such a delicate subject was extraordinarily forthright. Northcote, the Chancellor of the Exchequer, declared that Oriental peoples attached 'an enormous value . . . to very slight distinctions'. The Queen, he maintained, should not be forced to have her prestige suffer in India by the assumption of a title or 'use of language signifying that she holds a less exalted position than any other Sovereign'. The people of Central Asia, he went on to say,

> . . . are continually brought into close relations with the Natives of India, and throughout all those countries there is one Power in particular which exercises a great and deserved influence. Is it well that to the Emperor of Russia should be given in those countries a title which appears to the people there to be higher and greater than the title borne by the Queen? The announcement has been made that it is Her Majesty's wish to mark the visit of the Prince of Wales to India by taking some title which should seem to connect that country more closely with our own; and after this first step has been taken, will anybody be satisfied that she should adopt a title which may appear in the eyes of the people of India to be lower than the title of the Emperor of Russia?[31]

Disraeli openly stated the whole position on this point when he said,

> But while we have been pondering and legislating [in recent years on colonial self-government] . . . there have been greater changes going on in the very heart of Asia than even the conquest of India itself, or the foundation of all our colonies. There is a country of vast extent, which has been known hitherto only by its having sent forth hordes to conquer the world. That country has at last been

> vanquished, and the frontiers of Russia—I will not say a rival Power, but the frontiers of Russia—are only a few days march from those of Her Majesty's dominions in India. . . . But whatever may be my confidence in the destiny of England, I know that Empires are only maintained by vigilance, by firmness, by courage, by understanding the temper of the times in which we live, and by watching those significant indications which may easily be observed. . . . What was the gossip of bazaars is now the conversation of villages. You think they [the Indians] are ignorant of what is going on in Central Asia. You think they are unaware that Tartary, that great conquering Power of former times, is now at last conquered. No; not only do they know what has occurred, not only are they well acquainted with the Power which has accomplished this great change, but they know well the title of the Great Prince who has brought about so wonderful a revolution.[32]

In the Lords, the Earl of Feversham also gave expression to the fear of the Russian advance and the salutary effect of the new title in India.

> He would ask them [the Lords] to cast their eyes across the great Empire of India and observe the approach of the great Empire of Russia to our frontier. He did not say he was jealous of the approach of Russia, he believed the annexation of the barbarous countries of the East might tend to the civilization, or, at all events, to the increase of the trade and commerce of those countries, but he did not see why England and Russia—those two great Asiatic Powers—should not exist together upon terms of amity. But supposing the two Empires touched each other, or nearly so, would it not be an advantage that the people of India should be able to regard their supreme Ruler as occupying the same exalted position as the Emperor of Russia? It seemed to him that for this purpose it was desirable that our Sovereign should be styled 'Empress of India'.[33]

There is really no sharp and clear distinction which can be drawn between any one of these arguments and the others, for they all overlap and include one another. It is merely a question of what aspect of the Government's position the particular speaker chose to emphasize. In general, however, they all attempted to show that the new title would have a beneficial effect on the Indian princes and populace, would harmonize with their historical traditions and manner of thinking, and would bind them more closely to the Crown. It would also serve as a warning to European powers that England had no intention of giving up India, and it would certainly counteract the prestige and designs of the Russian Emperor in Central Asia and India.

There were four main arguments put forward by the Opposition against the Bill. (1) There was no precedent for it; thus it was against custom. (2) The titles of 'Emperor' and 'King' could not coexist, for the title of 'Emperor' would swallow up the title of 'King'; sycophants would use the title of 'Empress' even in the United Kingdom, where technically it was not to be used; and the attempt to employ both titles would only lead to confusion. (3) The major argument against the Bill was that the title of 'Empress' was despotic, military, and completely foreign and antagonistic to English feelings. (4) It was also argued that the Bill would be a slight to the colonies, since it incorporated India in the Royal Title but did not mention the colonies.

The first argument held that the Bill was without precedent and contrary to custom. On the very day that the Bill was introduced in the House of Commons, R. Lowe, who had been Chancellor of the Exchequer in the Gladstone Cabinet, 1868–74, attacked it vigorously. He asserted that George III in 1800 and Queen Victoria in 1858, both of whom had been advised by highly eminent statesmen, had rejected opportunities to assume the Imperial title. Both Palmerston and Derby in 1858 had

> . . . carefully considered the question and did not think it advisable to add anything to Her Majesty's title. In these matters, precedent goes for a great deal. . . . I question very much the expediency of breaking away from a custom established for so many centuries, in the matter of the title of our Sovereigns.[34]

In the House of Lords, the Duke of Somerset made more specific charges of this nature:

> I oppose this measure because I consider it contrary to the spirit of the Constitution. . . . I think it would be wiser to adhere to the Constitution. . . . Any change of the Royal Title ought to be carefully considered, and it ought not to be, as was one time said of a proposal of Mr Gladstone's, 'a fantastic innovation'. What is this addition to the Royal title but a fantastic innovation? Who has asked for it? Who wants it?[35]

The first part of the argument that the titles of 'Emperor' and 'King' could not co-exist was advanced by Gladstone. Conceding that there had never been any absolute diplomatic ruling on the relation of the two titles in regard to precedence, Gladstone declared that whenever the two titles had come into competition, 'King' had almost always been absorbed by 'Emperor' or had taken second place. Thus, as titles of the Emperor of Austria, 'King of Hungary' and 'King of the Romans' had almost always been subordinate to the title 'Emperor of Austria'. At present, the title 'Emperor of Germany' is ranked above the title 'King of Prussia'. When applied to the present question, Gladstone asked, shall it be that the sovereign of the United Kingdom shall take the title of 'Queen' from the superior, principal and central dominion [i.e. Great Britain] and the title 'Empress' from a secondary dominion?[36] The argument that sycophants would emphasize the title of 'Empress' rather than 'Queen' was frequently used, but never more bluntly than by the Duke of Somerset:

> Why, every sycophant will hasten to use the [new] title—we should somehow or other in the Act of Parliament provide that the title shall not be used in England. I do not believe its use can be so limited, and I can only say this—that one Peer at least shall raise his voice against a measure which cannot, in my opinion, have any other effect than the humiliation of the Crown.[37]

It was also urged in this connection that the titles 'Emperor' and 'King' could not co-exist for it would only cause confusion. Lowe maintained that the title 'King of England' already had an imperial character, and hence calling Her Majesty Queen in one place and Empress in another would mean calling the same thing by two different names—'To designate the same thing in different ways can only lead to confusion and mischief.'[38]

The major argument advanced by the Opposition, however, was that the title 'Empress' was despotic, military and un-English. Almost every speaker against the Bill used this argument in one form or another; it will, therefore, be possible to quote only a few outstanding examples. Lowe declared that the title 'King' carried the meaning that 'The King ought to be under the law for the law makes the King'; the title 'Emperor' such meanings as 'in all things the will of the Emperor is to be accepted', and that an emperor 'is one who has gained power by the sword, and that he holds it by the sword'.[39] George

Anderson, of Glasgow, stated outright that 'Empress' was a despotic title, and that he sincerely hoped no attempt would be made to add it to the titles of the Sovereign.[40] Gladstone believed the title 'Emperor' was stamped with bad associations—Emperors have been exempt from the control of law; Emperors were generally not hereditary monarchs like kings, but usurpers; Emperorship means despotism, 'the undefined exercise of will'.[41] Samuelson spoke vehemently on this point:

> The right Hon. Gentleman [Disraeli] had endeavoured to explain away the prejudices which existed against the title of Emperor, and had referred to the time of the Antonines. Instead of going back to that time, some 1700 years ago, it would have been much better had he devoted his attention to the events of the present time, when he would have discovered why the title of Emperor was not consonant with the feelings of the people of this country. He need not remind the House of the antecedents of the Second Empire in a neighbouring country in our own days—how it was founded in the orgies of the Camp of Satory—how it was confirmed by the slaughter and the barricades of Paris, and how it ended ingloriously in the catastrophe of Sedan. With regard to the German Empire, whatever might be the facts in reference to the policy of its creation it has been contemporaneous with an outbreak of religious strife between Catholics and Protestants.[42]

The un-English character of the title of 'Empress' was brought out with great force by Sir William Harcourt.

> He believed that the English nation would rather see their Sovereign the first and most ancient Queen, than the last and newest Empress. They might say, 'What's in a name?' In these things there was everything in a name. Association and sympathy gathered round these ancient names, and it was these things that constituted a national spirit, and the continuity of national life. Patriotism and loyalty, sentiments the strongest and the best in their nature, were made up of these ancient associations. It was for these things that the 'great men have been proud to live, and good men have dared to die'. . . . The English people were of a noble and a simple temper, and they preferred the substance of ancient greatness to the glitter of modern names.[43]

In a brilliant, and perhaps the most powerful of all the

addresses on the Bill, the Earl of Shaftesbury, in the House of Lords, declared:

> There are many things at the present time to gild the title of Empress. It would be held by an illustrious lady who has reigned for nearly forty years, known and beloved; it bears, too, an impression of feminine softness; but as soon as it shall have assumed the masculine gender, and have become an Emperor, the whole aspect will be changed. It will have an air military, despotic, and offensive and intolerable, alike in the East and West of the dominions of England. . . Why, here is a letter received only a day ago from a body of miners —'We may be,' say they—'Insignificant men, but we have sense of honour enough to hold in contempt which we cannot express, those who are endeavouring to attach the title of Empress to that of our Royal Queen'. . . . Loyalty is a sentiment; and the same sentiment that attaches the people to the word 'Queen' averts them from the word 'Empress'. We saw the force of loyalty exhibited in 1848. What Throne or Empire was undisturbed but the Throne of England? And why? . . . There were many agitators abroad who urged them [the people] to look across the Atlantic, and there see a Republic in the height of power, freedom, and prosperity. 'And why not here?' said they. 'No', replied the people. 'We hold to the traditions of a thousand years.' 'Kings have been our nursing fathers and Queens our nursing mothers'; the Crown of Alfred, the Edwards, Elizabeth, and George III, is worn now by Queen Victoria. ''We want none of your revolutionary doctrines', said they; 'and now', say we, 'we want none of your Imperial diadems of yesterday.' Destroy this sentiment and where are we?[44]

Conclusion

It has, I think, been shown that, although the whole background of internal, Indian and international developments prepared the way for the introduction and passage of the Royal Titles Bill, nevertheless, the actual discussion in Parliament centered about the symbol itself—whether the new title would evoke the proper and desired responses in England and India, and thus serve the larger purposes for which the Bill was originally introduced. The friends of the Bill endeavoured to show that the new title would serve as a warning to Russia and the other powers, and would not only harmonize with traditional Indian modes of thinking, but would also act as a unifying and stabilizing symbol in India. The opponents, on the other hand, drew their arguments from the English situation exclusively, attempting to prove that the word 'Empress' was a 'bad' word in England—that it was not in harmony with English modes of thinking and would thus evoke the 'wrong' responses, would have a disintegrating, rather than a unifying, effect. The Government, in reply, tried to show that the new symbol would not antagonize Englishmen, that it was not unprecedented, but connected with the historical traditions and rhetoric of the English monarchy. The Government's final victory was by no means overwhelming, and many members spoke and voted against the Bill even though they knew that the Queen herself ardently desired its passage. Victoria never forgave many of these members.

Notes and References

1 Hansard, *Parliamentary Debates*, Third Series, Vol. 227, pp. 424–25.

2 For both the expenditures on the army and the investment of British capital in India, see Leland H. Jenks, *The Migration of British Capital to 1975*, New York, 1927; for capital investment, Charles K. Hobson, *The Export of Capital*, London School of Economics and Political Science Studies, No. 38, London, 1914; for the economic development of India in this period, consult Romesh C. Dutt, *The Economic History of India in the Victorian Age . . .*, second edn, London, 1906; and Daniel H. Buchanan, *The Development of Capitalistic Enterprise in India*, New York, 1934.

3 Hansard, Vol. 228, p. 500; Disraeli.

4 Hansard, Vol. 228, p. 501.

5 See Kingsley Martin in the *Edinburgh Review*, Vol. 243, April 1926, p. 384; and for a more detailed analysis, Max Weber, *General Economic History*, New York, 1927, and *Gesammelte Aufsatze zur Religionssoziologie*, Vol. II; also, Hansard, Vol. 228, pp. 500–01.

6 For a brief description of how these factors operated, see Parker T. Moon, *Imperialism and World Politics*, Ch. II, New York, 1926.

7 See Carl A. Bodelsen, *Studies in Mid-Victorian Imperialism*, London, 1924.

8 Frank Hardie, *The Political Influence of Queen Victoria, 1861–1901*, London, 1935.

9 William F. Monypenny and George E. Buckle, *The Life of Benjamin Disraeli*, V, London, 1920; *Letters of Queen Victoria*, Second Series, Vol. II, New York, 1926.

10 Hansard, Vol. 227, p. 4.

11 Ibid., p.19.

12 Ibid., pp. 66–67.

[13] Ibid., p. 420.
[14] Ibid., p. 1724.
[15] Hansard, Vol. 228, p. 826.
[16] Hansard, Vol. 227, p. 1728; cf. Vol. 228, p. 90.
[17] Hansard, Vol. 227, p. 410. For further examples of this argument, see Hansard, Vol. 227, pp. 417, 420, 1727; and Vol. 228, pp. 88, 825–26.
[18] Hansard, Vol. 227, p. 420.
[19] Ibid., p. 1727.
[20] Hansard, Vol. 228, p. 129.
[21] Hansard, Vol. 227, p. 418.
[22] Ibid., p. 420.
[23] Hansard, Vol. 228, p. 135.
[24] Ibid., pp. 500–01.
[25] Ibid., p. 836.
[26] Hansard, Vol. 227, p. 1727.
[27] Ibid., pp. 1749–50.
[28] Hansard, Vol. 228, p. 836.
[29] Hansard, Vol. 227, p. 1727.
[30] Ibid., p. 1752.
[31] Ibid., pp. 1750–51.
[32] Hansard, Vol. 228, pp. 500–01.
[33] Ibid., p. 1080.
[34] Hansard, Vol. 227, p. 413.
[35] Hansard, Vol. 228, pp. 833–34.
[36] Hansard, Vol. 227, pp. 1741–42.
[37] Hansard, Vol. 228, p. 834.
[38] Hansard, Vol. 227, p. 412.
[39] Ibid., p. 413.
[40] Ibid., pp. 423–24.
[41] Ibid., pp. 1741–44.
[42] Ibid., pp. 1728–29.
[43] Hansard, Vol. 228, pp. 105–06.
[44] Ibid., pp. 1042–45.

The Agrarian Question and Development of Capitalism in India

Utsa Patnaik

As one re-reads Daniel Thorner's writings of the fifties and sixties today, one is struck by the remarkable insight they showed into the essential features of India's agrarian structure and growth problems.[1] I think this was because Thorner had that rare combination of a thorough knowledge of the theoretical debates over the peasantry and the agrarian question, which raged in Eastern Europe and Russia from a century ago to the twenties, and an intensive knowledge of India's economic evolution in the colonial period: a combination few academics can match to this day.

In the mid-fifties' lectures delivered in Delhi and collected together in *The Agrarian Prospect in India*, Thorner coined the term 'the built-in depressor' to denote that complex of agrarian relations which made it paying for landlords to live on extracting rent, usurious interest and trading profit out of an impoverished peasantry, rather than go in for productivity-raising investment.[2] In one way or another, the question of how exactly technical change and growth in agriculture are inhibited by the 'built-in depressor' (and the related question of the conditions under which the 'depressor' ceases to operate) has been the focus of much academic writing since then.

In the same book, Thorner suggested a three-fold classification of the rural population drawing a living from the land, into *mazdoor, kisan* and *malik*. The *maliks* he defined as those landed proprietors who derive their income by employing tenants or labourers, the *kisans* as those cultivators who 'live primarily by their own toil on their

This is the text of the First Daniel Thorner Memorial Lecture, delivered at the Nehru Memorial Museum and Library, New Delhi, on 20 April 1985. It was first published in *Economic and Political Weekly*, Vol. XXI, No. 18, 3 May 1986.

own lands', and the *mazdoors* as 'those villagers who gain their livelihood primarily from working on other people's land'. As he himself stated, 'the key to the division is the amount of actual labour contributed to the production process and the share in the product. The extent to which income is received despite lack of participation in agricultural work may well be an index of the severity of the agrarian problem.'[3]

Although Thorner was not one for labels, it would be true to say that what he was putting forward was essentially a Marxist concept of social class, in the emphasis he placed on possession of land and the consequent relations of labour-hiring and land-renting generated between the proprietory *maliks* and landless *mazdoors*, with the *kisans* occupying the classically intermediate Chayanovian space between the two.[4] What was missing was possibly a more detailed characterization within the broad groups delineated. Towards the last years of his life, Thorner's perspective on the agrarian question in India appears to have altered inasmuch as he advocated the applicability of Chayanov's category of 'peasant economy in India'. Nevertheless, I think Thorner would have been glad to know that attempts have been made, since he formulated his three-class typology, to operationalize the concept of class, that is, to capture it in an empirically applicable form in order to quantify class characteristics and eventually capture the structural changes of rural society.[5]

The insight which drew the greatest attention, however, was put forward by Thorner after a series of field visits to villages in 1966–67 when, in his own words, he saw 'new forces at work', 'a distinct emergence of a nation-wide class of capitalist producers'. Particularly striking, for him, was what he described as a veritable 'gold-rush to the countryside' of gentlemen-farmers, often from the professions, attracted by the high profit rate of capitalist agricultural production.[6] Incidentally, some researchers have subsequently argued on the basis of survey data that the proportion of such gentlemen-farmers entering agriculture from the professions was very small, for example, not more than 5 per cent in Punjab. The important thing, however, is that the very fact of the flow of non-agricultural funds into productive agricultural investment marked a qualitative shift in the agrarian cost–profit configuration.

When the discussion on the nature and the extent of the capitalist tendency had developed by the mid-seventies to a point where some participants were talking in terms of a 'green revolution', while others warned that the 'green revolution' might turn red if its gains continued to be inequitably distributed, Thorner retorted pithily that the colour of the revolution he saw was neither green nor red, but steel-grey. India was industrializing, and the agrarian changes were a consequence of this: again, a perfectly valid insight but one which perhaps required a much more detailed specification and analysis of the character of India's industrialization strategy and its impact upon agrarian relations. The paths of transition to capitalist industrialization are many, after all, and a single unique path is not predetermined by the initial conditions.

I would like to develop here some of these important themes which Thorner initiated: what has been the precise nature of the 'built-in depressor'; what have been the circumstances and the reasons for the cessation of its operation at least in certain cropping regimes in certain parts of the country; in what ways has the development strategy followed under the plans in the fifties, sixties and seventies impinged upon and altered agrarian relations; and what is likely to be the reciprocal effects of the way that agrarian relations have been affected upon the rate and structure of industrialization? At the end of some quarter century of the growth of the capitalist tendency in rural areas, where are we today with respect to the so-called 'mode of production' controversy? These are some of the questions which require to be raised, even though we may not yet be in a position to provide all the answers in a satisfactory manner.

The Rent Barrier

If the study of history is any guide, the process of growth of agrarian capitalism is seldom initiated by developments within a narrowly conceived agrarian sector alone; it appears to require also exogenous stimuli, of which the most important is the growth of the market. The sixteenth-century Tudor enclosures, and later the much more widespread eighteenth-century enclosures in Britain, were stimulated by the expanding export demand for wool and the growing internal demand for food respectively.[7] The striking feature of the seven decades before independence in India, for which data are available, is the remarkable stagnation of the domestic market for foodgrains which made up 80 per cent of agricultural production.

Foodgrains output overall virtually remained constant and per capita production declined—as did availability in every region, even in the most dynamic area, Punjab.[8] Only exportable primary products, including an exported foodgrain like wheat, registered a fair rate of expansion under the colonial government's policies of promoting exports as the commodity equivalent of the transfer abroad of a part of the taxation revenues.[9] The stagnation of the domestic market for foodgrains was a logical consequence of the colonial government's subserving of Indian interests to the requirements of Empire, to which end a specific set of domestic fiscal, monetary and trade policies were directed. Since every year a part of the taxation revenue was transferred abroad, in effect the government operated a surplus budget, with a consequent deflationary impact on the domestic economy, sustained year after year. Because exports represented tax-financed transfer of tribute, they had little or no multiplier effects on the domestic economy, especially since exportable commercial crops were not in addition to but largely substituted for foodgrains in the absence of adequate cultivable land.[10]

Given the very slow expansion of modern industry in an open colonial economy, the occupational distribution of the work force at best remained static and at worst changed to a slight proportionate increase in the burden on the primary sector.[11] The absolute numbers of people forced to draw a living from the land rose sharply, the land–man ratio declined, and an acutely underemployed surplus population was the result; which, as tenants, bid up the rents of land to hunger-rent levels, and as labourers, were forced to accept bare subsistence wages and debt bondage. The familiar pre-independence unholy trinity of the landlord–moneylender–trader (sometimes combining the three functional attributes in a single entity, as in the Trimurti of Brahma–Vishnu–Maheshwara, and sometimes remaining separate entities) acquired a strangehold over the peasantry. There emerged a formidable barrier to productive investment along capitalist lines, constituted by the barrier of precapitalist ground rent to capitalist investment.

Thorner's 'built-in depressor' operated in the following way. His *maliks* or non-cultivating proprietors concentrated some 70 per cent of owned area in their hands though they made up hardly 10 to 15 per cent of households. Such a landlord obtained on average about 50 per cent of the gross product as rent by leasing out to land-hungry tenants who bore all costs of cultivation. This rental income represented a 'return' to land monopoly *per se*, and had nothing to do with either any outlay of capital in the production process or participation in labour. At the same time the landlords were virtually the only people living off the land who had any liquid investible funds, which they put usually into trade and usury, and rarely into agro-based industry. In order to switch from leasing out and living as rentiers to direct capitalist cultivation, such a landlord would have to invest money in agricultural production, money which already got him a return elsewhere, and also withdraw land from tenants, land which already, without any outlay, got him a return by way of absolute ground rent.

It follows that by investing a given sum of money Rs M in direct cultivation of a unit of land it would not be enough if only the return Rs Pc at r_u per cent, which that sum would have otherwise earned (in usury, etc.) is obtained: a surplus profit over and above Rs Pc, equal at least to Rs R, the rent foregone on the withdrawn unit of land, is required. The rate of profit Pc in direct capitalist cultivation must therefore, *at least* be

$$Pc \geq \frac{R + P. \ 100}{M}$$

This represents a very high profit rate for precapitalist ground rent R is itself very large, representing usually the entire surplus product that can be wrung from a unit of land by the unremitting labour of the petty tenant.

Looked at another way, the constraint can be reformulated as follows:

$$Pc \geq r_t + r_u$$

where Pc is the profit rate in direct cultivation, r_t the rental amount payable expressed as a percentage of expenditures on cultivation by the tenant, r_u the return to money capital in the economy (to which the return to moneylending can be taken as the closest approximation in this case). The constraint is that by undertaking investment at the same technical level as (that operated by) the petty tenant, the landlord can at most hope to get a return $R/M = r_t$ on his capital (but in fact usually less, for costs of supervising hired labour and paying the market wage rate are likely to lower the surplus compared to what a small tenant underpaying family labour can obtain) but this sum Rs R the landlord has been getting anyway *without* any expenditure, and by virtue of his legal land title alone, as rent. For investing money in direct cultivation to make economic sense as compared to investing it elsewhere, therefore, the landlord must obtain not just r_u but at least $(r_t + r_u)$ on his capital outlay, that is, achieve a discrete rise in the surplus per unit of area. This is impossible unless the investment embodies productivity-raising new techniques, or better ways of organizing production, which raises surplus per unit of area by the required quantum. A quantum jump in yields is required for the rent barrier to be overcome, so that investible funds are directed into capitalist agriculture production.

Looked at in this way, that is, conceptualized in terms of a logical extension of Marx's argument on the barrier of ground rent to capitalist production,[12] the 'built-in depressor' is indeed seen as built into the agrarian structure of land monopoly and hunger rents: but, at the same time, under certain stringent conditions of technical change, it is capable of being overcome, initiating a narrowly-based tendency towards landlord capitalism, as has occurred in our country.

One fundamental way of not only overcoming but abolishing the rent barrier once and for all time, is through the doing away of absolute rent as a social category, as in an agrarian reform where the landlords' monopoly is broken through seizure of their land without compensation and its redistribution to the cultivating peasantry. This was the more revolutionary path of transition followed in the classic French Revolution and repeated in more modern times by the 1917 Revolution in Russia, in the Chinese land reform from the 1940s and, in a more attenuated form, in post-war Japan.

Landlord Capitalism

In India, however, it is the conservative path of Junker-style landlord capitalism which has been promoted in the three decades of agrarian reforms. Effective land monopoly has been preserved, while curbing the excesses of absentee ownership and illegal exactions, by allowing the ex-intermediaries to retain very large areas as their home farms or *khudkasht*, or by permitting tenant evictions on the pleas of direct cultivation through hired labour and conferring transferable ownership to these areas, while compensating generously with bonds and cash for the relatively small areas taken over by the state. Not the French model but the model of Meiji Japan, in which the feudal *daimyo* were compensated by bonds to emerge as 'financial magnates', and the village-level *oyakata* conferred ownership: this is the closest parallel to the Indian reforms. The big feudal potentates corresponding to the *daimyo* have gone into business, shipping and politics; the village-level zamindars are the modern landlord capitalists.

If the NSS data on land ownership for the 8th Round, 1953–54, and 26th Round, 1970–71, are compared, we find that concentration as measured by the Gini coefficients is unchanged: the value of the Gini coefficient was 0.676 at the earlier data and 0.675 two decades and many Reform Acts later. In certain states, notably Bihar, Punjab and Gujarat, ownership concentration had increased, while in others, notably West Bengal, Kerala and Karnataka, it had declined slightly.[13] The Gini coefficient, however, measures only the distribution of land over the set of recorded owners, and lack of change in it is consistent with an unfavourable change in the composition of the set itself. First, fictitious transfers and partitions have taken place; second, over the same time-period, the proportion of agricultural labourers in the total of cultivators and labourers has risen substantially (although a precise estimate is difficult because of underestimation of labourers in the 1951 Census and overestimation in the 1971 Census). If we accept Thorner's criticisms in his paper entitled 'India's Agrarian Revolution by Census Redefinition',[14] and put as he did the percentage of labourers in 1951 at somewhere around 28 per cent, then by 1971 it had risen to at least 35 per cent (though the 1971 Census yields over 37 per cent, this is widely thought to be an overestimate for definition reasons) and to 37 per cent by 1981. For these reasons the distribution of land ownership over the entire population dependent on agriculture is likely to have worsened slightly.

The series of evaluation reports sponsored by the Research Programmes Committee of the Planning Commission show, almost without exception, that mass evictions were the fate of the middling to poorer categories of tenants, a high proportion of whom had no cultivable land after eviction: they were either re-employed as unrecorded tenants-at-will or joined the ranks of wage paid labour.[15] At the other pole of the peasant class structure, a handful of the well-to-do, rich peasant owner-cum-tenants could raise the funds required to purchase ownership of land vested with the state, improve their economic position by expanding the scale of operation, and in many cases withdraw entirely from direct participation in labour.

Our land reforms have had the effect of redistributing some

land within the top two, at most three deciles of owners ranked by area, while augmenting through eviction, the class of rural labourers. In the process, at one pole of the village class structure, in some areas, the hitherto separate elements, the landlords and a section of the rich peasants, are being 'melted down and transfused'[16] into the as-yet-not homogeneous class which Thorner discerned in the process of formation, namely the rural capitalists; at the other pole, the traditionally landless, Harijan bonded labourers and the displaced poorer peasants form elements of a hesitantly emerging class, the rural proletariat.[17]

Since the more revolutionary path of overcoming the barrier of ground rent through the radical break-up of land monopoly has never been on the official agenda in our country, questions arise regarding the factors which have been conducive to the emergence of capitalist investment by landlords in direct cultivation with hired labour, and regarding the reasons for the extreme spatial unevenness of this capitalist tendency—which spawns academic models of 'semi-feudalism' from Bengal and roseate visions of generalized green revolution from Punjab.[18] Apart from the land reforms, there appear to have been two major sets of exogenous stimuli acting on the agrarian sector, particularly in the first quarter century after independence, 1950 to 1975: first, the marked expansion in the domestic market for foodgrains following large-scale state expenditures under the Plans, leading in turn to a shift in the agriculture–manufacturing terms of trade and a marked rise in the proportion of output marketed; and second, the complex of state-sponsored schemes for extending rural credit, disbursing at subsidized rates the new technology package involving fertilizer-fed high-yielding varieties under the 'new agricultural strategy' from the early sixties. While the consequences of both sets of stimuli are well known, a brief recapitulation from the point of view of their effects on the capitalist tendency, may not be out of place.

Impact of Development Strategy

The post-independence thrust of planned development, marked for the first time in India's modern history by a large increase in state expenditure and by deficit budgets, was analysed perceptively by the noted Polish economist Michal Kalecki. Writing and lecturing in Delhi during the mid-fifties, at a time when prices were still declining from the Korean war boom years, Kalecki warned that inflationary pressures were bound to emerge in the course of financing planned development in India, owing primarily to the class nature of the state. For a non-inflationary growth path initiated by state investment, it was necessary that agricultural production should grow at a commensurate rate and that investible resources should be raised through direct taxation of property incomes and indirect taxation of luxuries.

The state, however, would find it politically difficult either to reform drastically the agrarian structure and remove the fetters of landlordism on output growth, or to tax directly the incomes or indirectly the luxury consumption of landlords and capitalists to the required extent. The Plan expenditures, being initially in infrastructural and other areas with a high unskilled labour component, would generate a rapid expansion in the demand for necessities, while an unreformed agrarian structure would be unable to supply the most important necessity, foodgrains, at the required rate, leading to inflation in foodgrains prices in the first instance followed by inflation also in prices of manufactured necessities, the latter determined by the position with respect to excess capacity and supply of the raw material.

The Plan expenditures would therefore be financed in large part out of the forced savings of the wage earners and fixed income earners undergoing a cut in real incomes with inflation, while simultaneously the landlords and manufacturing capitalists monopolizing commodity sales would enjoy a profit inflation.[19] Kalecki's theoretical scenario has been fully borne out by the overall pattern of Plan financing in the last three decades, initiating an inflationary spiral from the Second Plan period.[20] Far from taxing property incomes or imposing indirect taxes on luxuries alone, progressively greater reliance has been placed by government on indirect taxation of necessities (all indirect taxes after the latest Budget account for over 85 per cent of tax revenues) and on inflationary credit financing, of which 'deficit financing' in the excessively narrow sense used in our country, forms only a part. An additional important factor, operative from the mid-sixties, has been the setting of administered floor prices to foodgrains by way of procurement prices by the Agricultural Prices Commission, which has reinforced the ratchet effect in price rise. Endemic inflation has been built into the structure of Plan financing, and so have the expectations of a continuing inflationary climate.

It has been argued that the very attempt to raise resources for the public sector by passing the burden onto the masses, rather than going for the harder option of tapping property incomes also has the unplanned effect of raising the private share of total surplus in the economy. An important distinction here is between tax-financed and credit-financed expenditures. While indirect taxes are highly regressive (the Indirect Taxes Enquiry Committee estimated that as much as 55 per cent of total indirect taxes in 1973–74 was paid by households with a monthly per capita expenditure of Rs 100 or less), such taxes do transfer purchasing power directly to the state at the expense of the mass of the people. But with credit-financed expenditures (which includes not only deficit finance in the technical sense[21] but government borrowing from the commercial banks), purchasing power is transferred from the mass of the people *via* inflation in necessities prices, to the landlords and the capitalists.[22]

Since a large part of the manufacturing labour force is unorganized, while agricultural workers are almost entirely unorganized, every theoretical consideration points to a worsening of income distribution, particularly in rural areas, over social classes.

The failure of the Indian state to raise resources for investment from the rural sector in particular is highly paradoxical in the light of the fact that for many decades before independence, indeed beginning from 1765, the transfer of a large part of India's taxation revenues (constituted then and up to the first war mainly by the land revenue) abroad served materially to finance Britain's Industrial Revolution and later helped her to maintain her world dominance in trade and capital exports. (Estimates by Sayera Habib and, following her method, by myself, indicate that between a quarter to a third of UK's domestic capital formation was financed by the Indian tribute during the crucial decade 1795–1804.[23]) Yet the national state in independent India is unable to tap the agricultural surplus for its own industrialization effort.

During the period of early industrialization in Meiji Japan, between 1873 and 1888, as much as 76.6 per cent of total state revenues was contributed by the land tax, while in the next fifteen years, 1888 to 1902, the proportion remained very high at 44.4 per cent.[24] In post-liberation China, direct taxation of the cooperatives and later of the communes, never fell below 15 per cent of gross output; in addition, resources were transferred by maintaining a more adverse rate of exchange of farm against manufactured products, than would have prevailed under free market conditions.[25]

In India, however, not only has effective land monopoly been deliberately preserved, but the landlords and rural capitalists have been absolved of all responsibility for financing development. All direct taxes on agriculture taken together accounted for less than 1 per cent of the net national product from agriculture and contributed only 3 per cent of tax revenues in 1974–75,[26] while the burden of financing investment has been passed on to the rural and urban poor, *via* the cut in their real incomes inherent in the combination of inflation owing to large-scale credit financing, and indirect taxation.

The rural poor, comprising the agricultural labourers and the poor peasants, and making up at least 60 per cent of the rural population, are heavily dependent on the market for necessities including food. They have suffered a severe cut in real incomes, for they lost out as commodity purchasers to a far greater extent than some of them gained as commodity sellers. A comparison of the Third and Fourth Rural Labour Enquiries shows that while money wages have risen during 1963–64 to 1974–75, when adjusted by the consumer price index for agricultural labourers, real wages are seen to decline drastically in the case of females. Since days employed annually have also declined, real earnings have fallen even more than have real wage rates.

Given that the rural labourers are already at the margin of subsistence, the implication of real income falls of this magnitude may well be imagined; the logical result, according to the data in the same Enquiries, has been a sharp rise in rural indebtedness, a higher proportion of the loans being taken from moneylenders.[27] While we do not have clear-cut information for the poor peasants as for rural labour, they must logically have suffered a slightly smaller order of real income decline. These findings relate to the average for the whole of India. If it is true, as many scholars maintain, that real earnings of labour in the Punjab–Haryana region had not fallen during this period, it follows that the real income decline in other areas must have been even more drastic. The steady flow of Bihari and eastern UP migrant labour to the western Eldorado indicates the operation of considerable real earnings differentials.

The somewhat fallacious argument is sometimes put forward that since agricultural labourers are paid a substantial part of their wage in customary kind forms, such as grain and meals, they do not to that extent suffer a real income decline with inflation. Everything else remaining the same, the argument would be valid; but it does not take account of the employers' ingenuity. In an inflationary situation it is obviously in the landlord-capitalists' interest to shift to cash wage payment, while the labourers resist this and demand their wages in kind. In the course of field-work we found that employers were resorting to ingenious variations on the traditional wage payments system to maximize their gain. They fixed the wage payable to contract labour and farm-servants in cash, but paid it out in a combination of cash and the commodity equivalent of the balance, which being evaluated at rising prices would be falling over time.

The labourers, agreeing to work for wage payment in kind and food security, ultimately got lower real wages: the *form* of the payment of wages in kind here disguises the fact that it is being treated as the commodity equivalent of an amount fixed in cash. In effect, landlords were found to be taking advantage of what might be called a 'grain illusion' on the part of the labourers, an analogy with the Keynesian 'money illusion', in order to lower real wages. A less polite way of putting the same thing is that they were swindling the labourers with impunity.[28]

While industrial workers and salary-earners who are organized can resist the onslaught on their living standards inherent in inflationary financing, the unorganized workers in urban and rural areas face immiserization, except in a few pockets of resistance where there has been a history of organization. Indeed the maintenance of rural real wage rates has little to do with the overall growth rate in the region concerned. Some areas of medium to low growth, such as Thanjavur in Tamil Nadu, Kerala and West Bengal have seen a much smaller erosion in real wages than have higher-growth areas, owing to the existence of some trade union organization of labourers. What is urgently needed today is the unionization of rural labourers to avert a continuation of their total immiserization, which will have drastic consequences in the event of any possible output shortfall of the magnitude experienced in the mid-sixties.

Nothing has occurred during the last decade from 1975 to alter materially the position of rural labour. The inflation in food prices, in a trend sense, continues, while outside Punjab money wages do not appear to be rising faster than the inflation rate.

Up to the mid-seventies, the agriculture–manufacture terms of trade show a steadily widening 'scissors' in favour of agriculture, taking 1960 as the base. A sustained profit inflation not only helped to stimulate some degree of productive investment by landlords turning capitalist, but also induced a flow of urban funds into agriculture, which Thorner had noted: the peak rate of inflation was attained in 1974–75, just prior to the imposition of Emergency. The 'dear food policy' effectively operating then did not draw forth any overt resistance from the industrial capitalists on the classical analogy of the anti-landlord Free Trade agitation in nineteenth-century Britain, because the classical model of a laissez-faire state does not operate in the Indian economy. Through budgetary and other transfers on a massive scale, the manufacturing capitalists were and are being more than compensated for the effects of food-price rise in raising the cost of labour power.[29]

After 1975, in the last decade, on the whole, manufactured goods prices have tended to rise at a slightly faster rate than agricultural prices, narrowing—but not reversing—the 'scissors' with base 1960, (while with a shift of the base year to 1970, terms of trade are seen to deteriorate by about 13 per cent from 1975 up to 1978 and hold fairly steady subsequently).[30] However, a range of direct transfers to the rural rich as well as state expenditures which are little different from transfers have in the meantime taken place, of which the provision of credit at negative real interest rates, subsidized inputs, guaranteed remunerative procurement prices, and expenditures on the NREP (National Rural Employment Programme), IRDP (Intensive Rural Development Programme), etc., are elements. The last-named expenditures, ostensibly meant for the rural poor, also have a substantial spin-off in benefits for the rural rich through the building of infrastructural facilities such as roads, and through the contract work for materials transport under-taken by the tractor-and truck-owning landlords as well as supply of materials like bricks from landlord-owned brick kilns.

Uneven Development of the Capitalist Tendency

This brings us to the question of the uneven development of the capitalist tendency. While the profit inflation inherent in the regressive, inegalitarian pattern of Plan financing has provided a general stimulus to the capitalist tendency in rural areas everywhere, by itself it would perhaps not have promoted a long-term shift from rent to profit as the main form of surplus appropriation. This is because the increase in money profit arising from price rise alone can be matched, even if with a lag, by an increase in rents paid by petty tenants cutting their subsistence. The rent barrier is not overcome by giving price incentives to landlords. The experience of Meiji Japan again bears this out. Periods of rapid inflation in rice prices enriched the landlords drawing rent in kind from small tenants and themselves paying a land tax fixed in cash, with no incentive to switch to direct cultivation.[31]

While the expansion of the internal market is a necessary condition, it does not seem to be a sufficient condition for such a switch where a formidable rent barrier is operative. The sufficient condition is provided by the feasibility of capitalist investment which embodies new, productivity-raising techniques which permit a quantum jump in the yield and surplus per unit of area. (It may be noted that techniques which raise labour productivity while leaving land productivity unchanged, will usually not do the job of overcoming the rent barrier —for labour is only one element of agricultural production costs, whose return is already depressed to a minimum: relative surplus cannot be raised to a sufficient extent by cutting labour costs.)

What is required is land-augmenting technical progress, and this is precisely the character of the Borlaug fertilizer-fed hybrid seed, which has been successfully introduced in wheat and rice production under controlled irrigation in climatic belts with low atmospheric humidity. With the recommended water and fertilizer dosages, yields could be doubled, and even trebled; short-duration varieties also permitted multiple cropping. The consequent quantum jump in yield per unit of area, if it could be realized in the field, permitted a decisive overcoming of the rent barrier. (The actual average rate of profit on capital advanced—excluding land value—for a set of 66 large farms intensively studied in 1969, worked out to as high as 49 per cent. If the actual rent received on land leased out is taken as the guide, the rental element out of this amounted to 28 per cent, leaving an average profit of 19 per cent on capital, which compares very well with the profit on capital obtainable in the non-agricultural economy.)

The operative constraint on the spatial distribution of 'green revolution' technology has proved to be that of controlled irrigation and the prevalence of low atmospheric humidity with not-too-long periods of cloud cover, since only under such conditions can experimental yields be translated into field practice on a wide scale within the existing set of technology options. Largely for this reason, the required quantum jump in yields in foodgrains production is so far difficult to achieve in the high rainfall, high humidity coastal regions which had hitherto dominated in food production, but whose weight is going down over time as capitalist production develops more rapidly in the north and west of India. Up to the mid-seventies, widespread investment in new technology was limited to particular climate–soil–crop regimes, namely wheat production under a combination of canal and tube-well irrigation in the 'green revolution' belt stretching from western Uttar Pradesh through Haryana and Punjab, down to Gujarat and Rajasthan. In the case of paddy, irrigated low humidity pockets in peninsular India showed a dynamic trend.

It is therefore no accident but a reflection of relative profitability conditions that Punjab, which was the region *par excellence* of petty tenancy, high *batai* rents and indebtedness at the time that Henry Calvert and M.L. Darling wrote,[32] saw in the fifties and sixties a drastic eviction process affecting seven out of eight tenants, which reduced the number of recorded tenants from over 6 lakhs to only 0.83 lakh by 1966, while further evictions subsequently have reduced the area under tenancy to comparative insignificance.[33] By contrast, in Bengal small-scale crop-sharing tenancy still accounts for nearly one third of the area under rice. For the last decade, the climate–soil regime of vigorous capitalism has remained unchanged, but rice has emerged alongside wheat as an important commercial crop in the 'green revolution' belt. As a consequence of the extremely uneven development of the tendency of capitalist production, a marked region-wise concentration of growth has emerged.

This is too well known to need recapitulation, beyond noting that of the total increase of 32 million tonnes in foodgrains production during the ten years 1973–74 to 1982–83 inclusive, as much as 62 per cent has come from only five states: Uttar Pradesh, Haryana, Punjab, Gujarat and Rajasthan, which have raised their share of total food production from 35 per cent to 44 per cent. One-third of the total increase in rice production also has come from these states, which account today for 23 per cent of the total rice output compared to only 13 per cent a decade earlier. By contrast, the traditional paddy areas of Bihar, West Bengal, Tamil Nadu, Karnataka, Kerala have together added only 14 per cent to the rice output, and their weight in the total rice production has dropped from 45.4 per cent to 34.8 per cent.

The class-wise concentration of market supplies from

agriculture is more difficult to estimate accurately since no direct data are available. My estimate,[34] now outdated, on the basis of conservative assumptions for 1960–61 indicated that the top one-eighth of rural households, ranked by area, contributed about two-thirds of the total marketable surplus of foodgrains. The degree of concentration is likely to have risen over the next two decades because the top one-eighth have added at a faster rate to their output and surplus than others. At least 70 per cent to 75 per cent of market supplies is now likely to be on their account alone. Assured and rising food prices primarily benefit this small minority monopolizing the lion's share of the commodity surplus and give them super-profits, since, with the application of modern technology, they have been able to lower the unit cost of production.

The same price, on the other hand, barely covers the cost of production, including the family subsistence, of the middle and small peasants. The big landlord-capitalists have consistently pressed for, and obtained, the inclusion of imputed rent on owned land as an element of return on outlays for the purpose of calculating a 'fair' procurement price. Apart from involving recognition of their land monopoly, inclusion of rent in price is highly undesirable from the point of view of the inducement to go in for productivity-raising technical change which has been operative for landlords in the past, only because of the necessity of overcoming the rent barrier. A dual pricing policy would be the logical solution to the problem that the same procurement price gives super-profits to one category of producers, the landlord-capitalists, while it barely allows a subsistence income to the mass of poorer cultivators.

For those who point to the difficulties of operating a dual pricing system, a study of the experience in Japan after 1941 might be instructive. In order to procure foodgrains smoothly,

> the government held its general rice-buying price to yen 55 per *koku* (=180.4 kilolitres), at the same time it granted production increase subsidies to producers when it purchased rice directly from them but gave no such subsidies when purchasing from landlords. As a result, the producer's price had reached yen 245 per *koku* by 1945. Without waiting for a land reform, the tenant farmer system had been reduced to a mere shell.[35]

Discriminatory pricing thus favoured the direct producers in the ratio of 4 to 1 by 1945 and this measure was undertaken by a state which was far from liberal or anti-landlord, owing to the overriding imperative of increasing production and the marketed surplus.

Implications for Rate and Structure of Future Development

Let us now turn to the important, and little discussed, question of the implications of the spatially uneven and socially narrowly-based tendency of capitalist production, for the question of the rate and structure of future development in the economy as a whole and its agrarian sector in particular. The implications can be looked at in terms of three interrelated processes: the tendency to raise the rate of surplus extraction, among other things by utilizing caste-based relations of domination and servitude; the tendency towards a narrowing of the rural market for manufactured products of mass consumption; and the tendency towards a widening of the gap between the potential and actual productivity of agriculture.

A central idea of the discussion in Marxist literature on the less revolutionary transition path represented by landlord-capitalism is that, first, it is more painful in preserving the servile character of precapitalist employer–labourer relations, and second, the transition is also slower and more long-drawn owing to its narrow social base. With regard to the first aspect, the proposition may be put forward that not only are the traditional caste-based relations of domination and servitude preserved but indeed are deliberately used by landlords to ensure tractability of the labour force and the raising of the rate of surplus extraction through methods of increasing absolute surplus value. History offers us not a few instances where the superimposition of commercialization, of production for the market, upon traditional exploitative social relations, tends to lead to a strengthening of these relations on a servile basis, rather than heralding a transition to greater freedom of the worker.[36]

This appears to have been the essence of the 'semi-feudal capitalism' that Lenin talked about in the East European context of the transition of the feudal lord to capitalist farming using former serfs' labour.[37] Elements of a similar phenomenon of semi-feudal capitalism are visible in India's villages today. Caste has traditionally represented, amongst its other facets, a system of fragmenting those engaged in the production process into discrete groups differentiated by minute gradations of rights and obligations. The modern landlord-capitalists treat the Harijan labourer on worse terms than the pauperized peasants, because the very fact of Harijan status entails customary disadvantages; they treat the labourers of tribal origin worst of all, and this applies also to the most advanced areas. Research into the conditions of work of Bihari migrant labour in Punjab show, for example, that the labourers of tribal origin are systematically subjected by their capitalist employers to physical chastisement, are locked into their quarters at night to prevent their running away, and are paid wages which are lower and are more in arrears, while non-tribal labour tends to be less subject to physical coercion of this crude form. In short, every avenue of raising the rate of surplus extraction is utilized.[38]

As the expansion of output with the adoption of the 'green revolution' technology raises overall labour demand and imposes more stringent requirements with respect to the time distribution of labour inputs, it becomes important for the landlords to have labour power 'on tap' in the same way that irrigation water is 'on tap'. Methods of labour control begin to change in the direction of longer-term contracts which carry, built into them, debt bondage of a new type.[39] Given the increasingly desperate condition of rural labour, debt bondage may be expected to increase, not decrease, as the capitalist tendency develops. A reinforcing of servility and bondage is a logical corollary of the socially retrogressive character of landlord-capitalism.

The extent to which landlords are prepared to go to maintain their overwhelming socio-political dominance against any stirring of protest, is attested to by the increasing incidence of violent confrontations ending in Harijan burnings in recent years. Behind the facade of caste conflict lie basic issues of minimum wages and of land. The attempt to press for the legal minimum wage, even the provision of house-sites or distribution of barren surplus land to labourers, are seen as a direct threat to their domination by the landlord-capitalists, who require for their functioning a docile and tractable labour force. While at the time that Thorner was writing, the phrase 'Harijan burning' conjured up the isolated image of village Kilavenmani in Thanjavur district of Tamil Nadu (where on Christmas Day 1968, landlords' men burnt to death 42 men, women and children in the *paracheri* following wage disputes), today the phrase has become associated with the names of innumerable otherwise obscure villages scattered throughout the country: Belchi, Sharupur, Dehuli, Golana, and many others.

When the capitalist tendency develops within a fundamentally unreformed hierarchical and exploitative structure, the result is a subversion of the personal, patriarchal relations of that structure in the interests of profit, without at the same time a sufficiently large-scale productive transformation occurring which can lift the mass of labourers and peasants out of the morass of economic deprivation and social degradation in which it is steeped. In the course of field-work we interviewed a very cooperative landlord of Nanjangud taluk in Mysore district of Karnataka, who had a request to us in return: could we obtain for him a special make of revolver from Calcutta, which he needed to deal with the shiftless Harijan labourers (including those who worked for him), who were in the habit of stealing from his crops at night?

On the proposition that productive transformation does not occur under landlord-capitalism, it may be argued that in terms of overall agricultural production, India has, after all, done quite well. Food output has trebled between 1951 and 1984, from around 50 million tonnes to 150 million tonnes. China with her extremely egalitarian agrarian structure does not seem to have performed all that much better, it could be argued: it too has just over trebled its total food out-put, from 112 million tonnes in 1951 to 350 million tonnes by 1983.[40] Certainly, it is true that viewed in the perspective of long-term stagnation during the pre-independence period, our post-independence record has been impressive; but it is far short of the potential that could have been realized by now, given our very low initial yield levels.

After two decades of 'green revolution' and technical change under the aegis of landlord-capitalism, Indian agriculture today produces per unit of area less than one-third of the Chinese foodgrains yield, and two-thirds of China's output per capita. Since China started with a higher initial base than did India with respect to foodgrains yield (in 1951 they were double the Indian level) the achievement of a similar growth rate as in India was for it a much more difficult task (especially in the absence of cultivable wastes which sharply limited area expansion)—how difficult, we are now in a position to appreciate in this country, as the stimulus of the first round of yield-raising Borlaug technology tapers off.

The basic problem with continuing land monopoly and the reliance on landlord-capitalism is that it requires continuous stimuli by way of successive rounds of feasible technical change which can raise surplus per unit area by discrete quanta. A small or gradual improvement in productivity is not sufficient to induce investment, unlike the case with peasant capitalism. Once the potentialities of one round of yield-raising technical change have been realized, productive investment tends to level off and investible funds tend to flow back into socially unproductive forms of investment or into amassing durable consumption goods. This is a fundamental reason for a slower long-term growth rate of production within an unreformed agrarian structure, compared to the alternative path of a socially wide-based tendency of capitalist production developing from within a peasantry after a radical land redistribution. Recent unpublished research offers support for the theoretical expectation of a 'plateau' with respect to private productive investment in agriculture and indicates that the major uses of surplus now are in bank deposits and other financial assets—housing, education investment and durable consumption goods.

The growing resource crisis of the state, leading to a cutback in real terms in the rate of capital formation, affects the agrarian sector primarily *via* irrigation investment, which is growing at a slower pace than is required to sustain past rates of growth. Private investment in irrigation appears to have been positively and strongly correlated with public investment in the past.[41] The components of the fairly respectable order of output expansion achieved to date have been expansion of cultivated area, which was relatively more important up to the mid-sixties, and the raising of yields, which has assumed a major role subsequently and is closely associated with the growth of area under irrigation.

With the near-exhaustion of the easy avenues of output expansion and the raising of the yield base, further output expansion in future is bound to encounter more severe constraints by way of a higher requirement of investment for a given increment of output. Irrigation investment in particular cannot be undertaken by landlords unless a further round of yield-raising technical change becomes feasible. Not only are the actual yields in our country amongst the lowest in the world, but the disconcerting fact is that the gap between potential yields (as measured by the achievements of Japanese and Chinese agriculture) and our actual yields is not narrowing, but has been widening over the last three decades.

As Thorner never tired of pointing out, 'the use of the comparative method in history and economics is fraught with risk, and it is the easiest thing to go astray'.[42] Nevertheless one is tempted to look afresh at the experience of our Asian neighbours, to see what lessons, if any, they hold for us.

In Japan, the major breakthrough in agricultural production came during and after World War II, with the effective abolition of the landlord–tenant system starting with differential procurement prices for rice earlier referred to, and culminating with the land reform under which resident landlords were permitted to retain only 1 *cho* (=2.45 acres) and absentee landlords no land at all, the rest being purchased by the state for sale to tenants. Tenant-cultivated land declined from 50 per cent to less than 10 per cent. A leading Japanese economist tells us that 'This stringent reform had the effect of rapidly increasing the productive capacity of rice-growing land . . . in the northeast half of Japan where landlords had been specially powerful.'[43]

China's experience cannot be duplicated without social revolution, but is nevertheless of immense interest. Not only was a radical land reform without compensation carried out, but with the formation of cooperatives and later the communes, a direct mobilization of underemployed surplus labour on a very large scale for infrastructural construction, especially irrigation works, was undertaken.[44] Despite low investment allocation in the central government plan to agriculture, a high rate of capital formation financed from within the collectively owned agrarian units took place, raising the proportion of area under irrigation from 26 per cent to 48 per cent; this, along with the spread of indigenously researched high-yielding varieties, permitted a substantial raising of yields over the already high base.[45]

The Chinese experience points to the fruitfulness of community labour for investment with the aim of raising productivity, the benefits of which can be shared by every member of the community. Since yields have reached fairly high levels, the emphasis in China now has shifted to output diversification towards orchard, livestock and aquatic products. With rising incomes for everybody—real income in rural areas is estimated to have doubled, and in urban areas to have risen by 43 per cent during 1979 to 1983 alone—there is today a consumption boom in China's rural areas. 'Agriculture-led growth' is a rational and socially equitable strategy in a large country with a potentially vast domestic market; we have a great deal more to learn from China in this respect than from Taiwan's 'export-led growth'.

To sum up the argument so far: land reform is usually thought of in terms of redistributive justice alone. History provides us with evidence, however, that it is equally necessary from the viewpoint of a faster rate of transition to higher productivity through rapid capital formation within the agrarian sector, which in turn affects the rate of industrialization through the rate of expansion of the domestic market for mass consumption goods and through the supply of wage goods and raw materials to industry. The shelving of land reforms and its reduction to a forgotten non-issue by policy-makers in our country implies that the constraints imposed by land monopoly upon the development of productive forces, are being deliberately preserved.

Language is an indicator of thinking: in officialese, there are no 'landlords' any more: there are only 'farmers', at most 'rich peasants'. Despite the result of large-scale sample surveys which show no decline in ownership concentration, our policy-makers have decided to undertake an 'agrarian revolution by category redefinition', to paraphrase Thorner. They have simply replaced the category 'landlord' by the category 'farmer'. The rigorous economic rationale for continuing to look upon a capitalist of rentier landlord origins as a landlord, as representing 'semi-feudal capitalism', is that he obtains a part of his surplus by way of a tribute imposed on society owing to the legal monopoly of land, and not entirely as a return on capital advanced in production. Continued land monopoly also implies continued land-hunger and landlessness at the other pole; the labour market is not free, labour mobility is restricted and wages depressed through the use of extra-economic relations.

In the course of field-work again and again one found that the dominant land-holding position in the villages was held by ex-intermediaries and ex-rentiers. Consider the owner of a 435-acre consolidated holding in a village of Mayavaram *taluka*. His family once held some 800 acres and now he double-crops his land with pumpset-powered irrigation employing more than 20 farm servants and the casual labour force of the entire village in the peak season, owns a petrol pump and cinema hall in the town and periodically visits Japan to study paddy culture. How has he ceased to be a 'landlord' and become merely a 'farmer'? Or, take the members of a former intermediary Thakur family of a village in Kaira district of Gujarat, who each now operate 50 to 60-acre holdings on an intensive capitalist basis, and who as a family still account for about 600 out of the 1,000-odd acres under cultivation, employing in all 45 farm servants. One wonders how they have ceased to be landlords.

Slow Expansion of Market

A serious implication of the inegalitarian financing of growth to date, combined with the slowing down of public investment, is the very slow expansion in the rural market for manufactured goods of mass consumption. This is a logical consequence of the fall in the real earnings of rural labour, making up 30 per cent of rural workers, and the stagnation in the real earnings of poor peasants and small peasants, making up another 25 to 30 per cent, at least, of all workers. A single-point study, with reference year 1972–73, of holdings below 15 acres and agricultural labourers in Haryana, shows that the small peasants, poor peasants and labourers, making up 60 per cent of the households, failed to reach the 'poverty level' as defined by the Planning Commission after a decade of 'green revolution'.[46] If this was the situation in one of the most advanced areas in the country, the position in the low-growth and stagnating areas may be imagined.

Corresponding to the stagnation in the market for goods of mass consumption, there has been an expansion in the market for durable consumption goods, on account of the increased incomes of the minority who virtually monopolize commodity sales from agriculture and engage in capitalist cultivation. Similar trends are observed in urban areas, where luxury consumption is burgeoning while mass consumption grows very slowly. The prolonged crisis of the cotton textile industry is in large part traceable to the long-term demand constraints which have lowered profitability and hampered modernization. The only dynamic sub-sector comprises the mills catering to the as yet primarily elite market for synthetics and blends. After three decades of development, the market distribution of effective demand ordains that the country's very poor, comprising at least 200 million people, should go about in the tattered remnants of the one or two garments they possess, while sick mills operate with excess capacity and many lakhs are spent in advertising to tempt the elite to add yet another synthetic garment to their bursting wardrobes. Anyone who has visited villages (and not confined the visit to a walk from the local official's jeep to the local landlord's house) can see that, except perhaps in the advanced areas of Punjab, hardly a single item of modern manufactured mass consumption good is to be seen in the majority of peasant huts.

Of course, the large absolute size of the Indian market implies that the expansion of elite consumption confined to the top 5 to 10 per cent of our population, still means that over 30 million people, indeed probably around 50 million, are spending much more than before. Further, this elite effective demand is concentrated in the urban areas and includes a substantial part of the landlords' consumption as well, conveying an impression of a dynamically functioning economy; while the nine times as many people who stagnate in thousands of atomistic, scattered villages and in urban slums, are unseen and unheard, except sporadically. For every laconically reported newspaper case today of a mother who kills herself and her children 'owing to poverty', there are a thousand who die slow unrecorded deaths from undernutrition and disease.

Some economists have informed us that up to 1981,

> there was no evidence that income distribution in India had worsened: what evidence there was suggested no change for better or worse. Even if there were [*sic*] such evidences, it is not logically true that a worsening of income distribution reduces the demand for industrial goods: in fact the reverse may be true.[47]

The proposition that income distribution has not worsened is the product of bad economic theory, combined with illegitimate inferences about incomes from empirical data on consumption which form the staple fare of poverty estimates. A basic proposition in macroeconomics is that in any economy where a minority of people are sellers of commodities produced with hired labour, and the majority are unorganized sellers of labour power, inflation in commodity prices redistributes income from the latter to the former through a profit inflation. The sixteenth-century price inflation in Europe is the earliest much-analysed case of such a profit inflation referred to by Keynes at length in his *Treatise on Money*, and by Marx in *Capital* in the context of primitive accumulation.

The more recent case of profit inflation discussed by Keynes relates to World War I, when the British government found itself faced with the necessity of raising the domestic rate of investment. Analytically speaking, this is similar to the problem of raising the investment rate in the process of planned development—Keynes' discussion of profit inflation merits attention for its relevance to our own experience. Thus, talking of the large increase in investment in arms entailed by World War I, Keynes pointed out that 'it exceeded the maximum possible amount of voluntary saving which one could expect', and therefore '*forced transferences of purchasing power* in some shape or form were a necessary condition of investment in the materials of war on the desired scale'. Logically, such a forced transfer could take place through one or more of the following methods: first, through taxation of incomes; second, through a cut in money wages; and third, through a faster rate of rise in prices relative to that in money wages. If the first method was used, 'the taxation would have had to be aimed directly at the relatively poor, since it was above all their consumption in view of its aggregate magnitude, which had somehow or the other to be reduced'. This was politically difficult, as was the lowering of money wages directly, in a situation where trade unions existed. Keynes was led to conclude that 'to allow prices to rise by permitting a profit inflation is, in time of war, both inevitable and wise'. So far, this is Keynes' well-known advocacy of taking advantage of 'money illusion' on the part of workers to cut their real consumption through a profit inflation, without the workers realizing the game of the state: but—and this is the important point—Keynes also advocated high taxation of profits at the same time.

> It is expedient to use entrepreneurs as collecting agents. But let them be agents and not principals. Having adopted for quite good reasons a policy which pours the booty into their laps, let us be sure they hand it over in the form of taxes, and that they are not enabled to obtain a claim over the future income of the community by being allowed to 'lend' to the State what has thus accrued to them. *To let prices rise relatively to earnings and then tax entrepreneurs to the utmost is the right procedure for 'virtuous' war finance, for high taxation of profits and of incomes above the exemption limit is not a substitute for profit inflation but an adjunct of it.*[48] (emphasis added)

In India, over the last quarter century, a policy of profit inflation has indeed poured 'the booty' into the laps of the manufacturing capitalists and the rural landlord-capitalists monopolizing commodity sales, thus restricting the rate of growth of mass incomes and consumption. But while the desirability of taxing profits was in principle accepted in the past, in the last few years a gradual shift has taken place with a progressive, shame-faced reduction of property income taxes culminating in the new policy embodied in the 1985 Budget, which now openly abandons 'virtuous' financing for the vicious course of giving up the state's claim, on the specious argument that it has been unable to enforce tax compliance in the past. The refusal to consider the imposition of an agricultural holdings tax to tap the rural surplus, combined with the slashing of corporate and individual taxes, means that the surplus wrested from the workers is being distributed with both hands to the private property owners—both through profit inflation following credit financing and through their exemption from the burden of financing public investment. The political economy behind this apparently suicidal course by the state is beyond the scope of this paper; for our purpose it is sufficient to note that the resource crisis of the state is bound to worsen following its latest fiscal measures, thus constraining more stringently the possible options regarding expenditures on employment generation and poverty alleviation.

Income Distribution

It is with these redistributive effects of inflation discussed by Keynes that we are primarily concerned: in any society where a minority of people monopolize commodity sales and a majority are sellers of only one type of commodity—labour power—it is crystal clear that inflation in prices of necessities would be in the interests of and constitute a profit inflation for the minority; while it would entail anything from real income decline (where labour is unorganized) or less-than-average real income rise (where labour is organized) for the majority working for wages. In rural areas, all available data indicate a high degree of concentration of cultivated area, assets value, output and the commodity surplus entering the market in the hands of a minority. In 1970–71, according to the Agricultural Census data, the top one-eighth of all rural households, ranked by area, accounted for 53 per cent of total operated area (this remains virtually unchanged in the 1976 Census), while the RBI Debt and Investment Survey showed the top one-eighth of households ranked assets value had 53.5 per cent of total assets. My estimate of marketable surplus for the year 1960–61 earlier referred to indicated that the top one-eighth of households, ranked by area, accounted for 52 per cent of total output and 66.7 per cent of total gross marketable surplus. At the other pole, the lower six deciles of households ranked by area in 1960–61 had 8 per cent of land operated, produced about 10 per cent of total output and contributed a mere 6 per cent of the aggregate marketable surplus. Since, according to every single one of a large number of district-level studies carried out in the sixties and early seventies, adoption of green revolution technology was found to be positively associated with farm size, the top groups have added at a faster-than-average rate of their output and marketable surplus. On the basis of plausible assumptions, drawing upon such data as we have on the differential rates of addition to output of different groups and their different degrees of market orientation, we can hazard a rough guesstimate that by today, with a doubling of total output and a 33 per cent rise in its monetization, the top one-eighth accounts for at least 75 per cent of total marketable surplus. (This in turn is likely to underestimate the extent of concentration of commodity sales by the landlords-capitalists, for acreage group is not coterminous with social class.) It is not merely the fact that the benefits of inflation in primary sector prices accrued to the minority in proportion to their command over total sales: simultaneously, the majority, wholly or mainly dependent on performing wage-paid labour for the minority, lost out from the inflation to a far greater extent than a few of them gained by virtue of selling commodities to a small extent (nearly three-fifths of the lowest six deciles ranked by area are likely to be labourers, the remainder being mainly poor peasants). As earlier noted, on deflating the money earnings data in the Rural Labour Enquiries of 1963–64 and 1974–75 by the Consumer Price Index for Agricultural Labourers, we find a drastic decline in real earnings over the period; since prices came down slightly in the Emergency period, a smaller order of decline is observed if the index for the two subsequent years (1975–76 and 1976–77) are applied to the 1974–75 money earnings data. The burden of real indebtedness has registered a rise over the same period. Given the fact that rural labourers are almost entirely unorganized and the poor peasants are wholly so, a substantial unfavourable redistribution of incomes over social classes is the logical consequence of inflation over the past quarter century.

Since 1975 to date, while inflation has continued, it has been relatively more rapid in the secondary sector compared to the primary sector. In short, in the course of overall profit inflation the balance with regard to the sectoral allocation of 'the booty' has tilted towards manufacturing; but this does not mean that the minority in rural areas have ceased to rake in their share of the booty: only that the share is somewhat less munificent than before. In the secondary and tertiary sectors the labour force is extremely heterogeneous with respect to levies of skills and extent of organization. While organized labour and the government-employed salariat is able to resist real income decline following inflation and even wrest some real income rise, unorganized labour in small-scale industry and the tertiary sector—several times more numerous than organized labour—is likely to have lost out to a greater or lesser extent.

While, on the above theoretical grounds, we may confidently state that an unfavourable shift in income distribution over social classes must have accompanied inflation, and particularly so in rural areas where labour is almost wholly unorganized, it does not follow that 'the data' as it is collected and analysed at present would necessarily show this. The reason is that such data bearing on incomes are generally not collected or analysed by social class. It may be noted that the only source of direct earnings data for a rural social class, the Rural Labour Enquiries, do show real income decline and rise in indebtedness as earlier mentioned. The indirect data are not by social class, and relate not to incomes but to the consumption expenditure of households ranked by per capita monthly expenditure levels; these consumption data have been made the basis for some quite arbitrary and illogical inferences on incomes by some authors in recent years.

First, in a number of studies using the NSS consumption data, the changing distribution of *nominal* consumption expenditure is made the basis for generalizations about levels of living and even of incomes, thus heroically abstracting from the differential impact of inflation on different social classes.[49] Second, even when real expenditures are sought to be calculated, the marked differences in the consumption baskets and prices paid by the different groups are not adequately captured owing to the failure to apply sufficiently refined differential deflators.[50] Third, the basic fact is ignored that workers (located mainly in the lower deciles of expenditure groups) consume all their income and some dis-save, while landlords and capitalists (located mainly in the higher deciles) have a high propensity to save, so that income distribution at any point of time is bound to be more skewed than consumption distribution. Fourth, and this follows from the previous points, the fact is ignored that a constant or declining concentration of expenditure (whether in nominal or real terms) is quite consistent logically with an increasing concentration of incomes.

Thus, in a situation of inflation in necessities prices, which simultaneously represents a profit inflation for producers of necessities as has occurred in India since 1960, nominal expenditures of the very poor (located in the lowest deciles of consumption expenditure distribution and with the highest proportion of necessities in total outlay) would have to rise faster than the nominal expenditure by the rich in order to maintain the same real consumption basket over time. (The poor would have to try to maintain their real consumption or they would die, since the initial level is already rock-bottom; hence, increased borrowing could be logically expected, as indeed is shown by the Rural Labour Enquiries.)

At the same time, profit incomes accruing to the rich in consequence of inflation would be almost entirely saved and not consumed. Therefore, nominal expenditure concentration may be expected to decline while real expenditure concentration remains nearly constant and income distribution worsens. Real expenditure distribution may even register a spurious improvement if, over time, the rich shift more to institutional forms of consumption (company or government flats and cars, expense accounts, costless financing of housing) which are not captured by household-centred consumption enquiries, such as the NSS, which, it is widely recognized, 'do not adequately capture the consumption profiles of the rich'.[51]

A recent rather more careful estimate of real expenditure changes over time, using appropriate deflators for different expenditure groups, finds that there has been no change in the concentration of real expenditures as measured by the Gini coefficient during the period 1961–62 to 1973–74. The absolute level of real expenditure of the poorest is such that the authors are constrained to remark that 'the subsistence level of consumption is so low that one may even doubt whether physical existence is at all possible at such a level', and note that 'the level of living of the poorest is found to be worse in 1973–74 than in 1961–62'.[52] At the same time, the rate of savings in the economy has been rising steadily; it has attained at least 20 per cent of national income by the late seventies and is projected to rise to 25 per cent in the Seventh Plan. The rise in the savings rate combined with unchanged real expenditure distribution on consumption, is a conclusive indicator of worsening overall income distribution under Indian conditions, where much of labour is non-unionized and fiscal policy has been regressive.

On the proposition that worsening of income distribution does not 'logically' lead to a reduction of industrial demand, it can and has been as logically argued that the shifting commodity composition of demand, with an increasing weight of luxury goods such as electronic products and automobiles at the expense of textiles and other necessities, will, by raising the import content of manufacturers, lead to domestic recessionary effects.[53] The composition of effective demand, and its growth, really forms the crux of the question of the political economy of agricultural development specifically and of the economy generally. Our basic proposition is that the socially narrowly-based path of landlord-capitalism combined with inflationary Plan financing leading to worsening income distribution, is simultaneously a path which generates a lower long-term growth rate of agricultural incomes and hence of industrial demand, than would a more egalitarian path initiated by a drastic land reform.

The strategy of relying substantially on a profit inflation has evidently 'succeeded' in curbing the rate of growth of mass incomes and mass consumption—for certain sections like rural labourers, to the extent of real earnings decline over certain periods—and has raised the savings rate in the economy. But the problem inherent in this same strategy is that of an inadequately expanding mass market for consumption goods. The distribution of effective demand has shifted markedly towards the labour-hiring classes and upper salariat whose burgeoning demand for import-intensive consumer durables—televisions, VCRs, electronic products, motor cars and motor cycles—for synthetic textiles and for real estate and housing, has been determining for some years now the directions of profitable investment. In the past the spontaneous pulls of market demand operated against barriers imposed by an apparatus of controls designed—whatever their actual effectiveness—to restrict monopoly, conserve foreign exchange for essential productive imports and prevent the penetration of foreign capital. While a shame-faced, piecemeal shift away from these priorities has been visible in official policy since 1980, the decisive break with the past has come, undoubtedly, with the 1985 Budget. This, along with a range of new policies including on monopolies and on foreign capital, clearly amount to an entirely new strategy of promoting elite consumption in the hope of generating growth (which is then expected to 'trickle down' automatically to the poor).

Work Programmes for Capital Formation

Where does a new economic policy leave the 300 million plus poor in the country who stubbornly remain poor despite sundry statistical attempts to push them above the 'poverty line'? There can be no doubt that it is the lack of purchasing power, or the limitation of mass effective demand with the poorer 50 per cent of the population, which accounts for their inability to absorb the bumper harvests of the last two years. The paradox of widespread hunger among the rural poor in particular, combined with unprecedented stocks of now over 29 million tonnes of foodgrains with government, some of which has rotted in monsoon weather for lack of adequate storage, is so striking that it has been noted by a number of observers of the economic scene. We may note that the per capita food availability and absorption in China today is somewhat over 50 per cent higher than in India; the argument sometimes heard, that we already consume as much as it is physically possible to consume, is simply not true. If the requisite purchasing power with the poor existed, a gross foodgrains output of at least 250 million tonnes, or 100 million tonnes more than the actual output today could be easily absorbed by the Indian population, as an output of 375 million tonnes (1984 figure) is absorbed by the Chinese population, which is a little less than one-and-a-half times India's. (Of course not the entire amount would be consumed directly as grain; some part would represent seed and some part animal feed, converted in part again to protein-rich foods.)

The obvious solution to our unemployment and poverty problem, which is at the same time a problem of inadequately growing mass effective demand for food and manufactured goods, is to use the unprecedented foodgrains stocks for an all-out attack on poverty by undertaking to supply food against work for productive capital formation, especially in rural areas, on a massive scale. What is required is the formulation of schemes for harnessing unemployed and underemployed labour in irrigation, soil conservation, terracing, afforestation, drinking water supply, rural industry and non-conventional energy projects. Instead of the present lackadaisical approach to 'poverty removal' as a system of doles to the destitute, from which petty functionaries and contractors filch at every level until only a fraction of the outlays reach the poor, what is required is a total restructuring of the administration of such employment generation schemes. Firstly, if the benefits of such schemes are to go to the rural poor comprising some 60 per cent of the rural population and not be siphoned off by the rural rich monopolizing land and assets, the institutional framework of cooperation among the rural poor becomes essential; work for building community assets will only be undertaken with enthusiasm if it is perceived to benefit every member of the community contributing the work, not merely in terms of the immediate wage payment alone but also in terms of the ownership of the productive asset created, be it reclaimed wasteland, afforested hitherto barren hills, a factory processing fruit, or a source of drinking water. Secondly, the administration of the schemes has to be not 'from above', but 'from below', by evolving suitable institutions, or perhaps utilizing existing institutions like the 'panchayats', provided these are made representative of the poor.

Such a large-scale programme of generating purchasing power in the hands of the poor and simultaneously giving a 'big push' to rural capital formation and essential social consumption with the assets created to be owned by the poor themselves, would require at least a five-fold expansion in the (unofficial) total Seventh Plan outlay of Rs 8,000 to Rs 10,000 crore. In short, an *annual* outlay of this order is required, which would imply an outlay per month of around Rs 30 per capita of the population in poverty.[54] Such a 'big push' in rural investment would generate employment and incomes, which through multiplier effects would rapidly expand the demand for manufactured products as well. The availability of large food stocks combined with excess capacity in textile mills implies that the inflationary potential of such a 'big push' can be kept to a minimum through a mix of suitable measures: payment of the remuneration to cooperative members largely in kind, extension of the public distribution of manufactured necessities (textiles, kerosene, etc.) against which the cash component can be exchanged; and a substantial stepping up of direct taxation to finance the outlays. An agricultural holdings tax on the top one-eighth of landowning households (who monopolize over half the total land and assets) and on traders would bring some 11 million households into the net of direct taxation; while enhanced corporate taxation and taxation of urban professionals with punitive measures for default, would be required. In the long run, the consumption of the poor cannot be increased without curbing the luxury consumption of the rich.

Such a 'big push' in rural areas to put purchasing power in

the hands of the poor and to enable them to own productive assets, would lead to a mass expansion of the demand for such wholly Indian-made goods as bicycles, radios, watches, plastic goods, textiles (including synthetics), etc., which in its aggregate expansionary impact would exceed by far the very dubious effects of the present policy of encouraging the demand for heavily import-dependent electronic goods and other durable consumption goods on the part of the rich.

A socially broad-based expansion of effective demand constituted by expanding purchasing power in the hands of the poor six deciles of our population, would not only lift the consumer goods manufacturing sector out of the doldrums but this in turn would extend its linkage effects to the capital goods industries.

The imperatives of economic rationality at this juncture are clear: whether the balance of social forces in the country will ever permit the policies consistent with economic rationality remains to be seen. As Paul Baran remarked long ago, just as whether meat is cooked in the kitchen is not decided in the kitchen, what happens within agriculture is determined outside agriculture.[55]

Mode of Production Debate

Finally, from the problematical present and the uncertain future, let us turn to a more soothing contemplation of more abstract questions. Where are we today, after a quarter century of the growth of the capitalist tendency, with regard to the 'mode of production' controversy? At the outset one should be clear that the debate of the early seventies, so cogently surveyed and discussed by Alice Thorner,[56] had more limitations than positive contributions to make to our understanding of India's changing agrarian structure. The positive contributions were, perhaps, to raise afresh the perennial questions of how 'capitalism' and 'feudalism' are to be conceptualized generally and in the specific context of an ex-colonial economy.

After that debate, for example, no one will rush to compute the size of the capitalist sector only on the basis of the area cultivated by hired labour, for this is a necessary but not sufficient index of capitalist production, as Thorner himself had pointed out. The limitations of the debate sprang from a lack of theoretical clarity regarding the use of concepts such as 'mode of production'. An analytical concept of Marxist theory tended to be used freely and illegitimately as a descriptive term, to the extent that people talked of 'the mode of production in agriculture', a logical extension of which could become nonsensical rubrics like 'the mode of production in West Bengal agriculture' or, worse still, 'the mode of production under the Akalis of Punjab'. New 'modes of production' started being invented to correspond to the empirical reality of particular social formations at a particular point of time, such as 'the colonial mode of production'. A major reason for my own non-participation in the debate after 1973, was the conviction that, methodologically speaking, it has gone off the rails.

In sum, I would consider it necessary and legitimate to employ the analytical concept of 'mode of production' developed by Marx along with its supportive theoretical apparatus; but would consider it illegitimate to reduce it to a term which is merely descriptive of specific empirical conjunctures in a given social formation in transition such as India is today. The very posing of the question—what is the mode of production in Indian agriculture?—is a theoretically impermissible use of the category. It is, however, perfectly correct to ask the question —what is the extent and nature of the development of the capitalist tendency within Indian agriculture? This is the question to which my paper has been addressed. My own tentative answer to this question has been advanced already: the capitalist path in India's agriculture is one dominated by a socially narrowly-based 'landlord-capitalism' with the semi-feudal feature of caste subordination of workers, which is capable of raising the level of productive forces only under certain exceptional conditions, and which acts as a long-run fetter on agricultural growth and hence on the overall growth of the economy.

Notes and References

1 D. Thorner and A. Thorner, *Land and Labour in India,* Asia, Bombay, 1965; D. Thorner, *The Agrarian Prospect in India,* Allied, Delhi, 1976, and 'Capitalist Agriculture in India', paper presented to the Modern Asia Studies Conference, Cambridge, 1968. This paper is reproduced in *The Shaping of Modern India* (Allied, Delhi, 1981), which also contains *The Statesman* (1 to 4 November 1967) articles on the growth of capitalist production. Similar views were put forward on the basis of secondary data by Sulekh Chandra Gupta: 'New Trends of Growth in Indian Agriculture', *Seminar,* No. 38, New Delhi, October 1962; 'Some Aspects of Indian Agriculture', *Enquiry,* No. 6, Delhi; 'India's Agrarian Structure', *Mainstream,* 1966.

2 D. Thorner, *The Agrarian Prospect in India.* 'Typically (the superior right-holders) found it more profitable to rent out their land than to manage

them personally . . . this complex of legal, economic and social relations uniquely typical of the Indian countryside served to produce an effect which I should like to call that of a built-in depressor.' (p. 16)

Similar ideas were expressed by Ranjit Dasgupta, who stressed the high return from leasing-out, moneylending and trading: 'Such a structure of rent, interest and trading profit operates against any productive real capital formation.' *Problems of Economic Transition*, Calcutta, 1970.

3 D. Thorner, *The Agrarian Prospect in India*, pp. 9–11.

4 Thorner played a major role in bringing the writings of A.V. Chayanov to our attention. Chayanov published two major studies. One was on peasant budgets: '*Byudzhety Kresty'en Starobel 'skogo Uezda*', Kharkov, 1910. The second was a theoretical work on peasant farm organization, which has been translated and published in D. Thorner, B. Kerblay and R.E.F. Smith (eds), *The Theory of Peasant Economy*, Homewood, Illinois, 1966.

5 One of the earliest attempts emanated from a leading political activist involved in the famous Telengana peasant movement. P. Sundarayya, in *The Land Question* (All India Kisan Sabha, 1976), gave the results of a classification of all households in two Andhra villages on the basis of detailed economic data, using the Leninist criteria of possession of means of production, type of labour use and viability. The classes were: landlord, rich peasant, middle peasant, poor peasant and agricultural labourer.

In an article entitled 'Class Differentiation within the Peasantry: An Approach to the Analysis of Indian Agriculture' (*Economic and Political Weekly*, Vol. XI, No. 39, 1976), U. Patnaik attempted to develop an empirical criterion, termed the labour-exploitation index, which was a shorthand form of the above three criteria, incorporating the questions of appropriation of surplus through hiring wage-paid labour and through leasing, compared to self-employment. This attempt was refined after taking account of criticisms by R. Sau ('A Theory of Rent and Agrarian Relations', *Economic and Political Weekly*, Vol. XV, No. 9, 1980), and applied to a sample of farms from Haryana. See U. Patnaik, *Peasant Class Differentiation: A Study in Method with Reference in Haryana*, Oxford University Press, Delhi, 1987. Although formulated specifically for Indian conditions, this particular method has been applied elsewhere as well. See Ednaldo Araquem da Silva, 'Measuring the Incidence of Rural Capitalism: An Analysis of Survey Data from North-East Brasil', *Journal of Peasant Studies*, October 1984; and Jose Ferreira Irmao, 'Agricultural Policy and Capitalist Development in North East Brazil', Recifc, 1984.

P.K. Bardhan has formulated another criterion ('Agrarian Class Formation in India', *Journal of Peasant Studies*, October 1982), using substantially the same idea of looking at the hiring in and out of labour relative to self-employment, put forward by U. Patnaik ('Class Differentiation within the Peasantry'), but rather surprisingly without any reference to that article or to the Indian work on the subject. However Bardhan does not take account of either simultaneous hiring in and out of labour by households or of rent exploitation, which would appear to limit the applicability of the index. Bardhan's failure to refer to the earlier Indian literature on the subject is perhaps owing to the fact that he bases himself exclusively on the work of Roemer (*A General Theory of Exploitation and Class*, Harvard University Press, 1982), which is a mathematical treatment of Marx from an anti-Marxist point of view. It is important to note that the formal similarity of the Roemer–Bardhan empirical index for demarcating agrarian classes to the indices formulated some years earlier by P. Sundarayya, followed by Patnaik, is compatible with totally dissimilar theoretical positions with respect to Marxism. Roemer finds 'exploitation' (in his sense) to exist without production of surplus, and the thrust of his work is to define 'exploitation' in socialist economies. See Roemer, ibid., especially Chs 1 and 2.

6 D. Thorner, *Agrarian Prospect in India*, p. 12.

7 R.H. Tawney, *The Agrarian Problem in the Sixteenth Century*; K. Marx, *Capital*, Vol. I, Part VIII; J.D. Chambers and G.E. Mingay, *The Agricultural Revolution, 1750–1880*, London, 1966.

8 S. Sivasubramanian, 'Estimates of Output for Undivided India', in V.K.R.V. Rao (ed.), *Papers on National Income and Allied Topics*, Vol. I, London, 1960. G. Blyn, *Agricultural Trends in India, 1891–1947*, Philadelphia, 1966. A.K. Bagchi, *Private Investment in India, 1900–1939*, Cambridge University Press, 1972.

9 Blyn estimates that while foodgrains production grew at a trend rate of only 0.11 per cent per annum, commercial crops expanded at 1.31 per cent annually. The difference would be even greater if exportable foodgrains were taken out of the first category and included in the second.

10 The question of the operation of multiplier effects is discussed in my 'Transfer of Tribute and Balance of Payments in the *Cambridge Economic History of India*', *Social Scientist*, No. 139, December 1984.

11 D. Thorner and A. Thorner, *Land and Labour in India*, Asia, Bombay, 1965.

12 In *Capital*, Vol. III, Marx discusses the way in which absolute ground rent constitutes a barrier to investment in capitalist society. This idea has been extended by myself to a consideration of how in an India-type economy, high levels of absolute ground rent will act as a barrier to the switch to capitalist production. See my 'Classical Theory of Rent and Its Application to India', in *Journal of Peasant Studies*, Vol. 10, Nos 2 and 3, January–April 1983, reprinted in T.J. Byres (ed.), *Sharecropping and Sharecroppers*, Cass, London, 1983.

13 These data are from A. Venkateswarulu, 'Regional Variations in the Agrarian Structure, 1953–54 to 1970–71', M. Phil thesis in the School of Social Sciences, Jawaharlal Nehru University, New Delhi; area adjustments have been made for states' reorganization, unlike in other studies. I am grateful to Venkateswarulu for permitting me to quote his results. V.S. Vyas ('Some Aspects of Structural Change in Indian Agriculture', *IAJE*) finds a slight decline in ownership concentration between 1961–62 and 1971–72, while H. Laxminarayan and S.S. Tyagi (*Changes in Agrarian Structure in India*, Agricole Publishing Academy, 1982) find the Gini-coefficient increased

between 1953–54 and 1961–62, and declined subsequently by 1971–72.

14 In *The Indian Economic Review*, Vol. III, No. 2.

15 For a discussion of land reforms and a useful bibliography, see P.C. Joshi, *Land Reforms in India*, Allied, Delhi, 1982.

16 To use the phrase employed by E.H. Norman, in 'Japan's Emergence as a Modern State', to describe the agrarian changes after the new land tax of 1873 (J. Dower, ed., *Origins of the Modern Japanese State*, Pantheon, 1975).

17 The customary social barriers between caste peasants and Harijans are seen to fall in specific situations of joint struggle, as in the Thanjavur rural agitations of the sixties. For an interesting account see D. Sivertsen, 'When Caste Barriers Fall'.

18 See A. Bhaduri, 'Economic Backwardness under Semi-Feudalism', *Economic Journal*, 1972. G.S. Bhalla, Y. Alagh and A. Bhaduri, 'Agricultural Growth and Manpower Absorption in India', in *Labour Absorption in Indian Agriculture, Some Explanatory Investigations*, ARTEP, Bangkok, 1978. This argues that high growth rates in the green revolution areas will generate overall growth rates in employment through a 'suction effect'.

19 Michal Kalecki: 'The Problem of Financing Economic Development', *Indian Economic Review*, 1955; 'The Difference between the Crucial Economic Problems of Developed and Underdeveloped Non-Socialist Economies', in *Essays on Planning and Development*, Centre for Research on Underdeveloped Economics, Warsaw, 1968; 'Problems of Financing Economic Development in a Mixed Economy', in *Selected Essays on the Economic Growth of the Socialist and the Mixed Economy.*

20 K.N. Raj, in his 'Price Behaviour in India, 1949 to 1966: An Explanatory Hypothesis' (*Indian Economic Review*, October 1968), takes the multiplier effect as changing investment as the main determinant of changing prices.

21 'Deficit financing' in India refers only to the government's borrowings from the RBI and drawing down of cash reserves, and excludes government borrowings from the commercial banks. It is, however, not clear whether purchases of central government securities by the banks is really any different in its impact from the narrower definition of deficit finance. The recently proposed change in the definition of 'deficit finance' does not deal with this problem.

22 P. Patnaik, 'Market Question and Capitalist Development in India', *Economic and Political Weekly*, Annual Number, August 1984.

23 S. Habib, 'Colonial Exploitation and Capital Formation in England in the Early Stages of Industrial Revolution', Department of History, Aligarh Muslim University. U. Patnaik, 'India and Britain: Primary Accumulation in Relation to Industrial Development', proceedings of seminar on Karl Marx and the Analysis of Indian Society, New Delhi, October 1983.

24 Calculated from J. Halliday, *Political Economy of Japanese Capitalism*, Pantheon Books, 1975, Table 2, pp. 49–52.

25 V. Lippit, *Land Reform and Economic Development in China*, New York, 1974.

26 U. Patnaik, 'Alternative Strategies of Agrarian Change in Relation to Development Finance', paper presented to ICSSR Seminar on Marx, Schumpeter and Keynes, New Delhi, January 1984.

27 These data have been summarized in my Introduction to U. Patnaik and M. Dingwaney (eds), *Chains of Servitude: Bondage and Slavery in India*, Sangam Books, Delhi, 1985. This material first appeared in *Social Scientist*, No. 122, July 1983, entitled 'The Evolution of the Class of Agricultural Labourers in India'.

28 Unpublished Ph.D. thesis, 'The Organizational Basis of Indian Agriculture with Special Reference to the Development of Capitalist Production', Oxford, 1972.

29 A. Mitra, *Terms of Trade and Class Relations* (Cass, London, 1977), stresses the imp-ortance of compensatory transfers.

30 Data for the period after 1970 provided by Chairman, Agricultural Prices Commission; see V.K.R.V. Rao , *India's National Income, 1950–1980*, Sage, 1983, which finds that for the entire period, primary sector prices rose at the fastest rate of 5.9 per cent per annum compared to 4.5 per cent for the secondary sector and 3.5 per cent for the tertiary sector.

31 E.H. Norman, 'Japan's Emergence as a Modern State'.

32 H. Calvert, *The Wealth and Welfare of Punjab* (London, 1936). M.I. Darling: *The Punjab Peasant in Prosperity and Debt*, Oxford University Press, 1928; *Rusticus Loquitur, The New Light and the Old in the Punjab Village.*

33 Planning Commission: *Progress of Land Reform*, Delhi, 1963; *Implementation of Land Reforms: A Review*, Delhi, 1966.

34 U. Patnaik, 'Contribution to Output and Marketable Surplus of Agricultural Products by Cultivating Groups in India, 1960–61', *Economic and Political Weekly*, 1975.

35 Takafusa Nakamura, *The Postwar Japanese Economy*, University of Tokyo Press, 1981, p. 19.

36 The role of commercialization in strengthening servile bonds was pointed out in the context of the 'second serfdom' in Eastern Europe, by Engels and Marx. Instances from European history have been adduced by M. Dobb in his *Studies in the Development of Capitalism* (Routledge and Kegan Paul, London, 1959). See also the well-known debate in R. Hilton (ed.), *The Transition from Feudalism to Capitalism.*

37 V.I. Lenin: 'The Land Question and the Rural Poor', *Collected Works*, Vol. 19; 'The Agrarian Question in Russia towards the Close of the Nineteenth Century', *Collected Works*, Vol. 17; 'The Agrarian Programme of Social Democracy in the First Russian Revolution', *Collected Works*, Vol. 13.

38 Manjit Singh, 'Migrant Labour in Rural Punjab', M. Phil. dissertation, Punjab University, Chandigarh. I am grateful to Manjit Singh for permitting me to consult his thesis. See, also, Manjit Singh and K. Gopal Iyer, 'Migrant Labour in Rural Punjab', in Patnaik and Dingwaney (eds), *Chains of Servitude.*

39 See Sheila Bhalla, 'Changing Relations of Production in Haryana Agriculture', *Economic and Political Weekly*, Vol. XI, No. 13, 27 March 1976.

40 U. Patnaik, 'Growth and Fluctuations of China', Working Paper, Centre for Economic Studies and Planning, Jawaharlal Nehru University, New Delhi, December 1984 (mimeo.). Data from the State Statistical Bureau of the People's Republic of China adjusted by excluding tubers for comparison with Indian foodgrains production data.

41 S.K. Rao, 'Regional Disparities in Growth of Income and Population in India, 1951–1965', Ph.D thesis, Cambridge University, 1971.

42 D. Thorner, *Agrarian Prospect in India*, p. 4.

43 Nakamura, *The Postwar Japanese Economy*, pp. 26, 28.

44 E.K. Wheelwright and B. MacFarlane, in *The Chinese Road to Socialism*, discuss the question of mobilizing surplus labour for capital formation in China. U. Patnaik, 'Alternative Strategies', attempts to contrast the Indian and Chinese experiences in this respect. For a vivid discription of labour mobilization in a Shansi village see W. Hinton, *Shenfan*, Chs 29–33, Picador, 1984.

45 In 1951 the Chinese foodgrains yield was already double that in India's. See U. Patnaik, 'Growth and Fluctuations in China'; Data from State Statistical Bureau of the People's Republic of China and Chen Nai-ruem, *Chinese Economic Statistics*, Edinburgh, 1966.

46 U. Patnaik, *Peasant Class Differentiation.*

47 A.V. Desai, 'The Slow Rate of Industrialization: A Second Look', *Economic and Political Weekly*, Annual Number, August 1984, pp. 126–27. See also A.V. Desai, 'Factors underlying the Slow Growth of Indian Industry', *Economic and Political Weekly*, Annual Number, March 1981. Desai relies for his conclusion on work using nominal consumption expenditures, by M.S. Ahluwalia (see note 49 below), who is quoted at length in turn, as is Desai, to support the proposition that income distribution has not worsened, by I.J. Ahluwalia, *Industrial Growth in India*, Ch. 4, Oxford University Press, Delhi, 1985.

48 J.M. Keynes, 'Treatise on Money: The Applied Theory of Money', *Collected Works*, Vol. VI, Ch. 30, Macmillan and OUP, 1971.

49 M.S. Ahluwalia, 'Rural Poverty and Agricultural Performance in India', *Journal of Development Studies*, 1977, whose work is invoked by A.V. Desai and I.J. Ahluwalia, to argue that income distribution has not worsened, does not himself put forward any such conclusion (which indeed would be logically quite untenable on the basis of his exercises with nominal consumption data). In fact he correctly states, though only in a footnote, 'Thus a decrease in inequality of consumption is consistent with an increase in inequality of income but *our focus here is not whether income inequality increased, which it probably did*, but whether agricultural growth produced absolute impoverishment' (fn 19, p. 322, emphasis added).

Ahluwalia wished to test the very strong proposition that green revolution is associated with an *increase* in the percentage of population in poverty: such an increase, however, is not a necessary condition for an increase in income equality. His results are quite consistent with increasing income inequality; and in fact they do not rule out increasing absolute impoverishment in certain regions either. Ahluwalia finds the following on fitting time trends to production data, and analysing trends to production data, and analysing trends in the incidence of poverty relative to production by states: (a) there has been 'stagnation in output per head' during 1957–58 to 1973–74 (p. 308); (b) 'the incidence of poverty for almost all states, using either of the two poverty measures, declines up to the early sixties and then begins to rise again, reaching a peak in 1967–68 or 1968–69, and declining again thereafter' (p. 304); (c) 'there is clear evidence of an inverse relation between rural poverty (add: incidence) and agricultural performance' at the all-India level using various indices of output per head (p. 310); (d) At the states' level, however, some of the fastest growing regions including the heartland of 'green revolution', show no decline in poverty incidence: 'Six states (Kerala, Orissa, Punjab and Haryana, Tamil Nadu, Uttar Pradesh and West Bengal) show significant growth in output per head. Yet, as shown in Table 4, none of these states shows a significant trend decline in the incidence of poverty . . . and West Bengal actually shows a significant trend increase' (p. 312); 'Finally, the most disquieting feature of our results is the evidence from Punjab–Haryana which does not support the hypothesis that improved agricultural performance will help reduce the incidence of poverty' (p. 315).

We have quoted at some length from M.S. Ahluwalia, so that the reader may judge just how misleading and disingenuous is the procedure of A.V. Desai and I.J. Ahluwalia, in invoking these results on poverty measured by consumption, in support of their proposition that income distribution has not worsened. The result that inequality in nominal consumption expenditure declines over time (which was also shown in a number of papers in Bardhan and Srinivasan, eds, *Poverty and Income Distribution in India*) is entirely consistent with increasing income inequality. Ahluwalia does not attempt to apply fractile specific deflators to nominal expenditures to get an idea of real consumption inequality (though recognizing the need to do so: p. 319); nor does he take cognizance of saving and dis-saving in the text when putting forward the (incorrect) inference that 'the view that agricultural growth within the present institutional constraints does not contribute to poverty alleviation, and indeed may generate absolute improverishment for the poor in the sense of *declining real income implies* that we should also see *increased relative inequality in the distribution of consumption*' (p. 318, emphasis added). In fact, increasing consumption inequality is logically *not* a necessary condition of increasing income inequality (as the author himself recognizes in fn 19 quoted earlier), nor is it at all unlikely that in India the very poor, already at a rock-bottom level, maintain real consumption despite falling real income, by borrowing. Hence Ahluwalia's result on declining nominal consumption inequality does not logically rule out absolute impoverishment, either.

50 A. Vaidyanathan, 'Some Aspects of Inequalities in Living Standards in Rural India', in P.M. Bardhan and T.N. Srinivasan (eds), *Poverty and Income Distribution in India* (1974), is frequently invoked by the 'no worsening in

income distribution' school. Vaidyanathan, in the absence of other indices, used the official wholesale price series to construct fractile specific deflators, obtaining the negligible differences in the prices paid by the lowest compared to the highest deciles. The obvious drawbacks of using wholesale prices rather than prices actually paid by consumers cannot as yet be rectified in aggregative analysis. Second, the official consumer price index is used for obtaining the value at current prices of a given poverty line expenditure in a base year, which is calculated using the budget weights of the 'average' household in the base year. This procedure too would tend to understate the price rise faced by the lowest expenditure fractiles.

51 N. Krishnaji, 'The Demand Constraint; A Note on Role of Foodgrain Prices and Income Inequality', *Economic Political Weekly*, Annual Number, August 1984, p. 1262.

52 N.S. Iyengar and M.H. Suryanarayana, 'On Poverty Indicators', *Economic and Political Weekly*, 2–9 June 1984, p. 901.

53 P. Patnaik, 'Some Implications of the Economic Strategy underlying the 1985–86 Budget', *Economic and Political Weekly*, Vol. XX, No. 16, 20 April 1985.

54 The actual outlay on all poverty alleviation programmes taken together during the Sixth Plan period did not exceed Rs 3,500 crore (Rs 1,000 crore under NREP, Rs 1,500 crore under IRDP and Rs 600 crore under RLEGP, with the balance distributed over other schemes). The maintenance of this level of expenditure in real terms over the Seventh Plan period would require a money expenditure of Rs 8,000 to Rs 10,000 crore.

55 P.A. Baran, *Political Economy of Growth* (Pelican, 1973), p. 308.

56 A. Thorner, 'Semi-Feudalism or Capitalism?' *Economic and Political Weekly*, 4, 11 and 18 December 1982.

Paper Laws

Atul M. Setalvad

At worst, and this is true often enough, 'paper laws'—meaning laws which are ineffective because they are not implemented, either because they are incapable of implementation or because no proper steps are being taken to implement them—are enacted to hide or cover up a problem. At even their best such laws do little more than give an impression of resolute action. They are, therefore, a sham, a deception.

Examples of paper laws are easy to find. Child marriages go on even though they have been prohibited for decades. Bigamy is prohibited for Hindus. Yet, well-known personalities go through bigamous marriages in a blaze of publicity and suffer no consequences.

The examples are not confined to reform legislation. Notwithstanding the enactment of laws against the adulteration of food, and their amendment to make the punishment more and more severe, adulteration of food goes on merrily. The adulterant may be a harmless substance (stone in rice); it is often lethal, as recurring instances of mass deaths or mass blindness show. Traders and merchants keep on selling adulterated goods as they keep on cheating on weights and measures. And the worst sufferers are the poor.

A glaring example is the law prohibiting dowries.

An ineffective law fails to achieve the objective for which it was enacted; the evil (adulteration of food, child marriages, etc.) continues. But that is not the only consequence. A failure of one law shakes the confidence of the people in laws in general, as they see malefactors going scot-free. If a prosecution is launched, and fails, people lose faith

This is the text of the Second Daniel Thorner Memorial Lecture, delivered at the Indian Merchants Chamber, Mumbai, on 3 March 1988. It was first published in *Economic and Political Weekly*, 16 July 1988.

in the courts and the judiciary even though the actual cause of the failure is a defect in the law or inefficiency or corruption amongst the enforcers. And the offender who has evaded one law is tempted to evade other laws.

Why do laws fail? Are our legislators who enact law after law aware of what is happening?

I think that parliament (and the state assemblies) takes the easy way out. Is there a problem? Very well, let us pass a law. Does the law already passed still not solve the problem? We will make the punishment more stringent. The belief, I presume, is that the very enactment of a law will achieve the result. And the politicians are not alone in this. Various pressure groups such as feminists or environmentalists clamour for more *laws* or more *stringent* laws.

What is lost sight of is that a law has to be implemented and enforced. Implementation requires an effective machinery which the state must set up. It also requires the support of a large section of the community as no governmental machinery can be all-pervading.

Dean Pound wrote as far back as 1917 that a law can but only deal with the outside and not the inside of man. A law can, at best, punish a man for doing something; no law can prevent him from *wanting* to do it; and if he wants to badly enough, catching and punishing him is going to be difficult.

Allott's comments are apposite: 'Laws are often ineffective, doomed to stultification almost at birth, doomed by the over-ambitions of the legislator and the under-provision of an effective law, such as adequate preliminary survey, community acceptance, and enforcement machinery.' (*Limits of the Law*, p. 55)

Evans lists the requisites of *effective* legislation (Gouldner and Miller, eds, *Applied Sociology*). These include:

1. The law must be practical, not utopian.
2. The rationale of the law must be compatible with established cultural and legal principles.
3. There must be sincere conviction in the enforcement agencies; they must be neither hypocritical about it nor corrupt.
4. The law must contain adequate sanctions and incentives, sanctions to deter the law-breaker and incentives for the victims to enforce the law.

To these I would add that the legislators must think as much of the enforcement machinery as they do of the object of the law and provide an effective machinery. There must also be more knowledge about the problem: why it goes on; how it goes on. After a law is enacted there must be *independent* surveys of how it is working, how effective it is. It is such independent surveys which can tell us whether the law is effective or not; and if it is not, the surveys will tell us why it fails.

Practical, Not Utopian

Take the first requisite listed above. A law must not be utopian. The most obvious example of utopian legislation must be the attempt to prohibit the consumption of liquor. It was first tried in the United States by a constitutional amendment. It was a disastrous failure. There were 60,000 prosecutions a year, property worth $205 million was seized and $75 million was recovered by way of fines and penalties. The quantity of illicit liquor seized was 40 million gallons (see Allott, p. 60). Yet people did not stop drinking. Almost everybody was willing to evade the law. And a whole tribe of smugglers and others grew who turned to other crimes when, with the repeal of prohibition, no money could be made from smuggling or illicit brewing.

The Gandhians in India learnt nothing from the American experience. They came from a middle-class background where drinking was rare. They ignored not only the old *rajas* and *girasdars* and others who drank but the so-called 'lower' castes who also drank and who represented the vast majority of the population. This has been as great a disaster in India as it was in the US. Regrettably, it has also bred the same evils: criminal gangs, corruption in the police, and so on.

The first requisite of a workable law is linked with the second; the rationale of the law must be compatible with established cultural principles. This problem is universal. When Kamal Attaturk, in his attempt to modernize Turkey, introduced both European commercial law and European family law, the former was a success but the latter was a near-total failure (Dorr, *Law and Social Change*, p. 96). Similarly, the attempt in a small and relatively homogenous country like Israel to fix the minimum age of marriage at 17 in 1950 was only a limited success; it resulted in marriages being celebrated without registration. This was because, as Dorr says (p. 97), 'Basic institutions rooted in traditions and values, such as the family, seem to be extremely resistant to changes imposed by law.'

Bigamy was legal amongst the Parsis. It was prohibited by

legislation in the nineteenth century at the instance of the community. The 'reform' has worked. It is hardly a success amongst the Hindus where leading lawyers and film actors have contracted bigamous marriages without any attempt to conceal the act and have not suffered either punishment under the law or social sanctions.

Lack of social acceptability will almost inevitably doom a law to be a paper law. I am not suggesting that a law must have majority support before it is enacted. Nor am I saying that social reform cannot be enacted by legislation.

The very enactment of a law has a symbolic value. Its rhetoric influences public opinion and gives it the desired direction. Several social reforms have been achieved by law. And in most cases such laws have been enacted as a result of the actions of a vocal and strong minority. But though the law has been brought about as a result of the efforts of a minority it would achieve the desired objective only if the majority find it *acceptable.*

Take the movement for equality for women. The movement for a vote for women was a movement of a small but very determined minority. It certainly did not command majority support. It worked as it was acceptable. But the next step, equal pay for equal work, has been much more difficult to achieve. This is because most employers and quite a few male workers have opposed equal pay for women. There is active opposition to the measure whereas there was little active opposition to giving women the vote.

As social acceptability is vital to make the law work one would have thought that the MPs who enthusiastically enact reform legislation would do something effective to make it socially acceptable. By doing something effective I do not mean making speeches or arranging for flashes on Doordarshan. I mean a sustained and systematic campaign to make the legislation acceptable. It means first understanding the problem, pointing out its evils, etc.

When the first of the laws prohibiting child marriages was enacted in 1929, the minimum age was 14 for females and 18 for males. It was later raised to 15. Still later it was raised (for girls) to 18. No argument is necessary to justify a law prohibiting child marriages. Raising the minimum age to 16 is consistent with the prohibition of *child* marriages. But when parliament raised it to 18 the step was sought to be justified as a family planning measure! On paper, India is well 'ahead' of Europe in this connection as marriages of girls over 16 are legal in Europe.

I say 'on paper' as *child* marriages go on. As far as rural India is concerned, the law has been virtually a dead letter. Marriages of girls of 10, 11 and 12 are common. And we have even heard of ministers celebrating such marriages of their children. Surely this has been so as nothing has been done to ascertain why parents are keen to marry off their daughters at so young an age, and to remove the *causes.* It could be just custom. It could be a reluctance to continue to bear the expense of maintaining her. It could be fear that once she passes puberty, problems may arise if she has an affair. Unless the underlying cause of child marriages is removed, they are going to go on, law or no law.

There is no *effective* propaganda or social education emphasizing the bad consequences of child marriage. And there cannot be as long as persons in a position of influence and power themselves continue to practise such marriages. The law remains socially unacceptable. And is, therefore, ineffective.

Enforcement Machinery

The third requisite of an effective law is a sincere and non-corrupt and, I would add, effective enforcement machinery. A sincere, non-hypocritical enforcement machinery would generally exist if the law is socially acceptable. Even our police are sincere in their attempts to catch murderers, though they often fail to do so. If, however, they have no sympathy with the law, their efforts are bound to be minimal. This is one of the reasons why the police are so 'ineffective' when it comes to laws against drinking or gambling. Again, a policeman who wants a dowry for his son or has married off his daughter at 13, is unlikely to be sincere in stamping out either dowries or child marriages.

The problem of a non-corrupt enforcement machinery is a much graver problem in India than in the west. Even laws that are universally acceptable are turning out to be almost wholly ineffective because the enforcement machinery is corrupt.

To discuss the *causes* of corruption in Indian public life is wholly beyond the scope of this article. The subject is, however, relevant because it exists. It exists in the sense of police officers and food inspectors taking bribes. It exists in the sense of politicians and ministers *permitting* sub-standard drugs to be produced and sold. The evidence before the Lentin Commission regarding the complicity of senior officers and politicians and ministers is symptomatic of a common trend. Whether the cause is monetary corruption or political pressure, the result is the same. The law is not enforced.

Another absolute requisite of an effective law is the need to set up an *effective* enforcement machinery. Under the Prevention of Food Adulteration Act, the enforce-ment machinery, essentially, consists of three elements: a food inspector, whose job it is to investigate offences and take samples; an analytical laboratory to test the suspected samples; and the ordinary courts where the accused is to be tried.

The Act has been repeatedly amended; the 1976 Amendment was described in the Statement of Objects and Reasons as a major offensive. Yet the number of inspectors is woefully inadequate. There are vast areas where there is none. And they are missing where they are needed most: in the villages or where the adivasis and the landless live. They are hardly trained and are not given the facilities they require and are poorly paid. A bribe is an almost irresistible temptation.

A trader is a big man in his town or village, able to command the support of the local corporator or member of the zilla parishad or village panchayat. To expect a food inspector, who is low in the official hierarchy, to vigorously tackle the problem is to expect the impossible.

The prescribed procedure is hopelessly cumbersome. Samples have to be drawn in three lots. One is to be sent to the public analyst. The accused can dispute the report of the public analyst and demand that the other sample be sent to the Central Analytical Laboratory. In a country of vast distances and poor communications, the result is not difficult to forecast. Months elapse between apprehension and trial. Samples get lost. They cannot be identified as the labels get torn or defaced. Samples deteriorate due to lapse of time. Wrangles go on, on whether the preservative added to the sample has affected the result.

The courts and lawyers play their part in making the law unworkable. There are endless adjournments and this discourages any honest citizen from agreeing to give evidence. The result is professional '*panchas*' amenable to bribes.

Sanctions and Incentives

The law against adulteration is a classic example, also, of the last requisite not being satisfied. There must be sufficient deterrent to the perpetrators and sufficient incentives to the *victims*. Though the law provides for a deterrent which on paper is severe enough, it rarely works. It is easy for a company or firm to evade the consequences by appointing a manager to be the 'person responsible'.

The law neither provides an incentive to the victim nor the inspectorate. Seizures under the Customs Act have increased remarkably in recent years because of the institution of a system of rewards proportionate to the value of the contraband seized. Similar schemes are in operation to avoid evasion of income tax or irregularities in foreign exchange. Why is such a scheme not introduced in respect of adulteration of food or the use of false weights? Is it because the government is not really interested in enforcing such laws? If persons who detect adulteration are rewarded will not there be many more cases being detected? No doubt there will be some cases of false and malicious complaints but would this not be a tolerable consequence if adulteration is substantially stopped?

Again, prescribing a minimum sentence of imprisonment no doubt sounds impressive and satisfies the instinctive reaction of all to the heinous offence of adulterating food. Its economic consequences are not, however, significant; if the proprietor can pass on the consequence to a helpless 'manager', it has no consequences at all. Why not, instead, a summary procedure, an automatic fine of say Rs 500 in rural areas, Rs 1,000 in small towns and Rs 5,000 in big cities, half the amount to go to the inspectorate, and the other half to the local community in some fund, *and the closing of the shop for, say, a month*? Would not this be a greater deterrent? If the consequence is not going to be deprivation of liberty, the existing paraphernalia of samples, laboratories and *panchas* can be simplified. Mobile teams, consisting of an inspector, a rudimentary laboratory and a magistrate can traverse the country on a random basis, testing and punishing as they go along.

Another aspect, wholly ignored in India at present, is that *all* legislation and all government policies must be directed to achieve the desired result. Today we have laws against adulteration of food and drugs. Yet our fiscal and industrial policies have the effect of making adulteration commoner and easier.

If more and more articles are processed and packed by large manufacturers the chances of adulteration or cheating in weights and measures would decline substantially. Not only are large manufacturers less likely to adulterate, their few factories are easier to inspect and supervise. An illiterate adivasi who may not be able to detect cheating in weighing tea or sugar is likely to be able to detect a torn package.

One would, therefore, expect a concerted government policy to encourage branded products, whether by private companies or co-operatives. One would expect a scheme to encourage the sale of packaged goods, by subsidies if necessary. We have policies which are the precise opposite. There is a greater excise duty on, say, packaged tea than loose tea! '*Masalas*' which are packed attract an excise duty, making them more expensive than '*masalas*' sold loose.

And, in the populist dislike of multinationals and big business, we encourage 'small-scale' industry. The consequences in the field of drugs are easy to see. The sale of sub-standard drugs is rampant, mainly to public hospitals and dispensaries. And virtually *all* the cases that have come to light relate to obscure small-scale manufacturers whose names become known to us only when the latest round of deaths takes place. There are believed to be 12,000 small-scale 'manufacturers' of drugs as against a few hundred manufacturers in the organized sector. Most of them merely formulate drugs; few of them have proper factories or quality control or testing facilities. They live by filling public tenders, compelled to underquote prices to survive.

Should not all our laws have the same direction? If we desire to stamp out adulteration of food or drugs, then our fiscal laws, our anti-monopoly legislations, our company laws—all must keep this objective in view.

We do not have an organized system of surveys. Though some legislation is preceded by, and consequent upon, a report by some expert body, even that is often not based on a detailed study. Much legislation is *ad hoc*.

After a law is enacted the legislators seem to lose interest. There are no independent surveys of its effectiveness. No doubt there are annual reports by the relevant ministries. These reports, compiled late and available even later, if available at all, are based on data available with the administration. The report relating to adulteration of foods will list the number of prosecutions launched, the number of convictions obtained, etc. But these figures tell us nothing of the extent of adulteration which has escaped detection altogether. And even when we know of the ratio of convictions to prosecutions, we are in the dark as to the causes of acquittals.

The officials whose task it is to administer a law do not have the time and objectivity to highlight the defects or lacunae in the law which makes their task difficult. They are unlikely to point to the corruption or inefficiency in their department. And they would have no knowledge of the 'cases' they are not aware of.

There must be independent surveys, whether by universities or other bodies, to tell us whether a law has achieved its objects; and, if it has not, why it has not. The expenditure on such surveys would be a negligible amount if one weighs it against the results it would produce.

Anti-Dowry Laws

I will conclude with a slightly detailed look at the laws against dowries. The parents of a girl have to pay dowry to the groom or his family. The amount depends on the social and economic status of the family and the prospects of the groom: a doctor commanding much more than a teacher. Though there are cases where the bride is harassed to extort higher amounts, leading to cases of suicide and even murder, for every one such case there are likely to be many more where such dire consequences do not result. The bride is reasonably happy. In such cases a dowry is more a way of life. The parents of the groom receive a dowry; they pay it when the sister of the groom has to be married.

Most of us would agree that a dowry is inherently objectionable. It is wrong that a girl cannot be married unless she or her family pays for it. It is, however, a much graver wrong, much more reprehensible, if the non-payment of dowry or a demand for more, leads to beatings or torture or death.

The distinction is important. The former is difficult to prevent by law, the latter is less difficult. The Dowry Prohibition Act, 1961, does not take adequate note of this distinction.

Dowries are rampant in India, reflecting the desire of parents of girls to get them married almost at any cost. Penniless girls could not easily get married in Victorian middle-class Europe and marriage settlements were common. The practice has almost disappeared in Europe not because it is prohibited by law but because a woman in Europe has attained considerable equality and economic independence. It is no longer a social imperative to get your daughter married; instead, she herself decides whether to marry at all and, if so, to whom. If our society still goes in for arranged marriages, if the parents of an unmarried daughter face social stigma, they will do anything to get the daughter married, including paying a dowry. No doubt the parents of the groom demand a dowry; no doubt (in many cases) they extort the money. But they do so because they are in a position of strength. Again, they are in a position of strength because they possess a commodity which the parents of the bride desire to secure almost at any price. The strength (and the evils of the dowry system) will go the instant the bride (or her parents) prefer non-marriage to the payment of a dowry. It is difficult to imagine how any law can stop dowries.

Parliament enacted the Dowry Prohibition Act in 1961. It was enacted to prohibit *the evil practice* of giving and taking of dowry. The Act, parliament was told, *ensured* that any dowry, if given, enures for the benefit of the wife. The Act defined dowry as property or valuable security paid in consideration of marriage. The giving or taking of dowry was made punishable by imprisonment up to six months. If, however, it was given, it was required to be transferred to the bride.

A number of questions come up. Why should the *giving* of dowry be punishable when the bride and her parents have to give dowry because of almost irresistible social pressures? Does this not equate the wrong-doer (the groom or his family) with the victim (the bride or her family)?

Apart from ethics, if the giving of information will expose both the giver and taker to punishment, will it not act as a disincentive to inform? Don't these provisions virtually ensure that no case of dowry will ever be reported except in cases where there is cruelty or violence? If the cases are not reported, the provision that the dowry will belong to the woman will not be effective. The hope of government in 1961 that the act would *ensure* that the dowry would enure to the bride remains just that, a hope.

The definition of 'dowry' in the 1961 Act and how it was enacted is itself interesting. The Bill excluded presents up to Rs 2,000 if in the form of clothes or ornaments. This was done to make the law 'workable'. The Parliamentary Committee scrutinizing the Bill objected as it felt, rightly, that it amounted to legitimizing dowry to the extent of Rs 2,000. The law, as enacted, permitted presents without any limit unless they were in consideration of marriage. The 1984 Amendment, designed to make the law more *vigorous*, made 'voluntary' presents of a 'customary' nature lawful if the value was not excessive considering the circumstances of the family.

Where does this take us? Money is wanted for what one can

buy with it. Clothes and furniture and ornaments are almost as good as cash. And how does one ever prove that it was *demanded*?

No wonder that the law has not worked. Would it not be better if the attack had been not so much at the institution of dowry but at the harassment of the bride or her family? The ordinary criminal law, with a few changes, might have achieved the result, particularly if provisions were made (as in the 1984 Amendment) enabling complaints to be made by recognized welfare institutions and organizations. The wider evil could then be tackled at source, by education and providing for the economic independence of women.

The Act makes no attempt to set up an enforcement machinery, trusting that the already overworked police and the overburdened criminal courts will be able to enforce the law. If the law is worth passing, if the legislators want to do more than merely pay lip service, one would expect the establishment of a network of welfare officers trained to investigate and report offences under the Act. The Act also offers no incentives at all to the victims; on the contrary, they are equated to the wrong-doers. Can you expect the bride to report the offence if the consequence will fall equally on *her* family?

We end up with a law which in its existing form is utopian, which is not socially acceptable, which has no effective enforcement machinery, which offers no incentives to the victims. Is it any surprise that the law is almost a total failure?

There must be a move to expose the whole sham structure of paper law after paper law which lulls the citizen into the false belief that something is being done; it not only does not achieve its ostensible object but, in the process, it discredits the whole legal system.

Postscript

Since this lecture was delivered in March 1988, parliament and the state legislatures continue to court popularity by enacting ambitious laws, and the executive continues to be hopelessly lethargic in implementing them. There has, however, been a very welcome development, attributable to the enthusiasm of the courts, led by the Supreme Court, to entertain 'public interest litigations', and the actions of many dedicated and public-spirited individuals and non-governmental organizations in moving the courts. In many decisions, in several fields, the courts have directed the executive to implement laws and also to monitor their implementation. Examples are court orders to ensure the implementation of laws abolishing forced labour and exploiting children, and laws designed to protect the environment. Such orders have made the 'paper' laws real laws. More and more public interest litigations and court orders, could, in time, solve the problem of 'paper' laws.

Land and Labour in India

The Demographic Factor

N. Krishnaji

During the 1960s Daniel Thorner travelled widely over the country and wrote extensively about the changes then taking place in Indian agriculture. We still read those writings of his for analytical insights into what was then described as the New Agricultural Strategy, now matured into the so-called green revolution. The observations he made watching that first scene have provided the seed material for two decades of scholarly effort by social scientists here and abroad. Likewise, his earlier studies of India on land reforms and the agrarian structure in general, have a quality of timelessness and generality that only a combination of scholarship and intuition can produce.

I refer to these works of Daniel Thorner because my own efforts during the last two-and-a-half decades to understand the Indian agrarian economy have roots in Thorner's writings. A tribute to Thorner must necessarily refer to themes close to his heart.

Among Thorner's foremost concerns was the distribution of land among landlords, cultivating owners and tenants. He was equally interested in the relative magnitudes of those who work on their own land and those who work for others as labourers. He attempted to assess the long-term trends in these distributions and compositions, paying attention not only to what published statistics actually mean but also to their theoretical and analytical significance. In this context, it is not clear to me from his work how much importance he gave to demographic factors. We know he had used Chayanovian ideas in

This is the text—slightly modified for publication—of the Third Daniel Thorner Memorial Lecture, delivered at the Centre for Economic and Social Studies, Hyderabad, on 9 March 1990. It was first published in *Economic and Political Weekly*, 5–12 May 1990.

formulating what he called the 'peasant economy' as a category in economic history and went on to summarize Chayanov's work as post-Marxian theory presumably of some relevance to India. On reflection, I think, however, that it will be wrong to infer that Thorner accepted the validity for countries like India of the so-called demographic differentiation arising from Chayanov's stylized description of the natural history of the family. Thorner has indeed noted in his introduction to Chayanov that the latter's theory may work well for thinly populated countries but would need serious modification for land-scarce economies. More directly, he analysed the impact of land reforms as well as other forces that shape the changes in land ownership on the processes of differentiation and the growth of agricultural labour in India.

It is not far-fetched, therefore, to imagine that Thorner's interest in Chayanov arose from and centred on the manner in which small peasants cope with an increasing family size, or how the small peasant economy has a tendency to persist in the face of capitalist penetration —slowing down the polarization process and giving it a specific character, with semi-proletarians, rather than those wholly divorced from the means of production, constituting a large section of the labour force. Among other factors, it is this kind of interpretation of Thorner that has promoted my interest in demographic questions posed in the context of a changing agrarian structure. In what follows, I want to make some observations on the deteriorating land–man ratio in India and the manner in which demographic factors induce changes in the distribution of land and thus in the ratio of agricultural labourers to cultivators. In doing so I will focus on inter-regional variations both in population growth and agricultural development and refer to the decisive role the state has played in promoting technological change and exacerbating regional disparities in the productivity of land which, along with the distribution of land, contributes significantly to the relationship between land and labour. I will indulge in some speculation about the shape of things to come during the next two or three decades.

I

The structural change in the Indian agrarian economy, as in other economies, has different facets: ranging from the growth of wage labour and the development of commodity, land and credit markets, to the links between agriculture and industry and further to the manner in which agrarian classes influence political and economic change.

A good deal of scholarly analysis of these changes has been set out in terms of how the capitalist mode penetrates into the agricultural sector. Unfettered capitalist development, based upon superior techniques of production and economies of scale, quickly puts the small farmer at a disadvantage. Not merely because of economies of scale but also because of the way the different markets—the land, labour and credit markets—tend to be interlinked to reinforce the differential advantage. The underlying processes are too well-known to be explicated here. It needs to be emphasized, however, that the processes of relative impoverishment of small peasants and the swelling of the ranks of agricultural labour are complementary to the process of capitalist and large-scale production. We may say there is only one process.

However, in retrospect, at least for the Indian case, we can recognize that the process has not been—and is not—an unfettered one. Indeed, why capitalist development in Indian agriculture is a slow process has been the subject of much discussion. I will not review this discussion. Instead, let me refer in brief to the role of the state.

The state has played a major role in the agrarian transformation in India in two distinct phases in the post-independence period. The first of these covers the implementation of land reforms—with varying degrees of success in the different regions of India. In this context, the elimination of zamindari and other similar types of tenurial relations is undoubtedly an important landmark in Indian agrarian history, but it has not led to the realization in full measure of the principle: 'land-to-the-tiller'. The structure that has emerged has left intact an extreme concentration in land ownership, with a small proportion of households claiming clear ownership rights to the major part of land in all the regions of India. Such a concentration meant that the large landholdings had either to be cultivated by wage labour or let out on lease on terms that changed with the times and to the advantage of the owners. And since the reforms concerning tenancy that followed had more to do with the regulation of the terms of tenure rather than with the total abolition of tenancy, land-leasing arrangements have continued to persist, although on a declining scale, with cultivation through wage labour becoming the predominant form in the large landholdings.

Associated with the historical emergence of a large concentration in land is the steady growth of labour households in the rural population. For the late seventies and early eighties it is estimated that about 37 per cent of Indian rural households earn the major part of their subsistence from wage work. This pool of labour is drawn from the landless population and other families who have only small bits of land. However, the proportion of landless households has decreased quite substantially, from about 23 per cent of all rural households during the early fifties to less than 10 per cent in recent years. This type of change suggests that increasing numbers of small peasants are seeking wage work to supplement their meagre incomes from land.

Along with the labourers at the bottom end of the land-ownership scale, small peasants owning less than 2.5 acres of land have continued—since the early fifties—to constitute over 60 per cent of all rural households. By the early eighties this proportion has increased to about two-thirds of the rural population. There is, of course, much regional variation behind this average: in states such as Kerala, Tamil Nadu and West Bengal, where the land–man ratios are very low, the proportion of such small holdings (in terms of ownership) is over 80 per cent. There is also the variation in productivity, so that small is not small everywhere. But even with fine adjustments, the fact that the majority is constituted by the landless and by those who do not own enough land for subsistence cannot be denied.

We know that the land ceiling laws exist merely in the statute books and that because of their poor implementation not much land has been redistributed. Therefore, it is likely that land reforms have made a contribution to the pattern of change in ownership described by published statistics, only to the extent that it is no longer possible to establish in the case of the big owners a clear identity between families and their holdings. However, family holdings hidden from view to evade the ceiling laws will probably be in the middle ranges and may not have contributed to the observed relative swelling of small holdings. Statistics, however, cannot reveal secrets.

In any case, we need to understand the persistence and growth of the small-scale farming economy, even during the phase of rapid technological changes and the emergence of relatively higher profit-making possibilities in the large-scale sector. To some extent, the second of the two phases of state intervention that I have referred to earlier, becomes relevant in this context. From about the mid-sixties, the state has promoted a massive technological transformation: not only through direct public investment in irrigation and infrastructure in general, but also through the provision of cheap credit and inputs and by buttressing agricultural prices through support operations. It is true that the benefits have accrued disproportionately to the surplus regions and to the large surplus producers everywhere. Nevertheless, support to agriculture in general—and this is a commitment that pervades Indian politics irrespective of political colour—must surely have provided some measure of protection to the small farming sector against the land-accumulating propensities of the rural rich.

It is difficult to provide a conclusive interpretation of the observed changes in land ownership, especially because, given the large regional variation, the answers could be different in different parts of India. Whether it is the growth of labour or the ability of the small peasant to survive by entering into wage work or other activities, or the adoption of technological change by the big owners, the underlying processes are complex and have strong regional–historical roots. I have no competence to make generalizations about these processes.

I want to restrict myself to demographic factors for two reasons. First, it is obvious that a deteriorating land–man ratio leads to increasing proportions of smaller holdings and, in the absence of compensating increases in the productivity of land in such holdings, induces wage dependence among the small peasants. Second, despite regional variations, demographic factors act uniformly, at least to a certain extent, and the outcomes are more predictable, in the short run, than the manner in which structural change takes place in agriculture.

II

Let me now consider some dimensions of population growth. In world history there are two conjunctures identified by unprecedented population increases in different parts of the globe. The first of these is Europe in the eighteenth and the first half of the nineteenth century, and the second is the contemporary third world. These two conjunctures have in common certain features: for example, a continuous rise—albeit at varying rates—in incomes and living standards, especially among the middle and upper classes, a falling death rate, and a high and fairly stable birth rate. But because the death rates in the poor countries have fallen dramatically in recent decades, population growth rates have been ranging above 2 per cent per annum in most countries in Asia, Africa and Latin America. In contrast, the growth rates in Europe in the eighteenth and nineteenth centuries were only of the order of 1 to 1.5 per cent per annum. The reasons are well known. The control and elimination of big killers such as malaria, cholera and smallpox, as well as the development of modern and effective methods of disease prevention and cure, are features more of the twentieth century—especially of the second half of it—than of the nineteenth century. The importance of declining mortality as a major determinant of a likely high population growth in the future lies in the fact that mortality rates would quite predictably decline further in the coming few decades in the poor countries, and, within them, especially in the poor regions and among the poorer classes characterized by relatively higher death rates even now.

Population growth in Europe and the west in general had begun to decline from high levels from about the middle of the nineteenth century. This decline had been brought about by a fairly continuous decrease in fertility (barring a brief period—the so-called baby boom period—after World War II). Without going into the very complex underlying causes, we may note that the prospects of a rapid fertility decline for the next two or three decades are not very bright for most countries in the third world, especially the big ones such as India and Bangladesh. The underlying difficulties are most sharply illustrated by the Chinese case. The promotion of the one-child family norm and the coercive methods used for its implementation—reminiscent of the Sanjay Gandhi times in India—have led to impressive declines in fertility and population growth rates in China during the seventies. But with the introduction of agrarian reforms in the most recent post-Mao phase, coupled with population momentum factors, birth rates have begun to increase once again even while death rates have tended to stabilize at the very low levels comparable to those in the rich countries. Some scholars suggest speculatively that the reasons could be purely economic and that they lie in the advantage of extra hands in the family, given the nature of the family production responsibility system. This is somewhat far-fetched because those who are born now will become helping hands only after a decade-and-a-half. Others refer in this context to cultural factors—such as the preference for sons—that are surfacing once again. Whatever the reasons, it is clear that the process of fertility transition can neither be hastened nor forced—beyond a point; it should not be forgotten that it has taken Europe and the west close to a century to achieve this type of transition during a period of rapid industrialization and all-round economic development, leading to both increasing living standards for workers and the provision of 'social security' (however understood).

One last point on the contrast with European history: the growing populations of Europe in the developmental phase were absorbed to a good extent by countries such as the US, Canada, Australia and New Zealand. However, nation-states have become stronger since those times and national boundaries are now virtually closed. Such scope as exists for international migration—whether for semi-skilled labour (as in West Asia) or for highly-skilled, technical and professional manpower (as in countries like the US or West Germany)—is wholly dictated by labour shortages of given types in the receiving countries. Regulated by strict quotas, the flows can hardly redress the international imbalances between resources and population.

Uneven regional development is, of course, at the heart of the matter in both the phases. The brute force of colonialism of the earlier phase has given way to economic power that underlies the present. Only the rules of the game have changed.

III

To assess the consequences of a high rate of population growth—likely to remain so during the next two or three decades in India—on the agrarian economy, it is necessary to look at the variations in the components of growth not only across the sub-regions of the country but also among the different agrarian classes.

Let me consider first the differentials between the poor and the rich. It is commonly believed that the poor are more prolific and that, as the Victorian epigram has it, while the rich get richer the poor get children. Despite its strong moorings within the western intellectual tradition—carried over to the educated middle and upper classes in the third world—the belief is based more on plain prejudice than on hard facts. Careful studies show that, under conditions of uncontrolled fertility—that is, in the absence of artificial means to prevent births—fertility levels tend to be somewhat lower among the poorer classes. This is generally true for the countries in the third world but is modified to the extent that the practice of birth control is slowly spreading. Reviews suggest that both an inferior nutritional status and a longer duration of breast-feeding (among other factors) contribute to such a differentially lower fertility among the poor.

The prejudice has probably spread because of what has

happened during the phase of demographic transition—the passage from high to low levels of fertility—in Europe (from about 1850). It was the educated and well-to-do classes who first began to practise birth control, which then gradually spread to the poorer folk. It is only during this transitional phase that fertility levels among the poor were higher.

Nevertheless, the mistaken belief has led to much theorizing about the supposedly higher reproductive capacity and its realization among the poor. A Marxist version of such a theory reads:

> When people are divorced from the means of production, they are left with only their labour to sell. To increase their income, the poor must produce more labourers per household. Thus while the rich can reinvest in capital and get richer, the poor can only 'get children'. High birth rates are therefore not the cause of continued poverty, they are a consequence of it. (Karen L. Michaelson [ed.], *The Poor Get Children*, Monthly Review Press, 1981)

Standing Malthus on his head in this manner is of course radical rhetoric at its best, but it shares with Malthus some mistaken notions about poor families. The formulation may at best be valid for the transitional phase, but it does promote prejudice.

For example, in India, agricultural labour families are small on average, ranging below 5, while for the rural population as a whole the average ranges above 5.5. Not only a somewhat lower fertility—by how much it is difficult to say—but also a higher mortality is responsible for this type of difference in the family size.

One of the important reasons why agricultural labour and small peasant households tend to be smaller on average is that they are always—in all regions of India—among the poorest. And, because poverty and undernutrition are associated with higher levels of morbidity and mortality, the proportion of children who survive beyond the age of five years in poor families tends to be smaller than in other groups of the rural population.

The implications of such demographic variation are obvious. As a consequence of narrow fertility differentials in the absence of deliberate control, and of higher death rates among the rural poor, agricultural labour and poor peasant populations are expected to grow at a somewhat lower rate than the rest of the population. However, they are not closed populations. Their numbers are affected by migration to some extent, but more importantly by the additions to the ranks of the poor through the pauperization process. Before we discuss these factors let me turn to a brief discussion on inter-regional variations in the demographic rates.

There is a considerable variation in these rates, especially in the rural parts of the country with which I am exclusively concerned here. Data relating to the late 1980s show, for example, that the crude death rate ranged from about 6 per thousand in Kerala to 16 per thousand in Uttar Pradesh. Among the states with high death rates are Bihar, Orissa, Madhya Pradesh and Rajasthan. The states of Maharashtra, Punjab and Haryana have relatively low death rates, although not as low as Kerala. In general, the poorer regions of the country experience higher death rates, for understandable reasons. This is even more sharply illustrated by the range in the infant mortality rate: it is about 25 per thousand live births in rural Kerala, as against an all-India rural average of slightly over 100 per thousand live births. Among the states with very high infant mortality rates are Uttar Pradesh (135), Orissa (130) and Madhya Pradesh (127) (roughly 5 to 6 times the Kerala rate).

Correspondingly, there is some variation in rural birth rates as well, but it is narrower. It must be noted in this context that there has been a marginal decline in the birth rate during the last two decades, the rural crude birth rate at the all-India level having fallen from about 38 per thousand to 34 per thousand. But the decline is unevenly spread and there is still much regional variation in fertility levels. The birth rates in rural Kerala and Tamil Nadu have come down sharply, to 22.2 and 24.4 per thousand respectively, whereas they continue to be at high levels of over 37 in Bihar, Madhya Pradesh, Rajasthan and Uttar Pradesh. Although the correlations are not perfect, generally high birth rates and high death rates go together and characterize the demographic picture of the poorer regions of rural India.

I have discussed these inter-class, inter-regional differences in fertility and mortality in some detail because they have clear-cut and quite predictable consequences for the land-to-labour ratios.

Consider mortality first. Kerala, including rural Kerala, has already attained a very low death rate (of about 6 per thousand, a level that prevails in the western countries). A further reduction in this rate may not be possible because, even as infant mortality can be reduced further, deaths occurring among the old may increase. The decline in death rates, which will surely come about in the next few decades, is bound to be more prominent in regions such as Madhya Pradesh, Bihar, Orissa and parts of Uttar Pradesh, and in general in the poorer sub-regions everywhere in rural India. And, within such regions, the decline would be sharper among the rural poor: agricultural labour and poor peasant families.

There is no undue optimism behind this prediction. It is based on a projection of our understanding of the history of demographic transition and also on the Indian experience during the post-independence period. The provision of clean drinking water, the spread of immunization practices, the control of infections, and other measures of public health and those for improving access to private medical care will continue on their upward course and bring down morbidity and mortality rates. To give only two examples, gastro-enteric diseases which take a heavy toll among children below the age of five are easily controllable at relatively low costs, as by oral rehydration therapy that is spreading in popularity. Deaths occurring among mothers and infants at childbirth will decline with the spread of hygienic delivery practices and the gradual replacement of the traditional *dai*s by medical and para-medical personnel. I mention these two examples because, for example, infant and child deaths account for about a quarter of all deaths and child survival beyond the age of five years is an important determinant of longevity. So, given the scope for a reduction in infant mortality and the likely course of public intervention in this sphere, there is no doubt that the death rates will decrease among the poorer classes all over rural India.

Turning now to birth rates, the decline in them has begun only recently in the rural areas, and it is likely that the process of demographic transition will take the usual historical course. Given the large differentials that exist between Kerala at one extreme and Madhya Pradesh, Bihar and Uttar Pradesh at the other, and given that fertility will decline further in Kerala, the transitional phase is likely to last several decades. But if history repeats itself, the practice of birth control will be led by the better-educated and well-to-do classes even in the countryside, and will spread to the poorer families only much later.

This means that the rural poor in the poorer parts of the country would be caught during the coming few decades in the same trap as the poor countries had been caught during the post-colonial period. This trap—I call it a trap deliberately because in the public domain we have to continue with measures for controlling morbidity and mortality—is the second phase of the demographic transition in which death rates continue to decrease while birth rates remain stable at their pre-transitional levels. This second phase will be experienced by the rural poor, even as the rural and urban rich go through the third phase, characterized by a low mortality rate and a falling birth rate. We must note in this context that in Kerala the conditions for decline in mortality and fertility have been created for all sections of the population more or less simultaneously, and that is probably why the Kerala case is such a dramatic incident in the history of demographic transition.

The implications are obvious enough. Even if processes that convert peasants into paupers are held in check so that net additions to the ranks of the rural poor do not take place from outside, the poorer sections will grow at a relatively faster rate, by virtue of a falling death rate among the poor and a declining fertility rate among the rich. In saying this I am not making a simple-minded projection of the past into the future. For, I have modified the transition model, taking into account inter-class differentials in demographic rates. Besides, we know that among the important correlates of both low mortality and low fertility are: a high rate of survival of infants and children; the spread of literacy and education, especially among females; a satisfactory living standard associated with expanding employment opportunities for men and women; and some provisions for social security for the aged. In the case of the rural poor these conditions are not satisfied. Therefore, while it is safe to predict that the demographic transition will encompass the poor as well ultimately, it can only be in the distant future—perhaps in the second half of the next century, if not later.

In the interim, populations of the poor countries, and of the poorer sections within them, will continue to grow. An idea about the magnitude of this growth can be had from the experience of Kerala, where demographic change has been the most remarkable in India. With birth rates still above 20 per thousand and death rates plunging to a very low level—6 per thousand—Kerala's population will continue to grow at between 1 to 1.5 per cent. Since conditions for a further decline in fertility exist and are being promoted assiduously and therefore will be strengthened, no doubt the rates of population growth in Kerala will come down even further and Kerala will be the first among Indian regions to achieve that demographic state of bliss:

zero population growth, i.e. a constant population that does not exert any pressure on the available resources. But even the most unbridled optimism cannot see this happening in the next couple of decades; it will take longer.

The poorer parts of India cannot, however, replicate easily the Kerala experience. Historical experience can perhaps be unwound fast by economists and historians to point to lessons to be learnt, but history itself cannot be speeded up. Kerala has had a long history—going back to the nineteenth century—of social involvement and state intervention in the fields of education and public means. And, after independence, the mobilization of the rural and the urban poor by the communists has led not only to the effective implementation of land reforms on a scale bigger than anywhere else in India, but also to a number of other measures that provide the so-called 'social security', recognized as a necessary condition for the transition to low fertility.

The conditions that promote a fertility decline will emerge only slowly in the rest of the country. The prospects in this respect—in the next few decades—are certainly not very bright for the poor in India in general. So, even as the population growth rates come down, mainly through the reduction in fertility among the middle and upper classes, higher growth rates are likely to prevail among the poor.

Population growth rates in any given region of course depend not only on the difference between the birth and death rates but also on net migration. However, the nature and magnitude of migratory flows within India are such that they hardly have a mitigating influence on the decreasing land–man ratio in rural areas at the state level. By far the most important of these flows is the rural-to-urban type of migration that does reduce the pressure on land. However, although such flows contribute to rapid increases in urban populations, they constitute only a small section of the rural population, so that the rural population in the total has declined only marginally from 83 per cent in 1951 to 76 per cent in 1981. Two further points on rural–urban flows:

1. They tend to be both localized and episodic as far as labour migration to industrial and mining centres are concerned and therefore their impact on the reduction in labour-to-land ratios can be more marked at the village or block level.

2. The rural-to-urban flows are of course limited not only by the development of urban work opportunities but also by the fact that migration is not cost-free and finding work is uncertain. It is no

wonder that within the rural-to-urban type of migration, crossing of state boundaries is a quantitatively insignificant phenomenon.

In contrast, rural-to-rural migratory flows are more prominent but they relate mostly to movements within the state boundaries. Indeed, by far the largest component of internal migration is that which takes place from one village to a neighbouring one in the same district. Moreover, labour migration accounts for only a small part of the flows, a good part of migration—that of women—arising from marriage and rules of residence.

I mention all this only to emphasize the importance of uneven regional development in agriculture (which I will discuss a little later). Inter-regional inequalities have grown and may continue to grow, but the redistribution of populations through migration does not—and probably cannot—take place on a scale big enough to bring even a marginal reduction in inter-state disparities. To give an example in this context: rural Punjab, which has prospered most in the country in recent times, has received during the decade of the 1970s less than half a million migrants from other states of the country. Likewise the out-migration from rural Bihar, which has done very badly in agriculture during the last two-and-a-half decades, is an equally insignificant flow in relation to its total population.

The situation is somewhat similar to the international imbalances between resources and population that cannot be reduced through migratory flows. While sub-nationalism within India is not yet strong enough to seal borders, there are both economic and cultural factors behind the relative immobility of the rural populations. The tenacity with which a peasant sticks to his native patch is, of course, an economic phenomenon, given that even a bit of land provides a secure, if insufficient, income, but it is hard to imagine a land-hungry Bengali or Malayali peasant migrating to Rajasthan in search of land that may be available there.

IV

During the period 1961 to 1981—on which I want to concentrate—land–man ratios have declined in all the major states in India. To assess this trend, if we look at the size of ownership holding per rural household, the decline in India as a whole is from about 4.4 acres to about 3.2 acres per household—a decrease of about 28 per cent. On the other hand, if we rely on gross cropped areas available per person in rural areas as an appropriate measure, the decline is from 1.03 acres to 0.79 acre per person—a decrease of about 23 per cent. I shall rely on this measure, i.e. gross cropped area per person, as well as the value of production per person in the ensuing discussion. The latter measure is relevant not only because it takes into account the differentials in cropping patterns and productivities of land, but also because it is a measure of per capita income from land—the most important determinant of welfare in the rural areas.

There is some variation in the decline in gross cropped area per person as between the different states. As I have remarked earlier, the rates of rural population growth have varied to some extent, and so have the rates at which cropped areas have expanded. But there are no systematic correlations between area expansion and initial levels of the land–man ratio, and similarly between rates of population growth on the one hand and initial levels of per capita production, rates of growth in productivity and per capita income on the other. This is only to be expected because any mutual adjustment that takes place between population levels and resource availability—through, for example, greater expansion of areas induced by fast deteriorating land–man ratios or through lower rates of population growth in areas experiencing stagnant or declining resource and income level—can only take place in the long run. More importantly, both population growth and area expansion have been governed by exogenous factors. In the case of population growth, the decline in mortality was the main regulating factor. In their spatial variation, death rates, and the decreases in them, do not bear a significant relationship with the availability of land. On the other hand, in this period, the expansion of gross cropped area has come about mainly through the development of irrigation, which had nothing to do with demographic factors or demographic change.

Irrigation expansion and the improvement in cropping intensities are two important components of the green revolution and we know that the most impressive increases in this respect have been largely in the north-west. It is true that private investment in irrigation has played a big part, but this would not have been possible without the intervention of the state through its diverse activities for promoting the green revolution.

The decline in land–man ratios at moderately varying rates in all the major states contributes directly to predictable changes in the distribution of land. Other things remaining the same, these declining ratios produce a proliferation of small holdings and a reduction in the average size of holdings.

The question of size of holdings is of obvious relevance to the determination of which households have to seek wage work within agriculture outside their own farms or in non-agricultural activities. What matters most is of course not the size of holding but whether it can generate subsistence for the peasant. The issue of increases in productivity, that could compensate for a declining size in holding, is thus crucial to the pauperization process.

Before I discuss the variations in productivity change, let me digress a bit and turn to other factors that shape the changes in the distribution of land ownership. Earlier I referred to the failure of land ceiling laws in leading to a significant redistribution of land. One must add, in this context, that some land has passed into the hands of the landless but it is too minuscule to have radically altered the distribution; moreover, much of such land is hutment land. In any case, the crucial issue concerns the passage of land from the poor to the rich—a phenomenon that lies at the heart of the processes of proletarianization and pauperization. It is difficult to get an idea about the extent to which it has taken place (from the landholdings data which, generally, show a marginal decline in the concentration ratio, perhaps because the largest holdings are not visible to the statistical eye; or perhaps a concentration in terms of surface area is not actually emerging). What is certainly true is that because the gains to the big farmers have in general been disproportionately larger, the disparities in incomes from land between the small and the big farmers are growing.

I have looked at some data (referring to 1971–72) on sale transactions in land to gain some insight into the land alienation process. Sale transactions appear to be generally minimal. At the all-India level only about one-half of 1 per cent of land has been transacted during one year. This means that if this annual rate is normal, about 5 per cent of the land changes hands every decade. More importantly, the data suggest that most of the transactions take place between and within the classes of middle and big owners. There is no evidence of a large-scale land transfer from the poor to the middle or upper strata. In any case, the poor, although constituting about a half of the rural population, have such a small proportion of the total land that the alienation of the land they own, at the observed rates, will not radically alter the overall distribution among other owners, although the ranks of the landless will swell in proportion. So, to the extent that the perceptible decrease in 'landlessness' among the rural households is not merely statistical but real, the data would suggest that small peasants have been able to cling to their tiny plots but are entering into wage work.

In saying this, I am not denying or even minimizing the historical importance of land alienation as a describing and governing factor behind the processes of proletarianization and pauperization. Indeed, apart from eviction of tenants by the so-called 'resumption' of cultivation by owners (on which Thorner has written much, referring to the fifties and sixties), alienation of land from peasants to landlords, moneylenders and traders—leading to the pauperization of the peasantry—is the very essence of Indian agrarian history. So also, alienation of land from 'tribal' populations is an important contemporary issue.

What I am suggesting, as a generalization of sorts, is that the models derived from our pre-independence historical experience cannot be carried over to the present, and that we must recognize the fact that small peasants have been able to hold on to their landholdings during the last two or three decades.

The staying power—the ability of the small peasants to survive—is no doubt derived in part from the support the agricultural sector receives through various measures, including those specifically meant to benefit the small farmer. But it is also derived from their increasing participation in markets as sellers of produce. The early debates on the relatively higher productivity of land in the small farm sector have clearly shown both higher labour intensities and higher-valued crop combinations as two of the most important features of small farm agriculture. However, whether it is the extent of family labour use or the crop combination, the choices at the household level are dictated by a largely unchanging resource base and constraints upon its use, and not—in Chayanovian fashion—by the calculations on the drudgery of labour within the family as an economic unit. But when families grow in size, as they surely do, and the resource base does not expand, wage work is the only option left.

This is admittedly a stylized description of structural change in Indian agriculture but it gives us some clues about the manner in which the components—the growth of labour, the pauperization process, the growth of commercialization and a slow process of polarization—are all linked to some extent through demographic factors.

The question of productivity change—to which I now wish

to turn—is more complicated. The most striking aspect of this is the widening of inter-regional disparities in agricultural productivity. This story has been told and retold several times, but mostly in terms of the productivity of land and its improvement during the sixties and the seventies, and not in terms of the growth of production in relation to the growth of population. It is only in north-western India (Punjab, Haryana, west Uttar Pradesh and Jammu and Kashmir) that impressive increases in per capita production have taken place during the sixties and seventies; in Andhra Pradesh and Gujarat the increase has been marginal. Maharashtra, Karnataka and Rajasthan present a somewhat stagnant picture. The rest of the country, covering the eastern region, Tamil Nadu and Kerala in the south, and Madhya Pradesh, has experienced a fall in per capita production—production not having kept pace with population.

The differences in population growth are not wide enough for demographic change to be cited as an underlying reason. On the other hand, we do know that an uneven regional development of irrigation and other resources has largely contributed to the region-specific nature of the spread of the new technology.

The importance of uneven regional development, as I have already suggested, lies in the absence or difficulty of matching population flows that can redress imbalances. Of course, it is true that regional self-sufficiency was never a clear-cut policy objective. In the agricultural sector, especially in the foodgrain economy, the guiding principle has been national, and not regional, self-sufficiency and the selected engine of growth is the well-endowed farmer. Referring to foodgrain production once again, we note that the widening regional disparities are sought to be mitigated through a public distribution system, so that one can read a measure of justice in the growth strategy. But the uneven potentialities for earning income from land that remain (despite the redistribution of food), generate a corresponding unevenness in the pauperization processes. I would like to repeat, in this context, that the poorer and hitherto neglected regions are likely to experience higher rates of population growth in the next few decades.

V

I have focussed on demographic factors in this note not to raise the Malthusian demons but to assess and describe the course of population growth and its consequences in a historical setting and within an analytical framework that are quite different from Malthus's.

Indeed, the demon of population adjustment through an increasing death rate has been exorcised by history. The most striking demonstration of this is the continuous fall in death rates all over India, despite much variation in the production and availability of food, with some parts such as the eastern region experiencing declining levels in foodgrain production per capita. The trends in the production of food and in population will take their future course largely independent of each other.

But the second Malthusian demon, of population pressure on land leading to an ever-widening pool of labour and a decline in real wage rates and the living conditions of the poor, is not so easily vanquished. These prospects cannot, however, be understood in terms of purely demographic factors working in combination, as in Malthus, with the law of diminishing marginal returns to land. They have to be understood in terms of the historical evolution of a high concentration of land and the manner in which it acts as a barrier to genuine land reform on the one hand and influences the nature of technological change on the other.

Famine Mortality

Elizabeth Whitcombe

In response to the alarming incidence of famine in the later nineteenth century and the escalation of its economic and social costs, the British government of India devised a systematic policy for the assessment and relief of famine and scarcity. Famine was determined by a specific sequence of events. Insufficient or untimely rainfall led to the failure of not one but a succession of harvests. Prices of foodstuffs rose, prompting government to predict that

> eventually prices will rise so high that the labouring classes cannot, with the wages they earn, buy enough food to keep sufficient health and strength for daily labour; then, unless assisted, they must gradually become weakened until they are unable to work at all and death by slow starvation follows; or if labour fails synchronously with the rise in prices, the same end results but more rapidly.[1]

The rise in prices was taken as the index of distress; and mortality, presumed to be the direct consequence of starvation, as the index of a famine's severity.

Government's intention was that measures for the relief of starvation should be implemented on receipt of notification of rising prices, to prevent, or at least limit, mortality. Assistance to the distressed was not to be provided in the form of foodstuffs, an interference with private commerce warranted only 'if the safety of the lives of the population is incompatible with the freedom of trade'.[2] Instead, district officers were to prepare programmes of public works with a scale

This essay is a revised version of the Fourth Daniel Thorner Memorial Lecture, delivered at the Indian Statistical Institute, Calcutta, in January 1991. It was first published in *Economic and Political Weekly*, 5 June 1993.

of wages such as would enable labourers to buy food. Camps were to be established to house the labourers and feeding-centres for the hopelessly destitute who could not work.

In the event, this policy did little to mitigate distress and less to prevent mortality. An explanation may be found in the events of the famine years; not merely in economic and social events, for which an impressive literature is now available, but in the peculiar and dramatic sequence of climatic events and the clinical and pathological history of famine years, which may be reconstructed from observations filed weekly by officers of the departments of revenue and agriculture, public works, and sanitation, of the provincial and central governments. The reconstruction of this famine history calls into question the assumptions upon which government's famine policy was based. Rising prices proved to be unreliable as a distress signal. The relation of prices to quantities of foodstuffs was never established; nor was the critical point determined which prices must reach for government to respond with the greatest efficacy. Relief schemes, therefore, could not but come into operation piecemeal, wherever district officers could convince their superiors, by the pertinence of their observations, of the necessity for intervention. Mortality, moreover, on the colossal scale recorded in famine years, was not simply the direct consequence of starvation but the outcome of a far more complex set of conditions than official policy allowed for. What these conditions were and how patterns of mortality characteristic of famine years were determined by them can be demonstrated by the history of Madras, 1877–78, compared with Punjab, 1896–97 and 1900–01. No wretchedness on such a scale has ever been better documented. It is possible, therefore, to conduct an autopsy of famine mortality, to clarify the nature of the problem in its complexity: who died, and where; when did they die and how, of what cause, and why.

Madras, 1877–78

The years of famine, 1877–78, were distinguished not by unrelieved drought but by months of drought succeeded by rain, tempestuous especially in coastal districts, from May to June, giving way to drought again in July to return from August at greater than average rate of precipitation (Table 1 and Figure 1).

By the beginning of 1877, scarcity had been officially declared

TABLE 1: ***Madras: Chronology of Events, End 1876–1878***

1876 end	Rains failed, loss of cattle
	Grain imports ↑
	Prices ↑↑↑—Food scarce—Distress: Kistna to Malabar
	Bellary, Cuddapah, N. Arcot, Kurnool: 7,50,000 on relief works
1877 Jan.	Relief Works: 902,629: Wages ↓: Stricter control of admissions
	Gratuitous relief: 80,834
Apr.	Temple reports situation worsening, especially in lower classes
	Relief works: ↓: Deterioration in labourers' condition
	Gratuitous relief: ↑↑: Special allowance for 'reduced' persons
May	Prices ↑
	Cyclonic storm: Madras, SE Coast
June	Rain: Initially general then poor
	Prices steady
July	SW Monsoon failed
	Prices ↑↑
	Relief ↑↑
Aug.	Rain
Sep.	Prices reach max.
	Rain good
	12 districts: 2,300,000 on relief
End Sep.	Prices ↓
	Relief ↓
Oct.	NE Monsoon: Good
	Storms: Tanjore, Tinnevelly, Madura
	NE Coast: Rain poor
	Relief ↓
	Prices ↓ Slow
Nov.–	
1878 May	Prices ↓
	Relief ↓
June	Rain poor
	Prices ↑
	Relief ↑
Jul–Aug.	Rain
	Prices steady then ↓
	Relief ↓
Oct.	Rain
	Famine 'practically over'
Dec.	Famine relief officially ends.

Sources: Government of Madras, *Review of the Madras Famine, 1876–78,* Madras, 1878; *Annual Report of the Sanitary Commissioner, Madras,* 13, 1876; 14, 1877; 15, 1878; *Report of the Revenue Administration, Madras,* 1876, 1877, 1878.

FIGURE 1: ***Madras: Rainfall, Monthly Averages, 1870–74, 1877, 1878***

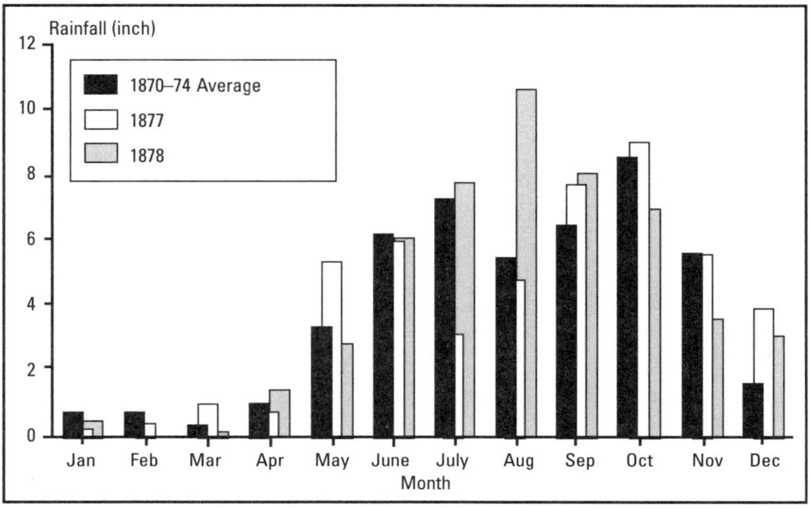

Sources: Annual Reports of the Sanitary Commissioner, Madras, 1870–79.

in Madras town and in seven districts: Nellore, Cuddapah, Bellary, Kurnool, North Arcot, Coimbatore and Madura. By March–April, prolonged drought converted scarcity, 'as evidenced by rocketing prices', into famine in South Arcot, Trichinopoly and Tinnevelly. Malthus's predictions were not borne out. The coastal, intensively irrigated districts of Tanjore, Ganjam, Godavary and Kistna, with populations of 540 per square mile and above, were prosperous and escaped, while famine ravaged the up-country districts where population barely averaged 150 per square mile.[3]

Drought, scarcity, hunger and the death of cattle compelled the villagers in the famine districts from late 1876 to migrate in search of food and work. They followed routes long established by seasonal migration: from Nellore, Chingleput and North Arcot in the direction of Madras; from north Nellore and Kurnool to the Kistna delta; from Coimbatore to Trichinopoly and Malabar. At the height of the famine, from April to July 1877, the migration was enormous, certainly tens of thousands, probably hundreds of thousands, of 'labouring poor'. Migration from Madura and Tinnevelly, for example, to the coffee estates in Ceylon and the Travancore hills more than doubled. Government policy encouraged migration to towns where foodgrains were stockpiled by private trade, at the behest of official policy, and to the public works and relief camps.[4]

The Madras famine was 'the first in which official arrangements were made for the systematic inspection of the distressed people'. In March, April, May and July 1877, the Sanitary Commissioner, Dr W.R. Cornish, toured the famine districts, making a clinical inspection of labouring gangs on the public works and the destitute in relief centres. Cornish physically examined some 3,000 persons. In March, he noted 'a general tendency to leanness of all classes . . . ribs, collar and shoulder bones are all unusually prominent. . . . But many had a fair amount of muscular development and clean, glossy skins.' Colonel (later Sir) Richard Temple, send from Bombay for famine duty in recognition of his expertise in the design and implementation of relief schemes, had toured the famine districts shortly before Cornish. Temple had been impressed by the muscular physique of the labourers. Concluding that the scale of wages was pitched too far above the bare necessity of relief, Temple had ordered a reduction.[5] Cornish, whose clinical eye had been caught by the incongruity of 'muscular destitution', took a history which showed the error of Temple's interpretation. Some nine-tenths of these labourers were 'of the animal food eating castes . . . [and] had largely subsisted on bullocks which had died or been destroyed on account of famine. In March, April and May, in many districts, beef was the cheapest food procurable.

The presence of these apparently well-fed individuals in the labour gangs caused superficial observers to draw wrong inferences as to the extent and severity of the distress amongst them. They ate meat because the famine had brought an abundance of it, temporarily, to their doors, and the food nourished them; but the supply was of very precarious and uncertain duration and the fact ought to have been accepted as a sign of the severity of the food dearth, instead of which there is reason to believe that the ruling authorities were at one time misled as to the real nature of the calamity, by glowing reports week after week of the physical condition of the labouring classes.[6]

Scarcity had already had severe effects on the old and young. Once the meat supply was exhausted, the condition of the labourers deteriorated rapidly. In Bellary in April Cornish found some 30 per cent of the gangs to be in a state of emaciation; in July, 'nearly all the people on the works were wasted'.[7]

His inspections provided Cornish with a superabundance of

the physical signs of starvation. *Wasting*, 'the most general physical attribute of the famine stricken', observed to follow a characteristic sequence: first, the loss of body fat, manifested in the disappearance of the rounded contour of the buttocks; later, the loss of muscle tissue from limbs and trunk, detectable in the abnormal protrusion of elbow and knee joints, in the wide spaces between closed legs, in the prominence of ribs. *Anaemia*, the characteristic pallor of mucous membranes of the eyes and mouth, cracking and ulceration of corners of the mouth and of the tongue, the sign of iron deficiency; the 'drawn' expression of women and children; the increase in heart-rate, 'the movement of the heart, knocking against the ribs, [visible] even at a distance of some yards'. *Scurvy*, observed in the early stages of the famine since green vegetables had disappeared from the markets before foodgrains, and in March already, in North Arcot and Cuddapah, the heart of the famine tract, the normally ubiquitous lime had become unprocurable. The characteristic deep, purplish-blue discoloration and thickening of the gums, ulceration, bleeding and loosening of the teeth were repeatedly found on physical examination. '*Famine skin*', 'dirty-looking', scaly, degenerate epithelium; and a striking reddish pigmentation of the hair, now known to be indicative of *kwashiorkor*, hypoprotein-anaemia. By July, Cornish estimated that some 60–70 per cent of the labouring population of the famine districts were suffering from scurvy, anaemia and generalized wasting. The physical signs of starvation, he noted, were 'significantly absent in cooks and others employed in camp kitchens'.[8]

In women and children, in addition, there were the signs of arrested growth and development. Children born in the camps had 'the wizened and spider-like appearance of the half-starved', from defective nutrition *in utero*. Of girls aged twelve to fourteen, barely 20 per cent had reached puberty. Menstruation in young women was scanty and irregular, and in severe emaciation, ceased altogether. The population of pregnant women was remarkably low. These findings were confirmed in the decline in birth rate: in 1877, 25 per cent, in 1878, 50 per cent below the average of the two previous years. Analysis of the breast milk of mothers in the camps showed it to be no more than a thin, watery secretion, deficient in solids, salts and casein.[9]

Starvation was unmistakable, widespread and unmistakably severe.

At the height of the famine, from April to July 1877, 'the

labouring poor, destitute of food and work, forsook their village homes to an enormous extent'. Government also saw in migration the prospect of relief, and actively encouraged it. Attempts were made to open up new routes from the famine districts, from Bellary and Cuddapah, for example, to the Buckingham Canal works on the Nellore coast. Government and the migrants were deceived. The drought which had driven them out deprived them of food, and water, on the way to the towns and camps. Foraging killed the migrants, the necessity to 'resort to unusual—repulsive and noxious—kinds of food': the result, diarrhoea and death from dehydration. Wells and tanks had long dried up. Such water as was available was mostly contaminated: the risk of drinking it, diarrhoea and death from dehydration. The excessive heat of the famine months heightened the risk of dehydration. The planned migration to the Buckingham Canal served merely to demonstrate the cruel futility of the expedient. The 'line of migration' selected was 'out of the usual course', understandably, since it lay 'across a barren mountain range'. 'The experiment had ultimately to be abandoned as unsuccessful and full of disaster to the people.'[10]

Most of the migrants were the able-bodied poor. How many died *en route* will never be known. These deaths went for the most part unregistered. Circumstantial evidence suggests many thousands. Of those who survived the journey, hundreds of thousands were to die at their destination, 'victims', as Cornish put it, 'of the circumstances of the food dearth [which brought] the people under peculiar insanitary conditions . . . Hundreds of thousands of destitute poor crowded the relief works and centres and towns where food is to be had; all this contributed to disorders of digestive functions, often with fatal consequences'. The principal cause of death and disease was the 'deterioration' in the water supply:

> The usual surface wells and tanks have dried up and the sources that are available are so much polluted, that even persons who are particular about the quality of their water are unable to procure a wholesome supply. When the people, therefore, are accumulated by thousands on various road works and the wells were few and far between, it was no cause for surprise that sudden explosions of cholera occurred amongst them.[11]

An abundant water supply and efficient 'conservancy' were provided for in camp plans. Estimates of the population to be provided for were wretchedly inadequate. Camp facilities were overwhelmed from the outset. Explosions of cholera were recorded early in the famine, declining by March, when migration intensified, to be overtaken by other diarrhoeal diseases with similar fatal outcome. 'Some form of bowel disorder', Cornish estimated from the weekly returns of camp hospitals, accounted for at least three-quarters of the mortality.[12]

Post-mortem evidence substantiated Cornish's estimate. From December 1876 to July 1877, 3,250 persons were admitted to the hospital of a relief camp on the outskirts of Madras; of these 1,117 (34 per cent) died. Porter, the medical officer in charge, performed 459 autopsies. The bodies were 'greatly emaciated':

	Average Ht	*Average Wt (lb)*	
		Normal	*Autopsy*
Tamil men (181)	5′ 7″	110–120	54 –113
women (121)	5′ 2″	95–105	40–102

The skin was dry and scaly. Most bodies slowed oedema—swelling due to the accumulation of fluid—of the feet; some, generalized oedema. The internal organs were 'wasted'; the brain markedly atrophic and reduced in weight. The most significant changes were found in the gastro-intestinal tract: loss, and in many cases ulceration, of the mucosal lining, a gross reduction overall in the absorptive surface of the intestine. Porter identified some cases of cholera; most he diagnosed as 'terminal dysentery and diarrhoea of famine'. The pathological appearances he describes are consistent, in a modern interpretation, with bacillary dysentery, the immediate cause of death being gross fluid loss.[13]

Registration, while approximate and inaccurate in detail, provides an adequate source for overall estimations of mortality by region, principal cause and by season.[14] Mortality during the months of drought, from late 1876 to July 1877, the mortality, principally, of migration and of towns and camps, of diarrhoeal diseases, famine mortality in the strictest sense, may have amounted to some three-quarters of a million, a provisional estimate based on camp and municipal returns. The total mortality for 1877, however, was officially estimated at 1.5 million and calculated by Cornish to be in excess of 3 million. An examination of the monthly returns for the famine years shows not one but two phases (Figure 2). 'Phase I', mortality of the months of drought, to July 1877, was the mortality from cholera and bacillary

FIGURE 2: ***Madras: Registered Mortality, 1877, 1878, Monthly Distribution***

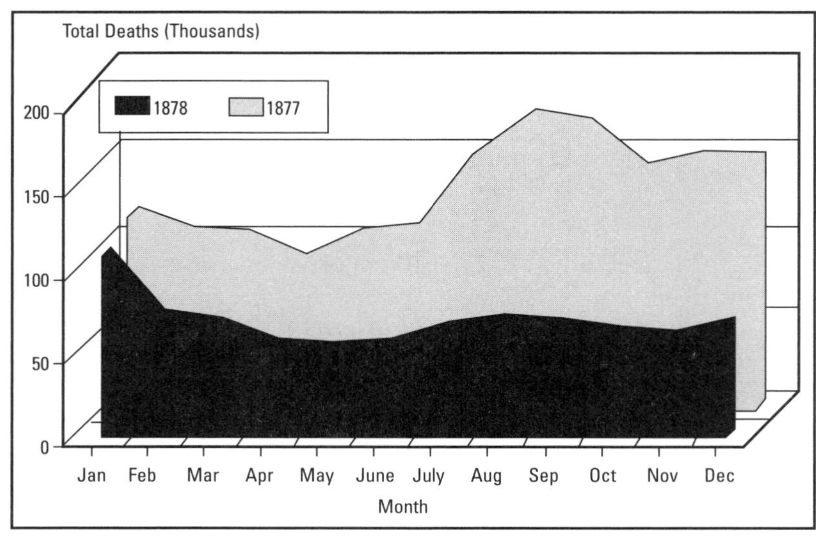

Sources: Annual Reports of the Sanitary Commissioner, Madras, 1877, 1878.

dysenteries, the diarrhoeal diseases, for which the focus was the towns and the famine camps. This was far exceeded by the mortality of 'Phase II', from August–September, distinct not only in the season of its predominance but also in its principal cause, 'fever' (Figures 3 and 4).

This fever, described in the field observations of medical officers in 1877–78 as 'predominantly of the malarious type', was the greatest single cause of mortality in Madras in all years (Figure 5).

The mortality curve of the famine years differs not in seasonality, nor in principal cause, but in amplitude. In 1877, mortality in Phase I, mainly from diarrhoeal diseases, at a record level, was succeeded by a huge epidemic wave of malaria. The following year, characterized by a more equable rainfall, there were far fewer camps and most closed by the third quarter. Cholera and the dysenteries were much less in evidence in the mortality returns; smallpox, always associated with drought, was negligible; the autumnal wave of malaria returned to near-normal proportions.

Early in the famine in 1877, medical staff remarked on the significant absence of the 'usual' amount of intermittent fever in the famine area. It remained absent 'as long as the drought continued'. As late as in May, no case of 'ordinary intermittent fever' had been recorded throughout the famine camps and hospitals. But after the heavy

Table 2: *Madras: Selected Relief Camps.**
Registered Mortality, January–July 1877: Principal Causes

District	*Total Deaths*	*Cholera*	*Smallpox*	*Fevers*	*Bowel Complains*	*Other***
Madras	1756	82	44	43	1070	5177
Chingleput	1304	46	18	44	1124	112
Trichinopoly	1171	186	67	–	888	30
Madura 1	831	327	45	242	217	–
Madura 2	1029	26	18	23	780	182
Cuddapah 1	770	25	42	130	378	195
Cuddapah 2	4196	–	5	11	2986	1194
Bellary	239	15	2	8	126	88
Salem	3890	9	11	7	2944	919
Coimbatore 1	589	20	4	101	252	212
Coimbatore 2	975	–	3	7	785	180
Coimbatore 3	379	1	1	4	1773	160
Total	17129	737	260	620	11723	3789

* Camps for which most returns are available.
** Defective registration: no cause certified.

Source: A. Porter, *The Diseases of the Madras Famine of 1877–78*, Madras, 1889, Appendix C.

Figure 3: *Madras: Registered Mortality, 1877, 1878, Principal Causes*

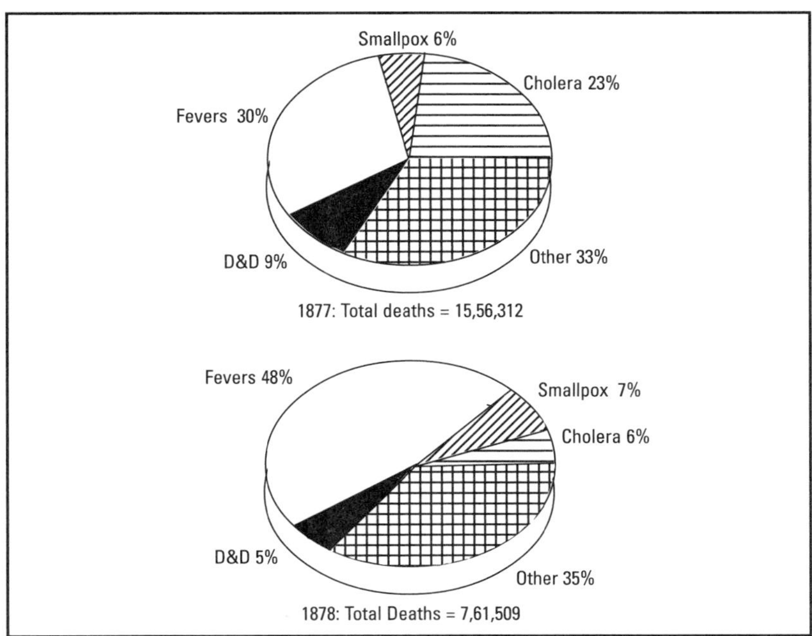

Sources: Annual Reports of the Sanitary Commissioner, Madras, 1877, 1878.

FIGURE 4: ***Madras: Registered Mortality, 1877–78, Principal Causes: Monthly Distribution***

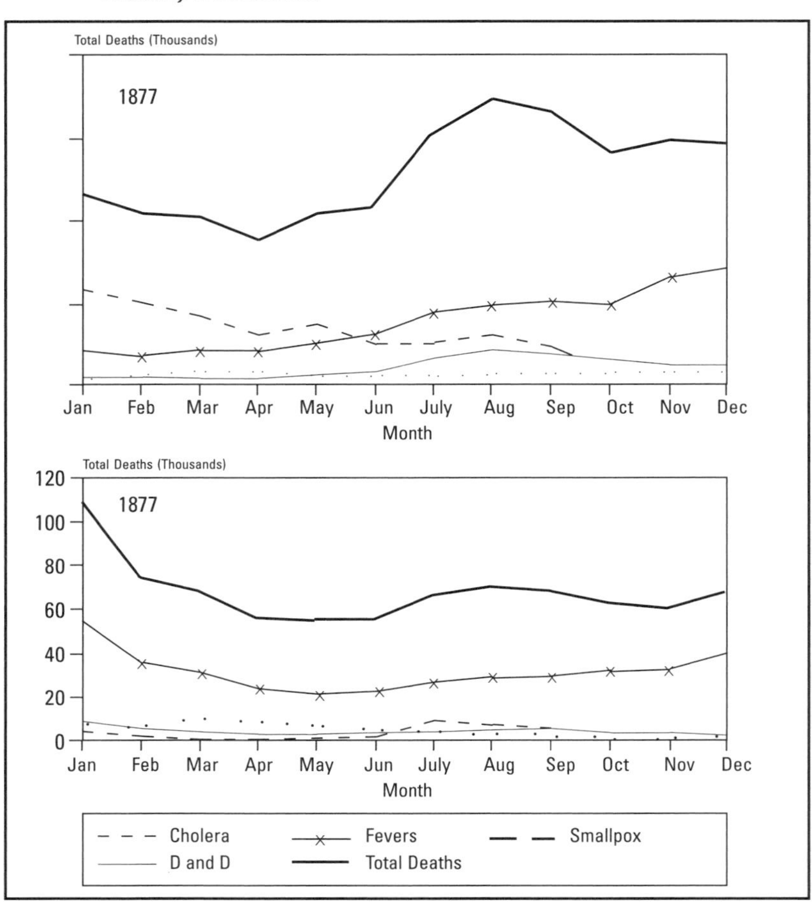

Sources: Annual Reports of the Sanitary Commissioner, Madras, 1877, 1878.

cyclonic storm at the end of May, 'agues' characteristic of malarious fever were widely reported. In September and October, 'the long delayed rain fell in unusual quantities and . . . febrile affections, always of the malarious type, either intermittent or remittent, were exceedingly prevalent, especially in the famine districts': fever of ten to fifteen days' duration, exacerbated at night, complicated by dysentery or oedema, followed by recovery or more often death within a month. All classes of the population were vulnerable. In Kurnool and Cuddapah, 'public business nearly collapsed on account of the subordinate classes [of officials being] stricken with fever'. Throughout November,

FIGURE 5: ***Madras: Registered Mortality, 1866–78, Principal Causes***

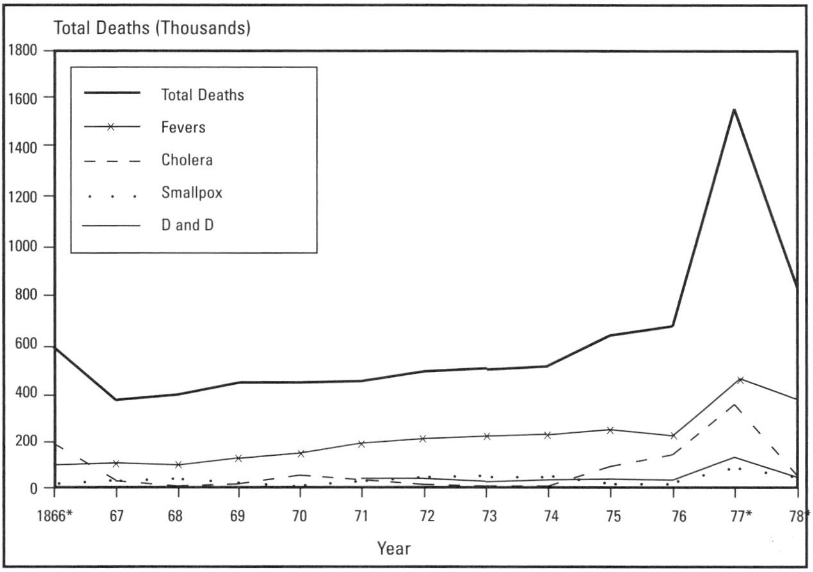

* Famine Year

Sources: Annual Reports of the Sanitary Commissioner, Madras, 1866–78

December, January, temperatures high by day and low by night 'favoured the infection'; 'thousands of the half-starved survivors of the worst period of the famine fell victims to the fever'.[15]

Neither the climatic conditions which characterized the years 1877–78 in Madras nor the catastrophic consequences were isolated events. Cornish warned, from long experience and examination of the historical record, that 'malarious fevers on an exaggerated scale' must always be anticipated in India where long droughts 'were, as often, succeeded by inordinate and tempestuous rains': as in Rajputana in the famine year 1868; in Tonk in 1869, when an estimated 25 per cent of the population had died, 50 per cent of these from 'the fever that followed the rains'; in the central provinces the same year, 'the exceptional mortality' was reported to have begun 'just when the famine ended; the scourge of the times was "fever"'.[16]

The association of drought, excessive rainfall and epidemic malaria was thus well known. A noxious miasma, malaria, exhaled by saturated soil was generally believed to be the cause. Cornish subscribed to this opinion and assumed that saturation of soil overheated by prolonged drought must intensify the exhalation. But he made a striking observation which was incidental to his analysis of fever mortality, and irrelevant to the ruling miasma theory: 'malarious fevers following on famine are just as much natural phenomena as the enormous development of insectivorous life after prolonged drought'.[17] Insectivorous species throve on the enormous proliferation of insects, amongst them the mosquito, unleashed in the intense humidity when the rains broke the drought. Two years after the Madras famine, Laveran in Algeria identified the malaria parasite, *plasmodium spp*. In 1896, Manson predicted that malaria in man would prove to be transmitted by the mosquito. In 1898, Ross established by experiment that malaria in man was vector-borne, transmitted by the bite of the female anopheline mosquito, and determined the phases of the life-cycle of the parasite plasmodium in the vector anopheline. The vector was the key to the relation between climate and malaria, demonstrated by the catastrophic events in Madras in 1877–78.

The years of famine were distinguished not by drought alone, but by drought and episodic, often tempestuous, rainfall. Drought and the scarcity of food resulted in widespread starvation, confirmed by clinical examination, in migration and overcrowding in towns and camps where conditions favoured contagion and thousands died of dysentery and diarrhoea. This was the classic mortality of famine, provoked by starvation and aggravated by precisely those measures devised by government to relieve it. But the greatest mortality in the famine years came after the drought had broken, from epidemic malaria.

Is this pattern of climatic conditions, not unrelieved drought but prolonged, intense drought broken at its height by rain, and this biphasic pattern of mortality, seasonal and skewed heavily to the third and fourth quarters of the year, to be found in other great famine years distinguished by colossal mortality? Evidence from Punjab, from two years, 1896–97 and 1900–01, when scarcity and famine were officially declared, proves instructive.

Punjab

1896–97

The famine year 1896 in Punjab was a dry year, a year in which drought was widespread and persistent, and rainfall, particularly in the crucial third quarter, significantly below the average for the decade (Table 3 and Figure 6).

In the course of the year, prices rocketed in response to the drought and the export trade in foodgrains. Government set up public works camps in the worst-hit districts, Lahore, Hissar, Gurgaon and Ferozepore. Migration, however, was reported to be modest and to have tailed off before the hottest months.[18]

Conditions in Punjab in 1896 differed strikingly from Madras in 1877. So did the seasonal distribution of mortality (Figure 7). The highest incidence is recorded early in the year, with no late peak. The figures for 1897, when the climate returned to 'normal', show the pattern of seasonal distribution characteristic of 'normal' years, and similar, in the shape of the curve for the later months, to the catastrophic year in Madras, 1877.

An examination of the distribution of mortality in Punjab by principal cause is illuminating (Figure 8). Smallpox, the disease most

TABLE 3: ***Punjab: Chronology of Events, 1895–1897***

1895 Jan.–May	Crop ↑
	Wheat exports ↑↑
	Prices ↑
June	Rain ↑
July	Rain ↓
Aug	Rain moderate—heavy
Sept	Rain ceased
	SE, SW: Crop failure
1895 Dec–1896 Mar	Rain ↓
	Crop ↓↓
	Prices ↑
	Wheat exports ↓
	Lahore Relief works
May	Rain—slight
June–July	Rain ↓
Aug	Rain ↓↓
	Temperature ↑
Sept	Rain ceased
	Crop failure
	Prices ↑↑
	Scarcity general + Famine, Delhi division, Gujarat
Oct–Nov	↑ Temperatures and hot winds
Dec	No rain
1897 Jan	Rain: Late, unusually prolonged
April	Crop ↑
	Prices ↓

Sources: *Report of the Revenue Administration*, Punjab, 1895–1898; *Report of the Sanitary Administration*, Punjab, 1895–1898.

FIGURE 6: ***Punjab: Rainfall, mean per quarter: average 1889–99, 1896, 1897***

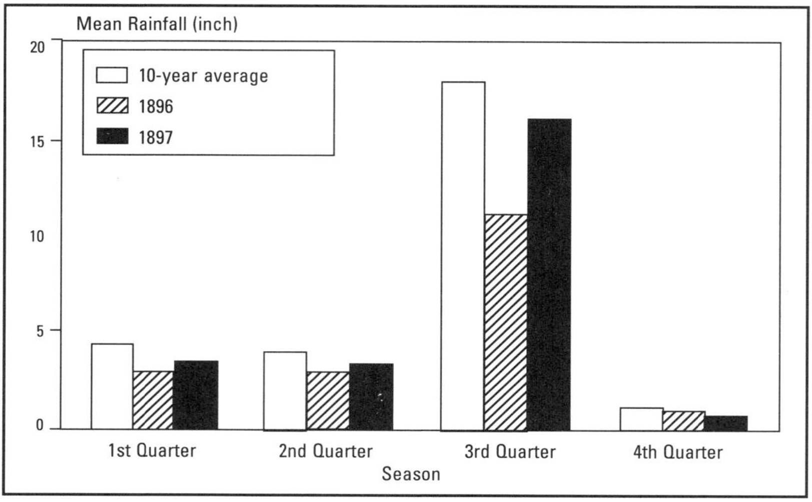

Sources: Report of the Revenue Administration, Punjab, 1889–1900; Reports of the Sanitary Administration, Punjab, 1890–1900.

FIGURE 7: ***Punjab: Registered Mortality, 1896, 1897, Monthly Distribution***

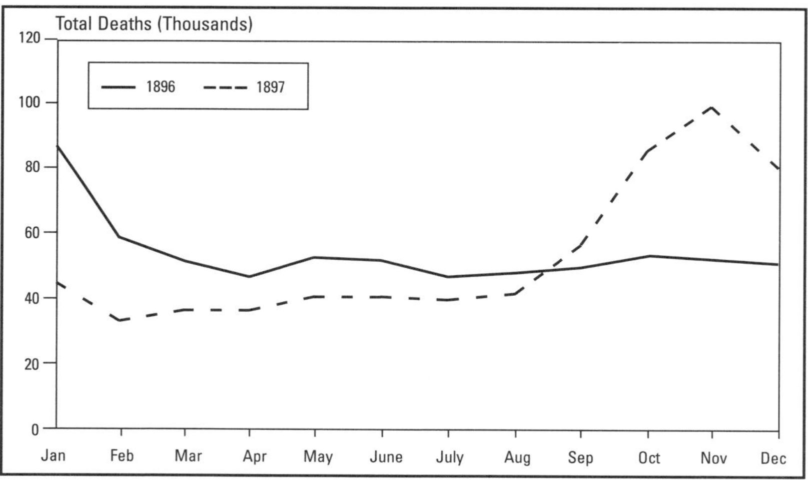

Sources: Reports of the Sanitary Administration, Punjab, 1896–98.

characteristically associated with drought, reached record levels in 1896. The 'famine diseases', of overcrowding, cholera and diarrhoeal diseases, were relatively insignificant. 'Fever' accounted for the overwhelming majority of deaths in both 1896 and 1897, as in every year in Punjab. The seasonal distribution of total mortality follows the curve

FIGURE 8: ***Punjab: Registered Mortality, 1896, 1897, Principal Causes***

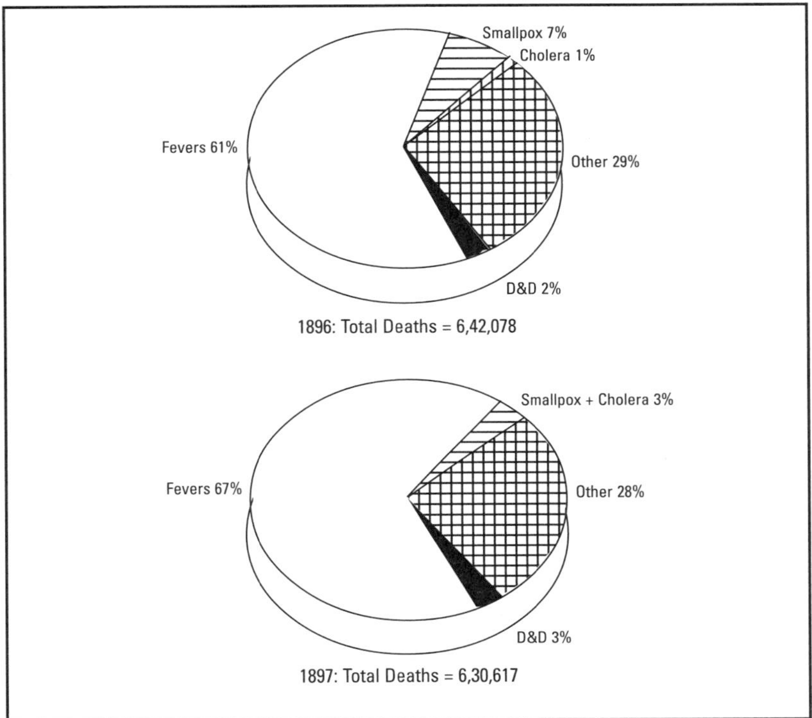

Sources: Reports of the Sanitary Administration, Punjab, 1896–98.

for 'fever' mortality closely (Figure 9). 6,42,078 deaths were recorded for the famine year 1896, in Punjab, 6,30,617 for the following year, a rate of 31.5 per mille, shockingly high; but significantly lower than the average death rate for the decade, 39 per mille.

The observations of the Sanitary Commissioner provide an explanation. Cholera, he reported, had been 'introduced into many localities but conditions favourable to the growth and virulence of the micro-organism were wanting in most places'.[19] Four years earlier, epidemic cholera had swept through Punjab, accounting for nearly a third of the total mortality for the province in 1892, at a rate of 49.5 per mille. In 1896, the contagion was somehow contained. Relief camps were fewer, confined largely to the Delhi division, and wound up after a few months. The provision of disinfectant, potassium permanganate, for municipal water supplies may have been effective. The level of immunity in survivors of the recent epidemic was no doubt high.

FIGURE 9: ***Punjab: Registered Mortality, 1896, 1897, Principal Causes: Monthly Distribution***

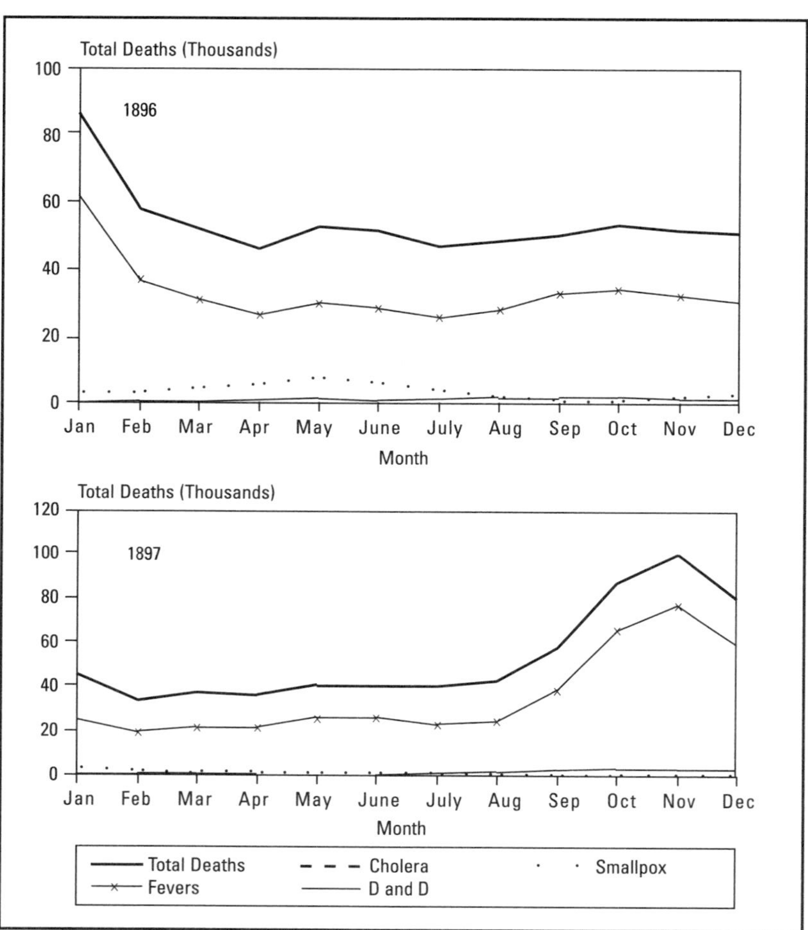

Diarrhoeal diseases accounted for no more than 0.68 deaths per mille, for similar reasons.[20] Conditions, that is, drought, were eminently favourable to the transmission of smallpox. Mortality, at a rate of 2.19 per mille, was reported in a characteristic seasonal distribution, maximum in May at the height of the drought, minimum in September–October.

As in every year, so in 1896, fever was the largest single cause of mortality: over 3,90,000 registered deaths. But the rate of 19.15 per mille was more or less equivalent to that recorded for 1895, markedly less than the rate in 1894, 25 per mille, and far below the decade average, over 29 per mille. The figures for 1896 came as no surprise to the Sanitary Commissioner.

> In this Province (and generally in India), a deficiency of rainfall and a low death-rate from fevers are almost invariably associated . . . whereas heavy rainfall, followed as it is by the swamping of low-lying places, great floods, and excessive moisture in the soil is almost invariably followed by high fever mortality . . . the curve generally falling during the rain, while in the succeeding dry weather the cases increase. The rise and fall of the ground water, by causing variations in the amount of moisture present [in the soil] evidently plays an important part in producing or controlling outbreaks of paroxysmal fevers. . . . With a permanently lowered sub-soil water the general health of the population living on the land remains good.[21]

In 1896, rainfall was deficient throughout Punjab and the groundwater level low in most parts of the twenty districts of the plains. In ten districts, high groundwater levels persisted even in the driest years: three in the submontane region to the north, and five plains districts, much of them low-lying, with extensive perennial irrigation from high-level canals. Marsh and waterlogging were familiar features in these districts. And in these districts, and these alone, the death rate in 1896 was the highest in the province, and fever mortality far in excess of the provincial average. The highest death rates from fever were recorded in the districts served by the lower reaches of the Western Jumna Canal. In less than a decade after its opening in 1820, this stretch of the canal had become notorious for persistent waterlogging from seepage and obstruction of natural drainage, and a persistently high incidence of fever. Clinical surveys were carried out along it in exhaustive detail in 1846–47, and thereafter at intervals throughout the nineteenth century. Successive attempts were made to remedy the 'unhealthiness' associated with the canal by realignment and surface drainage cuts. The canal however flowed through a shallow basin. The natural disadvantages of drainage were not only not relieved but compounded by the surface cuts, which tended to become pools of sluggish or stagnant water. Drought and famine in the early nineteenth century had in part prompted the construction of the Western Jumna Canal.[22] In the drought and famine year of 1896, mortality in the Karnal and Delhi divisions of the canal was the highest for Punjab, and fever was its principal cause (Figure 10).

FIGURE 10: *Punjab: Western Jumna Canal, Karnal and Delhi Divisions, Registered Mortality, 1896, 1897, Principal Causes*

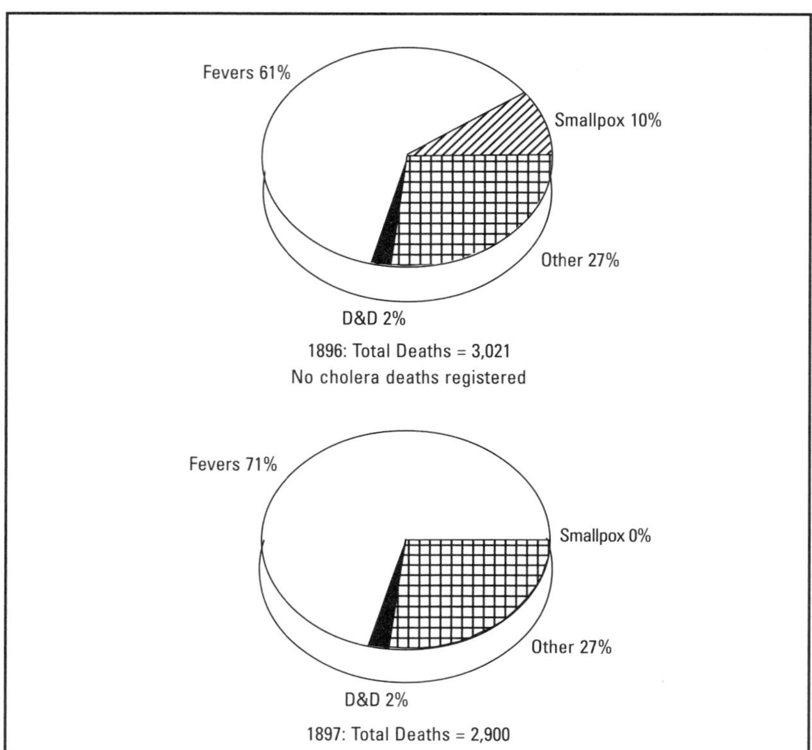

Sources: Reports of the Santitary Administration, Punjab, 1896–98.

Quinine was now officially recognized as an agent of prophylaxis. But the prospect of prophylaxis was wrecked on the rocks of administration. An experimental system introduced in Delhi division, by which quinine was to be sold through the post office, had proved a failure.[23] No alternative scheme was prepared.

1900–01

The famine year 1900 was marked by a catastrophic coincidence of drought and rain, conditions starkly reminiscent of the great famine year 1877 in Madras and reflected, as in Madras that year, in the scale and the pattern of mortality (Table 4 and Figure 11).

'The year 1900', Dr Bamber, the Sanitary Commissioner reported, 'will long be remembered as one in which the Province suffered severely from famine, then cholera, and lastly malarial fever' (Figures 12 and 13).[24]

Cholera struck hardest where famine struck hardest, in the southeastern districts of Hissar and Rohtak, a continuation of an outbreak in 1899. The spread of the disease could be mapped with precision, from the movements of labourers to government's relief camps. On 13 December 1899, a tank used by famine relief labourers in Hissar was reported to be contaminated. Some of the labourers moved on to neighbouring Rohtak, where the first case for the district was reported

TABLE 4: ***Punjab: Chronology of Events, 1898–1900***

1898 May–June	No rain
July	Rain, but ceased early
Aug–Sept	Rain ↓↓
	Crop ↓↓—Wheat exports ceased
	Impending famine—
	Hissar: Relief Works
Oct–Nov	No rain
Dec	Rain patchy
1899 Jan–Feb	No rain
Mar	Rain patchy
	Crop ↓
May	Temperature ↑↑
June	Rain ↑↑
July–Sept	Rain ↓↓
	Crop ↓↓
	Prices ↑↑
Oct–Nov	Unusually dry
Dec	No rain
1900 Jan–Feb	Rain ↓↓
	Crop ↓↓ Wheat exports ↓↓
March	Temperature ↑↑
April–May	Fodder ↓↓—Cattle mortality ↑↑
	Delhi, Lahore divisions:
	Famine conditions ↑
	No state relief found necessary
April	West: Rain ↑↑
	Crop ↑
May–June	Temperature ↑↑
July–Sept	Rainfall ↑↑↑
	Crop ↑↑
Oct–Nov	Dry
	Prices ↓
Dec	Rain: Timely, sufficient
1901 March	Prices ↓

Sources: *Report of the Revenue Administration, Punjab*, 1899, 1900, 1901; *Report of the Sanitary Administration*, Punjab, 1898, 1899, 1900, 1901.

FIGURE 11: ***Punjab: Registered Mortality, 1900, 1901, Monthly Distribution***

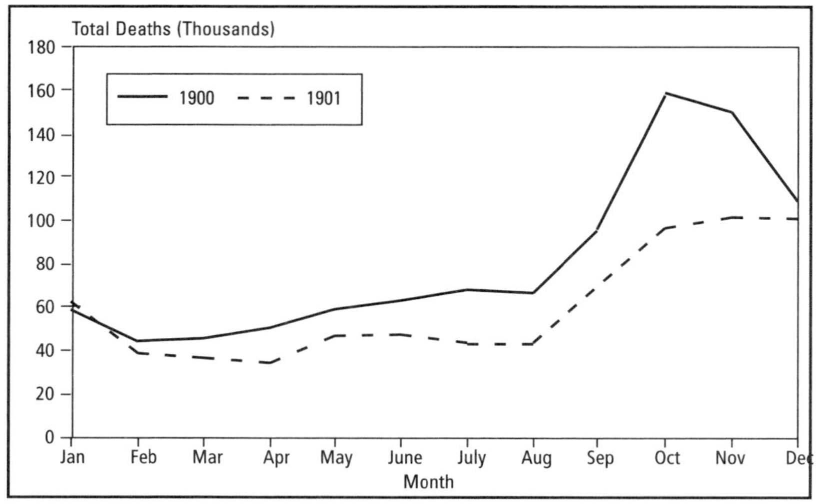

Sources: Reports of the Sanitary Administration, Punjab, 1899–1901.

FIGURE 12: ***Punjab: Registered Mortality, 1900, 1901, Principal Causes***

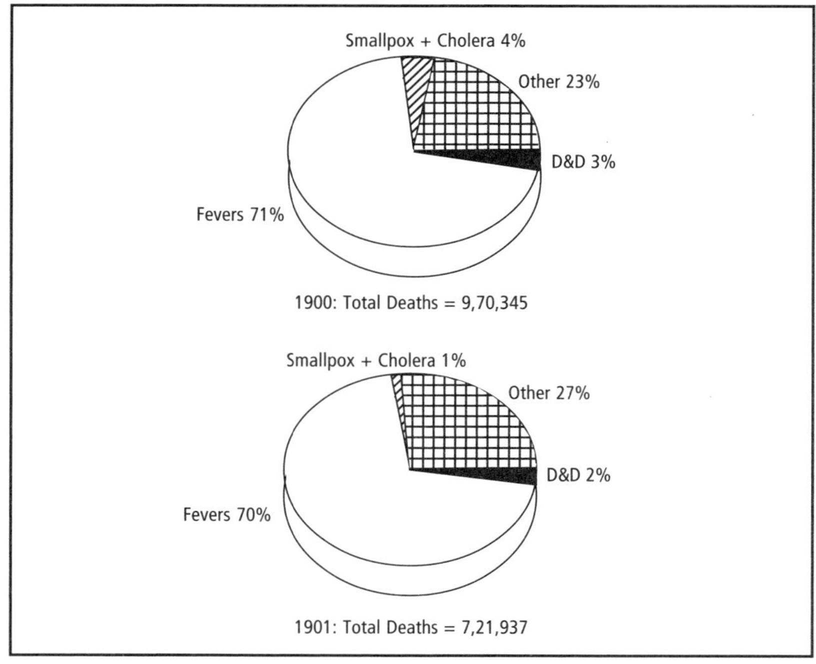

Sources: Reports of the Sanitary Administration, Punjab, 1899–1901.

FIGURE 13: ***Punjab: Registered Mortality, 1900, 1901, Principal Causes, Monthly Distribution***

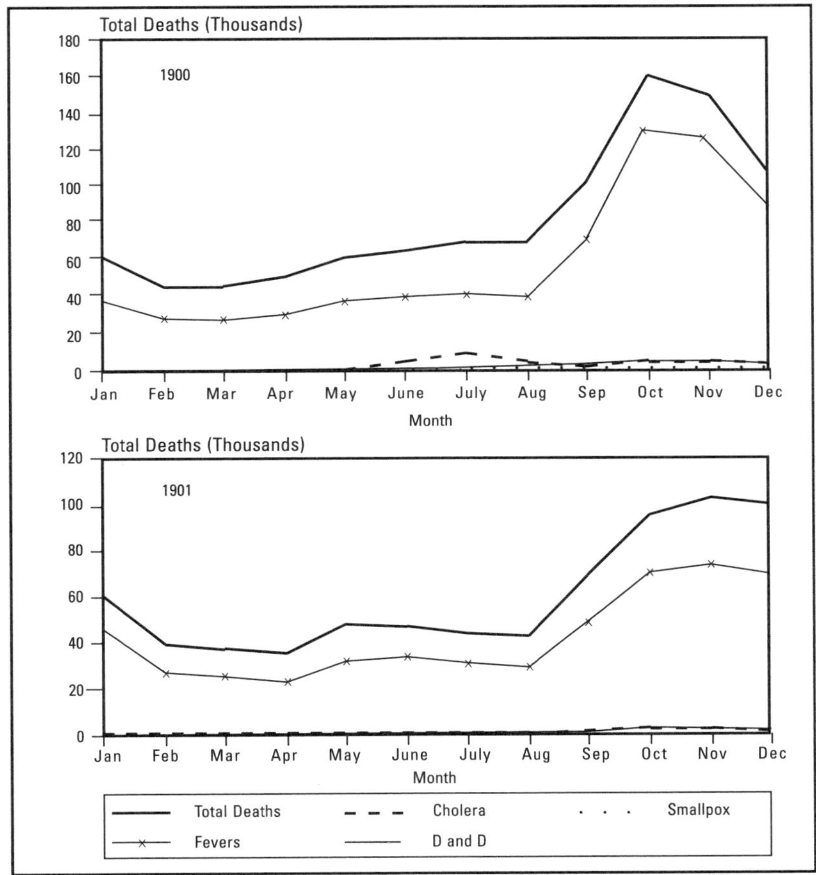

on 19 December in a family of labourers on the relief works. On 10 April 1900, an outbreak of cholera was reported in a famine relief camp at Delhi, amongst a gang of chamars 'imported from Rohtak'. The medical officers of the sanitation department understood the situation perfectly and, since contamination of the camps' water supply could not be prevented, knew that they were powerless to change it. 'If the landless labourers resorted to relief camps', Dr Derbyshire observed, they 'stood a greater risk of dying'. Cholera raged on in the southeast, reaching its highest incidence in July. By November the epidemic had, characteristically, 'lost its virulence'. By December it had virtually disappeared.[25]

In 1900, severe drought was followed by unseasonably heavy rainfall. 'Fever' then far outstripped cholera. Conditions in Ferozepore district were typical: epidemic malaria, following the very heavy rainfall late in September. Malaria accounted for nearly 6,86,000 deaths throughout Punjab in 1900, a rate of more than 33 per mille. Rainfall led to persistent waterlogging and its noxious effects. Mortality, pre-eminently fever mortality, was again maximal in the districts served by the lower reaches of the Western Jumna Canal, bad in a dry year, and catastrophic in a wet one. Reviewing the mortality returns, the Sanitary Commissioner called again for attention to be paid to prophylaxis. Mortality in this famine year was the mortality of each and every year, writ large: 'As fever causes more than two-thirds of the mortality in this province annually, I am strongly of the opinion that some special arrangements should be made for the distribution of quinine in all parts of the province.[26] In the Sanitary Commissioner's budget for that year, expenditure per district on quinine supplies came to Rs 60.

Why Malaria?

'Malaria reaps the harvest prepared for it by the famine', or so it seemed to the distinguished malariologist, Christophers, commenting on the Punjab epidemic of 1908.[27] A crucial part of the explanation lies not in 'famine' as such, but rather in the peculiar climatic character of the famine years marked by greatest loss of life, years not of drought alone, as in Punjab in 1896, but of extreme drought and of rain, as in 1900 in that province, and in Madras in 1877. Christophers described the characteristic patterns of rainfall, temperature and sub-soil moisture associated with endemic and epidemic malaria.[28] His colleague Gill identified climatic factors which were critical in transmission: pooling of fresh rainwater, which provided the anophelines' breeding-places; and atmospheric humidity, which regulated the longevity, and therefore the breeding-time, of the vector. A level of atmospheric humidity of 63 per cent, Gill suggested was critical; below this, the anopheline could not breed.[29]

In 'normal' years, the persistence of high temperatures during the rains regularly created conditions which favoured the proliferation of the vector, and a 'normal' autumnal wave of malaria regularly followed. In years of drought, high temperatures with little or no rain drove atmospheric humidity well below the critical breeding level; the incidence of malaria and annual mortality fell below 'normal' levels. The history of Punjab in the famine year of 1896 demonstrates precisely this: mortality in the drought-stricken districts of the plains was below the average for the decade, while mortality in the perennially waterlogged and 'pestilential' districts of the Western Jumna Canal, by contrast, was far in excess of provincial rates. In the famine years of greatest mortality, the association of prodigiously high temperatures with 'unseasonable' rain greatly increased the level of atmospheric humidity and prolonged it, creating the optimal conditions for a massive proliferation of vectors and an uncommon increase in their longevity, signalled by that 'extraordinary development of insectivorous life' which Cornish had observed in Madras 'whenever unseasonably heavy rain followed drought'.

Proliferation of anophelines on such a scale favoured an increase in infectivity sufficient to destabilize the precarious equilibrium between infection and immunity which obtained in areas where malaria was endemic in 'normal' years. The intense and prolonged drought so characteristic of these famine years may also have played its part in destabilization. In 'normal' years, anophelines feed on cattle, in addition to human, blood in a ratio of perhaps 3:1 blood-meals. It has been observed that outbreaks of cattle plagues, of rinderpest for example, with its huge cattle mortality, were followed not infrequently by an epidemic of malaria.[30] Deprived of cattle, anophelines fed increasingly on humans, thus increasing the rate of transmission of the parasite. In the months of drought in famine years, cattle died in far greater numbers than from plagues. The vector population, swollen by the enhanced rate of proliferation induced by the heightened humidity when rain followed the drought, fed almost exclusively on humans. Cattle mortality in all probability contributed significantly to human morbidity and mortality in these catastrophic years.

These factors alone may have been sufficient to overwhelm host defences. The relation of infectivity to the nutritional status of the host is even today obscure. In the months of drought and worsening scarcity, the incontrovertible physical signs of starvation were repeatedly observed. Drought and starvation drove the labouring poor into the insanitary conditions which took so great a toll in the famine. Here, in the first of the two great phases of famine mortality, 'it was not the heat of the sun which scorches, but the sand which is heated by the sun'. The risk was recognized. Kipling's heroic 'William the

Conqueror' organized the distribution of his foodgrains in the famine, very possibly the Madras famine of 1877–78, by carts amongst the villages precisely to minimize the risk of contagion associated with famine camps.[31] In the camps, rife first with cholera and then other diarrhoeal diseases, no case of fever—malarious fever, the greatest killer in the famine years as in all years—had been reported as late as July. In Madras, in 1877 and 1878, and in Punjab in 1900–01, but not in 1896–97, a huge rise in mortality came with the huge increase in the incidence of malaria, from late August through September, October, November, December. Malaria took its toll on all classes of the population. It is conceivable that the starving poor were less susceptible to malaria than the well-fed, as the Woodhead Commission was to suggest in reviewing the evidence of the Bengal famine of 1943. Such observations are consistent with Murray's recent hypothesis, from field studies in Africa, that 'refeeding' may enhance susceptibility to malaria.[32] The traditional practice of treating malaria by *lunkernam*, starvation, or, more properly, abstinence, as surgeon Sturmer, for example, observed in Nellore in 1877,[33] may well be pertinent. How precisely the fasting, or starving, state may protect the host remains to be determined. It is conceivable that anaemia, an inevitable concomitant of famine, could play a specific part, perhaps by denying the parasite its required nutrient in its passage in the red blood cell.

The picture which emerges from this brief sketch is frightful. The giant misery of starvation was compounded by the appalling conditions of migration and overcrowding into which the starving poor were driven, often literally to death, conditions exacerbated by the official measures devised for famine relief. Worse, in the great famine years, by perhaps the cruellest of the many cruel ironies of famine history, rain which might have been expected to bring respite to the survivors of the drought, instead intensified their suffering: epidemic malaria took its colossal toll. In other years drought, where it persisted, ironically limited mortality. But this saving grace was denied to the wretched populations of the submontane marshland and the water-logged districts along the lower Western Jumna Canal where irrigation, intended to solve the problem of famine, added its quota to the principal cause of famine mortality, malaria.

The history of famine mortality raises many questions. The search for answers should lead to an understanding of famine more commensurate with its complexity. The observations set out here are not unique. Outbreaks of famine in every province of British India were documented. While few observers may have possessed the acumen of Cornish and his pathologist Porter, all reported in detail the manifestations of disease and the physical conditions associated with them. The overriding importance of malaria in famine years is well described, notably in the extensive review of famine demography of Dyson.[34] With such groundwork, an epidemiological history of famine in South Asia becomes not merely desirable but a practical proposition.

One cannot but marvel at India's instructiveness: so terrible a history but one which can be known better than any other by reason of the incomparable wealth of its documentation. No one appreciated better the richness of India's record than Daniel Thorner, nor better understood how to use the lessons of its past to illuminate the present. His explorations, with Alice, of modern India are informed at every turn by history, every observation sharpened by comparison with the written record. Their work is honoured in the way they best deserve, in the inspiration given to others to continue it, many with the help of this great scientific institution, the Indian Statistical Institute, many with the active encouragement of Daniel and Alice. Our debt to Alice is beyond measure, for her generosity in keeping this great friendship with India so wonderfully alive.

Postcript

The argument of this paper is that the pattern of mortality characteristic of the great famine years of Madras and Punjab—its principal causes, seasonality and amplitude—reflects the extraordinary climatic events of those years. This argument serves as a hypothesis for a systematic exploration of mortality, principally from cholera and malaria, in association with conditions of the monsoon environment reconstructed *en longue duree* from the exceptionally comprehensive and detailed records of the British Government of India's departments of public health, revenue and meteorology. The practicability of such a large-scale reconstruction has been confirmed by a pilot study of monthly mortality and meteorology in Madras and Punjab 1866–1910, funded by the Office of Global Programs of the National Oceanographic and Atmospheric Administration of the USA, which was completed in December 1999. This has shown a highly significant association between the seasonal pattern of mortality and the variability of the monsoon specific to Madras and Punjab respectively in this period. A largescale three-year study, extending this pilot to the whole of British India for the period 1860–1940, is expected to begin by the autumn of 2000. The aim of this is to use monthly observations from British Indian technical records of public health, climate and ecology, which are unique in their range and reliability, to establish the pattern, seasonal and regional, of mortality from cholera and malaria and of the variability of the monsoon together with the nature and the significance of their association over the seven decades from 1860, a period before significant intervention in public health was practicable. This study is designed to deepen scientific understanding of long-term trends in patterns of climate and disease and their inter-relation in the monsoon environment of South Asia, and thus provide a precise and comprehensive basis for prediction so that intervention may be better directed, in the interests of public health.

My most grateful thanks are due to Lola Nathaniel, who compiled the tables and figures; to the Welcome Trust, for the research grant which made it possible to draw on Lola Nathaniel's expertise; to David Arnold, for providing an introduction to the famine literature of Madras; to David Bradley, for an introduction to the epidemiology of malaria; to Harold Lambert, for advice as to the interpretation of medical observations; to Tim Dyson, for assistance with demographic records.

Notes and References

1 Government of Madras, *Review of the Madras Famine, 1876–78*, Madras, 1878, p. 73. Hereafter, *Review, 1876–78.*

2 Ibid.

3 *Annual Report of the Sanitary Commissioner, Madras*, 15, 1878, p. lxxiv. Hereafter, *Annual Report, Madras*, 15.

4 *Review, 1876–78*, p. 26.

5 Ibid., pp. 27–32.

6 *Annual Report, Madras*, 15, p. xi.

7 Ibid., p. xi.

8 Ibid., pp. x–xxiv.

9 Ibid.

10 Ibid., p. lxxxv.

11 Ibid., pp. xxv–xxvi.

12 *Annual Report of the Sanitary Commissioner, Madras*, 14, 1877, sec. 457. Hereafter, *Annual Report, Madras*, 14.

13 *Annual Report, Madras*, 15, pp. xii–xiii, xxxvii–li.

14 *Review, 1876–78*, Appendix B; and see T. Dyson, 'On the Demography of South Asian Famines', *Population Studies*, 45, 1991, 5–25 at p. 10.

[15] *Annual Report, Madras*, 15, pp. xxvii–xxviii.

[16] Ibid., p. xxix.

[17] Ibid.

[18] *Report of the Sanitary Administration, Punjab*, 1896, 1897; Government of India, *Revenue and Agriculture (Famine) Proceedings*, Punjab, December 1896, Nos. 121–22.

[19] Government of Punjab, *Home (Medical and Sanitation Department) Proceedings*, 12 July 1897, No. 682 S; *Report of the Sanitary Administration, Punjab*, 1896.

[20] Ibid.

[21] *Report of the Sanitary Administration, Punjab*, 1896, sec. 42; Appendix, Proceedings of the Sanitary Board, 1896.

[22] On the history of the Western Jumna Canal, see E. Whitcombe, 'British India: The Costs of Irrigation—Waterlogging, Salinity and Malaria', in D. Arnold and R. Guha (eds), *The Environmental History of South Asia*, 1993.

[23] *Report of the Sanitary Administration, Punjab*, 1896, sec. 43.

[24] *Report of the Sanitary Administration, Punjab*, 1900, sec. 1.

[25] Ibid., sec. 23.

[26] Ibid., sec. 42.

[27] S.R. Christophers, 'Malaria in the Punjab', *Scientific Memoirs by the Officers of the Medical and Sanitary Departments of the Government of India*, N.S., No. 46, Calcutta, 1911, p. 109.

[28] Ibid., pp. 90–104.

[29] C.A. Gill, *The Seasonal Periodicity of Malaria and the Mechanism of the Epidemic Wave*, Churchill, London, 1938, pp. 48–49.

[30] David Bradley (personal communication).

[31] R. Kipling, 'William the Conqueror', in *The Day's Work*, Macmillan, London, 1899, pp. 170–214 (reference from Harold Lambert, personal communication).

[32] M.J. Murray et al, 'Refeeding-malaria and Hyper-ferraemia', *Lancet*, 22 March 1975, pp. 653–54.

[33] *Annual Report, Madras*, 15, p. xxix.

[34] T. Dyson, 'On the demography of South Asian famines', 5–25, 279–97.

Colonialism and Environment in India

A Comparative Perspective

Jacques Pouchepadass

Current anxieties regarding our dwindling capital of biomass resources at the world level have brought to the fore the question of the relationship of rural societies with their forest environment. The social perception of nature has always been a central preoccupation of social anthropologists. But students of peasant societies have long considered the forest as of peripheral importance, probably simply because it was situated at the periphery of the cultivated space. Agrarian history, both western and non-western, has up to now largely been a study of techniques, yields, appropriation patterns, taxation, commercialization, social stratification, peasant resistance. It has too rarely examined from a truly ecological standpoint the effects of land colonization, agricultural and animal husbandry practices, hunting and gathering by peasants, and the functioning and crises of agro-systems (except in the special case of famine). The opening chapters of many books of agrarian history are geographical presentations of the areas of study which convey the impression that the natural setting of agrarian life is a timeless framework of unchanging biophysical conditions. Any static conception of the relationship between human communities and their environment is of course misleading, as an agro-system is usually the outcome of a long history of ecological disruptions and adaptations. As long as it functions, it necessarily remains in a state of dynamic and unstable equilibrium. In particular, the inter-relationship between agriculture and its forest 'frontier' is often ignored in these studies, or treated marginally. As a rule, the agrarian historian has left the forests where they were, on the distant horizon, or as dark wild patches in the

This essay is a revised version of the Fifth Daniel Thorner Memorial Lecture, delivered at the Madras Institute of Development Studies, Chennai, on 16 March 1993.

midst of the humanized artificial land-scape of peasant life and activity. The origin of the word 'forest' is a Latin word, 'foresta', most probably derived from the adverb 'foris', which means 'outside'.[1] In leaving the forest outside his purview, the agrarian historian in fact adopts the point of view of the state, or more accurately, the point of view of his sources, that is to say, official records which relate mainly to the cultivated area, that produces revenue.

The conception of the forest by the peasant himself was of course quite different. The accessible forest was a central element in the organization of traditional agriculture, a sort of wooded extension of the cultivated space, often crisscrossed by pathways, and daily frequented by village people who came to graze cattle, to hunt, and to collect fuel, timber, litter, green manure and all sorts of other vegetable produce which often constituted important adjuncts to their diet or to their sources of monetary income. Prompted by the current fears of an impending world ecological crisis and by the widespread indictment of thoughtless deforestation, the agrarian historian is now reversing his perspective, and forest history has been developing rapidly over the last few years.

My purpose here is to explore briefly the colonial phase of the history of Indian forests, and this in a comparative perspective. As everyone knows, it is in the tropical world that ecological devastation is most dramatic today. The biological wealth that is being destroyed here is both the most abundant and the most vital to the future of the human species. And it is here that its destruction seems most difficult to control. The forests of the tropical zone entered for the first time into a phase of common history on a world scale when they were all brought under more or less simultaneous attack during the age of the capitalist expansion of Europe. The phrase 'imperialism and the natural world' has become paradigmatic these last few years for a new and growing range of historical problems and research. The details of Indian forest history during this period are now being gradually unearthed from the forest records by historians. I would like to review these data in the light of current general views on this new aspect of the history of European expansion.

It is commonplace to say that, in the countries which underwent European colonization the colonial period normally represented a very important phase from the standpoint of the destruction of the natural environment. However, let us not be overly Eurocentric here.

This phase of destruction was not the first in history. The desertification of Mesopotamia, the depletion of the cedar forests of Lebanon from the time of the Phoenicians, the massive fellings in Roman North Africa, the extensive hill clearings in the Southern Maya Lowlands of Mesoamerica, the ecological decline of the classic Khmer empire, the over-exploitation of forests and consequent energy crisis in Tokugawa Japan, the almost complete denudation of China for agriculture by its own peasantry, are only scattered dramatic examples of a general historical phenomenon, the gradual depletion of the world's forest cover for the needs of agricultural expansion and urban development. India, also has not been spared by this general trend and evidence is not lacking, for instance, on the impressive rate of forest clearance throughout the Gangetic basin during the medieval period. Also, considering what followed it in many countries, the colonial phase of environmental disruption has not everywhere been the worst. But it undeniably set in motion processes (economic, demographic, social, administrative, legal) that stimulated the overuse of natural resources and have proved difficult to reverse. On the other hand, the colonial period was often marked, in the countries involved, by the inception of conservation policies, even though these policies reflected the needs of the state rather than any strong concern for the welfare of the local populations. The overall picture is thus dark, but not entirely black.

Colonial Factor in the History of Environment

The historians of the 1960s waged a long war against the structuralist notion of 'societies without history' (or rather, against the distinction which Levi-Strauss made between 'cold' and 'hot' societies, which was in fact misunderstood, historicity being mistaken for history). A similar struggle might well have to be launched to combat the notion of 'nature without history'. There is, after all, a connection between the two notions. Societies without a history, in the common erroneous interpretation of the phrase, were believed to have remained outside the mainstream of history because of their total immersion in the unchanging rhythms of a natural environment which was thought to determine them completely. While historians have rightly refused such an idea, we must also reject the idea that colonization everywhere struck the first blow against natural states of equilibrium which had remained intact since primordial times. The myth of primeval nature is found everywhere and at all times. In Europe, medievalists long thought that the massive clearings of the ninth to the twelfth centuries had been done at the expense of forests which had been untouched until then, and they believed this on the basis of the medieval chronicles themselves. Now, wherever precise archaeological enquiries have been carried out, they demonstrate that on the site of many of these medieval forests there had been intensive human occupation during protohistorical or Roman times. Everywhere in the tropical world, for accidental reasons like the construction of roads, remains of very ancient (not infrequently neolithic) human occupation are found in the midst of supposedly virgin forests. Palynological and palaeobotanical studies of quaternary sediments within the dense forests of peninsular India show evidence of clearances and of the practice of agriculture from the beginning of our era. It is common knowledge that the terai forests of northern India contain innumerable remains of fortifications and shrines, of canals, of deserted village sites. We know, for instance, from the evidence of Chinese Buddhist pilgrims, that the Gorakhpur forests were the site of flourishing towns before the fourth century which lasted at least until the seventh century. In Sri Lanka, the forests of the dry zone, where by the beginning of the colonial period only groups of hunters and shifting cultivators remained, were actually not more than five or six centuries old. They had succeeded, after the twelfth century, to a long phase of prosperous agriculture supported by a highly developed water-supply system. Vestiges of pre-Colombian agricultural practices are found in the Mexican forests. Bantu expansion colonized many parts of central African forest long before European colonization. Historians have formed the hypothesis that vast teak forests discovered by the Dutch in the centre and west of Java in the seventeenth century were the result of plantation carried out at the beginning of our era. In India, similarly, the 'jungle' was not infrequently man-made, as when local kings planted forests or allowed their spontaneous regrowth in order to protect their territories against potential invaders: we have precise examples of this from Saurashtra, for instance. One could go on indefinitely with examples of this kind. It must be noted, incidentally, that the western myth of the 'virgin forest' carried with it, in the colonial context, important legal and economic implications. Since by definition the untouched primordial forest belonged to no one, it seemed only logical that its control should vest in the colonial government.

Similarly, the societies which lived in and from the forest when the Europeans arrived were not isolated communities preserved from all outside influence from the beginnings of history. In India, the relationship between the forest tribes and the sedentary populations of the plains was constant and diversified, and the myths of the former show how deeply the latter formed part of their cultural universe. Many forest societies of the tropical world were in fact peoples from the plains who had been driven into the forest by force or had had to take refuge in them. Many societies of hunters–gatherers have been shown to be former societies of settled agriculturists who were at some point driven out of their habitat and forced into the forest where they adopted a different mode of subsistence, based on the natural resources of the forest. Godelier has interesting examples of this to offer from New Guinea and elsewhere.[2] Similarly, the nomadic herdsmen of Mongolia are not originally people of the wilderness, primitive hunters grown into pastoralists, but peasants who gave up the insecurity of dry-farming in a most difficult environment for a more reliable and, in their eyes, noble mode of subsistence.[3] Shifting cultivation, contrary to a widespread cliché, was in fact not necessarily associated with insulated and primitive ways of life. It was occasionally compatible with a market economy, with land ownership and taxation, and it has at times supported urbanized civilizations, such as that of the Mayas.[4] In addition, many products gathered in the tropical forests had been items of long-distance trade long before the advent of the Europeans. So, western colonial expansion did not necessarily disturb or destroy primordial states of ecological equilibrium, nor any original harmony between societies and their natural environments. At best, it destabilized *relatively* stable situations, which were the last stage of long histories of successive disturbances and adaptations.

The nationalist myth of the precolonial golden age survives today in the oft-stated view that indigenous societies, before the advent of colonialism, were able to maintain a state of ecological homeostasis with their natural environment. They achieved this equilibrium, it is said, thanks to their immemorial knowledge of the natural world and to the innate wisdom of their self-managed local communities, which were spontaneously inclined to nature conservation and practised collective self-restraint in the utilization of its resources. There is no denying, of course, the marvels of ethnoscience, but such pronouncements imply more dubious value judgements which have unfortunate implications. They in fact resuscitate the Eurocentric narrative according to which the history of the non-western world was set in motion by the disruptive impact of western expansion (beginning with the 'Great Discoveries' of the late fifteenth century). They implicitly postulate that the access to natural resources was equally open to all, and ignore the facts of power and inequality in the structure and functioning of precolonial societies. They give a new span of life to old opposition between tradition and modernity, an ideological construct which was believed to have foundered with modernization theories. They seem to disregard the evident material fact that the collective preservation of a natural resource base requires no particular ecological ethos as long as population density remains low, and that it is the scarcity and overuse of available resources that generate the impulse towards conservation. They also do not raise the basic sociological question of the relationship between symbolic norms and actual behaviour or practice, and especially of the efficacy of ethical rules when individual interest, pressing necessity or strategies of survival run counter to them. This is not to detract from the value of the various experiments in joint management of forest areas by local populations and the forest departments now going on in India, or to deny the virtues of communal control of common property resources, as it is urgent in any case to do away with the abuses of exclusive state control of the forest biomass. But the emotional reference to what is in essence the western phantasm of 'the world we have lost' is scientifically unsound and probably only serves to make the necessary political compromises more difficult.[5]

This does not mean that we should systematically minimize the importance of the colonial impact on natural environments. From many points of view, it represented a radically new phenomenon. First, it was an attack on a world scale, corresponding to the phase of expansion of western merchant and industrial capitalism. Second, the intruders had means of conquest at their command which were generally out of all proportion to those of the local societies. Third, the offensive was backed by a conquering modern ideology according to which nature ceased to be the sacred order of things or the abode of the gods (as Marx said, it was 'disenchanted'). It had become an object to be mastered, exploited, transformed and commoditized, a means of speculation, a merchandise (and there is no need to lay the blame for this promethean and deprecating attitude to nature on the tradition of

Christian anthropocentrism, as has sometimes been done[6]). Fourth, the colonizers carried with them techniques and tools, introduced crops and forms of animal husbandry, opened up routes for diffusion and exchange, which irreversibly altered the local socio–ecological configurations. And finally, to serve their own interests, they set up everywhere an increasingly efficient framework of governmental control, which gradually denied the local populations free access to their traditional natural resource bases, at a time when their numbers were beginning to increase. Although the ecological stresses and traumas resulting from European colonization were not by any means the first events of their kind in the tropics, the scenarios for the first time were modern, representing the onslaught of commercial and industrial capital on the natural resources of the world at large.

Domestication of Tropical Nature

Cultural perceptions of the forest are always ambiguous. On the one hand, the forest is a generous provider of plant and animal resources, a space for freedom, pleasure and adventure, a refuge against the evils of war or the contradictions of society, and a place of spiritual retreat, of regeneration, of salvation, where saints choose to reside and where, according to the Hindu model of *ashramas*, men ideally should retire as *vanaprasthas* (forest-dwellers) at the end of their life. On the other hand, the forest is viewed as a land of the unknown and the unpredictable, inhabited by outlaws and wild tribes, and a haunted space, an abode of threatening and undominated forces, demons or the spirits of the dead. It is the 'other side', against whose dangerous intrusions men and communities have to protect themselves. One of the major responsibilities of the *raja* in Hindu tradition was to extend his domination over these wild areas, to placate the uncontrolled powers inhabiting them and thus to protect his people against them, while displaying his own superior might.[7] Guardian gods and goddesses in the Indian countryside are placed at the outer limits of the cultivated space, facing the wilderness. One could characterize the social perceptions of the desert in equivalent terms.[8] In one form or another, this kind of interplay between the geographical and the symbolic occurs in all cultures. The colonial perception of the tropical forest was no exception. On one side there is 'the emerald forest', the fantasmatic illusion of a pure virgin nature in all its profusion and beauty; on the other there is the 'green hell', a tentacular and entangled plant world, essentially hostile, where invisible dangers lurk.

The perception of animal life was more ambiguous because of the anthropomorphic characterizations of animal behaviour, which projected onto it all the ambivalences of the human soul. This is particularly obvious in the vast colonial literature of hunting stories and memories. In the ideology of the colonial hunt, besides the quest for adventure and prestige, there is on the one hand a fascination with natural beauty, and on the other a sort of urge to exterminate symbolically the dark side of human nature, that is to say, human defects which are attributed to animals, such as cruelty, cunning, treachery, thieving or murderous instincts. The hunt is also a symbolic re-enactment of the victory of the forces of civilization over savage nature.

Finally, even human societies of the forest and of the savanna were commonly stylized, according to a sort of brutal naturalist reductionism, into elementary essentialist characterizations. The aborigine in the bush or the forest was described as childlike, ingenious, unpredictable, potentially dangerous, and he was seen as a survival of primal human savagery, entirely determined by the ecology of his habitat.

Ideology of Exploitation

Everywhere in the colonies, the forest was at first considered as an obstacle to the rational and profitable use of land. Colonization bred the emblematic figure of the pioneer, whose symbols were the axe and the gun, both tools of destruction whose ultimate purpose was to substitute civilized order for savagery. And the aborigine himself, whenever organized and productive exploitation of natural resources became the order of the day, often came to be seen as standing in the way as a troublemaker who had to be displaced, uprooted or neutralized. It should be plain, however, that the will to clear, dominate and exploit wilderness was not by any means a cultural specificity of the western colonizer.[9] Even in Hindu culture, which lays a stronger stress than most on the necessary conformity of the human order to nature, the duty of kings, as set out in the *Arthashastra* for instance, is to extend their kingdoms both by military conquest and by clearing and colonization of virgin land. But the colonial onslaught on the forests was worldwide, and it was carried out by Europeans with powerful technical means, so that its effect was unprecedented.

The agents of this development were colonizers who, so to say, 'carried their ecology with them'.[10] They renamed regions, trees, animals and landscape elements after those with which they were familiar in their countries of origin. They were bent on applying western principles and techniques of cultivation in non-temperate environments to which they were not adapted, at the cost of repeated failures. They were culturally biased in favour of settled agriculture or cattle-raising and against itinerant lifestyles such as shifting agriculture, which was considered wasteful and unproductive. As far as forestry was concerned, their ideal was the plantation—which is a domesticated, rationalized, optimized form of the forest. Colonial forestry, as a rule, was mainly concerned with a few commercially valuable species, while the species commonly used by the local populations were extremely numerous. The ideal of the foresters in French Africa or Indochina, according to the principles that were taught at the school of forestry at Nancy, was homogeneous populations, closed formations, and tall, straight tree growth. The German tradition of forestry, which spread to the Dutch and British colonies, was no less single-minded. In India, as elsewhere, the foresters sought to increase the commercial profitability of the more accessible forests through the systematic plantation of a very small number of species, such as conifers in the Himalaya and teak in south India, species which were of little use to the local populations, as contrasted to many other species which were eliminated.

The application of these eco-ethnocentric concepts overseas led to the destruction or reshaping of landscapes and the displacement of indigenous populations. As always, human intervention in natural systems determined a transition from complexity to relative homogeneity. The main trend was towards the substitution of single-species cultivation for natural diversity, the replacement of prolific generalized ecosystems by specialized ones (and especially agro-systems). This was often done on the basis of an inadequate knowledge of the environments involved, leading to spectacular failures. For instance, there was an erroneous belief, particularly in the first phases of colonization, in the exceptional fertility of tropical soils, based on the luxuriance of spontaneous vegetation. Knowledge of the dynamics of tropical forest ecosystems was extremely scanty; a high rate of failures in these conditions was inevitable.

Features of Tropical Ecocide

It was normally in its initial phase that colonization of natural environments was most carelessly destructive. The process began with the conquest itself, when deforestation was part of military operations. Defensive forests were as common in the tropical world as they had been in ancient and medieval west. Muslim chronicles in India often refer to the forests that the armies of the sultans or the Mughals had to chop down in the course of their campaigns against rebel chieftains. Even in the 1850s, at the time of the Sepoy Mutiny, most of the 159 strongholds of the *taluqdars* of Oudh were mud forts bordered by ditches and surrounded by 'jungles'.[11] A forest was an obstacle to the movement of armies; it could easily become a base of resistance or guerillas; it provided a convenient refuge to criminal elements; that is, it stood in the way of political hegemony, and it also formed a barrier to agricultural expansion. Forest destruction was consequently a common feature of the colonial conquest in south Asia as elsewhere. It is known, for example, that the forests which protected the kingdom of Kandy in Ceylon were razed at the time of the British onslaught.

In the first phases of colonization, forest exploitation was generally extremely improvident and wasteful. The scenario was more or less the same everywhere. The vastness and abundance of the forests encouraged the illusion that they were inexhaustible. The most accessible stands, close to the coast or to river banks, were attacked first, and they were destroyed without a thought for their regeneration, thus creating increasing difficulties, costs and delays (in transport, floating, etc.) for later exploitation. The forest was gutted to procure a small number of precious species. Dozens of trees were damaged in the process of felling a few. Massive felling was done just in order to extract some 'minor products', as in Java, where sometimes several hundred camphor trees would be sacrificed in order to find one containing crystallized camphor. It must be added, however, that in this regard, as in the case of military deforestation, colonization did not mark an absolute beginning but often an acceleration or systematization of earlier practices, made easier by the introduction of more effective techniques and tools. Everywhere the export of valuable woods or 'minor forest products' had started long before colonization.

More radical was the razing of forests to the ground with the consent of the colonial authorities, in order to develop plantations, commercial cultivation or animal husbandry. The most spectacular ecological transformations of this kind were those which took place on islands such as New Zealand, the Canaries or New Caledonia. New Zealand was almost entirely deforested by the European agricultural settlers in a little more than a century, and most of the wood was burnt on the spot because the overproduction was such that it had practically no market value. In New Caledonia, which became a French colony in 1853, the Kanak agricultural system, which was based on a delicate balance between forest, grasslands and horticulture, was driven back by European cattle-raising. The cattle were introduced by the white settlers in the hope of repeating the Australian 'miracle'. The Neo-Caledonian savannas were more or less similar to those of eastern Australia, and as J. Barrau says, 'with their historical experience of livestock farming, Europeans could not see these grasslands without immediately thinking of cattle'.[12] Land was taken from the Kanaks and where necessary it was deforested and converted into pastures. The bovines had been introduced in the 1850s. By the late 1880s, there were close to 90,000 of them on the island, roaming freely everywhere, trampling down and destroying the elaborate irrigation and drainage system of the Kanak horticulturists, breaking up their gardens and endangering their very subsistence. Then, as the soil was in fact poor and had become subject to erosion, and the grass overgrazed, these pastures soon became unproductive and the yield of the cattle farms went down. This prompted the settlers to take more land from the Kanaks. In the end, they were confined in a few tiny reserves encircled by huge cattle farms, where each bull enjoyed much more living space than each individual Kanak in his reserve.

This phenomenon was universal, though in differing degrees, throughout the colonial world, because exploitation of land was one of the main reasons for colonization as such. Let us remember that the Permanent Settlement of Bengal was designed, among other purposes, to induce the *zamindars* to increase the profitability of their lands: the revenue being fixed once for all, any increase in their rent rolls would remain exclusively theirs. This of course represented a powerful incitement to the clearance of forest and jungle on their *zamindaris*, and in this way the Permanent Settlement became an engine of deforestation in eastern India.

Local contractors and timber dealers often played an important part in the deforestation. For instance, local merchants and proprietors carried out reckless exploitation of the forest of the western ghats during the first half of the nineteenth century before the advent of strict government control, and private contractors (almost all Indians) were prominent in the harvesting of the 'sal' and 'deodar' forests of northern India for railway construction.[13] The building of the huge railway system of the Indian empire was a major windfall for the Indian timber business. The story of railway deforestation is well known, and need not be repeated here.[14] Let it only be said that railways required more than one million sleepers every year in the 1870s, each sleeper lasting normally twelve to fourteen years. One average mature tree (sal, teak and deodar being the only species of appropriate strength) could provide seven sleepers. Until the 1890s, when the use of coal begun to become general, the forests also had to provide for railway fuel. The way in which the Indian forests were being worked by private enterprise was, as a rule, extremely wasteful. This is one of the reasons for the creation of the forest department in 1864, as it appeared necessary to protect the forest capital of the empire more effectively in order to cater to the needs of the railways. In Sri Lanka, Ceylonese timber merchants (who, in addition, had a stake in coconut and rubber planting on the deforested areas) played a decisive role in the deforestation of the island. So did Indonesian and Chinese entrepreneurs in the Indonesian archipelago, and Chinese dealers in timber and forest by-products in French Indochina. Yet the main agent of environmental transformation was the European colonizer. The local merchant or contractors who took part in the process operated within an economic framework which had basically originated in the colonial situation.

The extent and methods of colonial deforestation all over the world have been the subject of active research for several years now. The accounts of the martyrdom of colonized nature in the tropical world are sadly repetitive, and I will not dwell at length on this aspect. Because of the lack of scientific knowledge the fellings led to massive and irreparable ecological mistakes. Even past experience did not always restrain destruction, because the quest for short-term profit led to disregard of long-term consequences. One significant example is that of the extensive fellings carried out in Ceylon by the first generation of coffee-planters, who were but adventurers looking for quick profits at all cost and who were ready to abandon their lands as soon as they were exhausted, as the cost of virgin land at that time did not exceed a few shillings per acre.[15] Once they had left, however, the ecological damage remained and the local populations had to put up with it. Actually, in the colonizing countries also the disadvantages of too-intense deforestation were well known. England and the Netherlands had lost almost all their forest cover when they started exploiting that of their tropical colonies. In France, the forestry school at Nancy was created in 1827 in response to the need for careful management of what remained of the forests in the country. But nowhere in the colonies was any serious attention paid to the necessity for scientific working of forests before the second half of the nineteenth or the beginning of the twentieth century. Indigenous practices for the management of the natural environment were unknown or ignored. In pastoral zones, overgrazing was the great danger. Thus in the South African veldt the grass was overcropped by the sheep of European settlers, whereas in former times the indigenous Hottentot farmers used to migrate with their cattle at the very first indication of decline. The same was the case with the rapid degradation of the grasslands of New Caledonia, which had been mistaken by the European settlers for rich natural pasture, and which, besides losing their fertility through soil erosion, were soon overgrown, because of selective grazing by the cattle, by unpalatable grasses and various introduced weeds.[16]

One of the main reasons for these ecological failures was the fragility of specialized agrosystems which took the place of destroyed generalized ecosystems. The more an agrosystem is specialized, the more it is rigid and vulnerable and the greater are the efforts necessary to protect it and to maintain its productivity. As a rule, the replacement of a diverse biocenosis by a monoculture activates predators and parasites who live at the expense of the cultivated species and whose impact was previously limited. The expansion of open, disturbed habitats favours the proliferation of weeds (many of which were unwittingly introduced by western man himself, particularly from the New World). Such ecological mechanisms soon lead to difficulties in maintaining the artificial ecosystems, and sometimes to total failures. To give only one Indian example, one may cite the case of the coffee plantations in Coorg. Coorg had been occupied by the British in 1834 and was still covered with dense evergreen forest or (to the east) thick jungle twenty years later. It was only after the advent of the European coffee-planters that the large scale felling of forest began. The first European plantation was started at Mercara in 1854. Land being cheap and profits substantial, a veritable rush developed during the following years. Thus 20,000 acres of dense forest were cleared in a little more than a decade. But within a few years, the coffee trees began to suffer from bug, leaf rot and leaf disease, and they became prey to a devastating pest, the borer. A commissioner was appointed in 1868 to investigate the ravages of this insect. The felling and burning of extensive areas of forest had destroyed a great deal of the surface soil. Then the practice of exhaustive weeding, designed to show a clean surface (a clear case of imported ethno-ecological prejudice), increased soil erosion. Forest destruction caused recurrent failures of drainage and also induced unforeseen imbalances in the fauna. All this largely explained the proliferation of the borer. An increasing number of estates were abandoned, especially after a commercial slump had set in because of competition from Brazilian coffee. And to crown it all, the abandoned estates were soon overgrown by lantana, a shrub introduced in 1863 by local British settlers for their gardens, which proliferated across the hillsides in the form of a dense scrub.[17] This kind of ecological blunder, due to the underestimation of the vulnerability of artificial mono-cultural ecosystems, occurred everywhere in the colonial tropics. The reforestation with single species led to similar difficulties. Drastic changes in vegetation and mistaken agricultural practices such as total removal of grass-cover or down-slope drainage, had destructive effects on soils: erosion, leaching, laterization. In nineteenth and early twentieth century Sri Lanka, deforestation by coffee, tea and rubber-planters caused heavy soil erosion. Streams and rivers were increasingly blocked by alluvial deposits; they became unnavigable and subject to sudden flooding; peasant irrigation systems and rice fields on the valley floors became silted up. In 1931, when a soil erosion commission was finally set up, the director of the Kew Botanical Garden wrote to the government of Ceylon that 'this island seems to be dissolving in water'.[18]

I will only mention in passing the question of the extent to which deforestation affects climate, and especially rainfall patterns, as this question, which has been a subject of speculation for two centuries, is still controversial. But it is highly probable that the effect was not negligible. It was also injurious to the health of human populations, as in Sri Lanka, where recent research seems to show that the spread of plantations (for reasons which are still debated) has aggravated the incidence of endemic malaria.[19]

The European onslaught on the natural and especially forest resources of the colonies entailed the disruption, at least partial, of the mode of life of the indigenous societies of the areas concerned. It is the heavily unequal balance of power and the establishment in the conquered countries of a modern type of centralized rule, which made possible the displacement or the forced adaptation of these societies, whose former relations with their natural environment were more or less brutally shattered. I would thus like to turn to the attitudes of the colonial states, particularly of the British colonial state in India, towards nature, its exploitation and conservation.

Colonial States and Nature Conservation

Exploitation/Protection

In the colonies, as a rule, the military administrations which took over immediately after conquest were gradually replaced by governmental structures inspired by those of the colonizing countries. Whatever the official policy pronouncements, the conquered territories were generally organized empirically, according to immediate needs and without any very strong predetermined plan. Yet there was at the background the general conception of government implicit in the modern western liberal ideology, which is that government must be rational, autonomous and uniform. In this sense, the colonial governments represented to some extent attempts to adapt to exotic circumstances and conditions the processes of institutional development that the colonizing nations had experienced a little earlier, or were experiencing at about the same time. The institutions of government created in the colonies were not, however, as in the home countries, the outcome of endogenous historical processes. These institutions had no roots in the culture of the colonized societies, and they often did violence to them. The establishment of state controls over the natural environment must be seen as part of these general processes of institutional growth. It went hand-in-hand with the extension of governmental structures and regulations into all domains of public life (or more exactly, with the expansion of the public domain and the creation of a new distinction between public and private). In India, for instance, the imposition of colonial state control over the forests during the second half of the nineteenth century was only one aspect of the all-round expansion of the modern state which characterized the post-Mutiny period of Indian history. Custom was being codified and ambitious modernizing laws were passed. The colonial administrative network was growing and coming closer to the people. India was entering the statistical era, and it was being exhaustively surveyed, described and inventoried by way of maps, censuses, gazetteers and ethnographic compilations. Customary rights and practices in all walks of economic life were being listed, sifted, redefined and recorded for fiscal and judicial purposes. Road communications were being improved and the railway was casting its net over the subcontinent. In short, an attempt at the restructuring of Indian society according to the requirements of the modern state was underway. The seizure by the state of the natural resources it needed for its own reproduction and expansion was similarly on the agenda.

There are instances of royal or aristocratic monopolies over natural and especially forest resources in all great civilizations since very ancient times, and India is no exception to the rule. The prescriptions of the *Arthashastra* regarding the establishment of forest reserves for the protection of elephants, which were a basic component of the military strength of the Maurya sovereigns, are often cited in this regard, as well as the forest rules laid down by the Marathas in the eighteenth century to cater to the needs of state naval construction. What the ruling powers required everywhere for civil and military building and for their navies was high-quality timber of large diameter, usually provided by species of slow growth, which had to be efficiently preserved by successive generations. This was the prime motive behind Colbert's Forest Ordinance of 1669 in France, which organized forest reserves on the basis of growth cycles of 120 years. Forest (and game) were also commonly protected to permit the proper accomplishment of an important ritual, the royal hunt, and of its more modest replicas at the level of local princes and lords. The attempts of the ruling classes to control forest resources are thus, in most areas, a very old story.

What seems to have been lacking behind these efforts before the eighteenth century, as R. Grove has shown, is an explicit theorization of the finite character of the earthly stock of natural resources and of the vital need to organize its conservation.[20] The consciousness of the risks consequent on centuries of overuse of forest resources was however present in seventeenth-century Japan, when the Tokugawa rulers decided upon increasingly restrictive forest legislation to avert the impending scarcity of timber. The fact that Confucianism, which stresses the notion of harmony between nature and society, was then the dominant political ideology in Japan, may have contributed to the emergence of this policy.[21] Yet ecological problems of comparable magnitude in early modern China do not seem to have evoked the same kind of governmental response.[22] The genealogy of modern European conservationism both in Europe and in the colonies from the seventeenth to the nineteenth centuries is now known, thanks to the work of R. Grove.[23] It was strongly influenced by the realization of the fragility of overexploited forest ecosystems in several tropical islands colonized by the French or the English, combined with the pre-romantic idealization of nature. In France, the rigorous forest legislation of the Revolution and the Napoleonic Empire, completed and reinforced by the Forest Code of 1827, marked the end of the extensive utilization of the forests by the peasants and the confining of agriculture within strictly circumscribed spatial limits. The French National School of Forestry was created at Nancy at about the same time (1824). Nature had then come to be perceived not only as a vulnerable provider of precious resources but as a public heritage to be preserved. This conception arose simultaneously with the idea of the monumental or architectural heritage. The phrase 'historical monument' was coined in the early nineteenth century.[24] Both the vestiges of the national past and the remnants of supposedly unspoilt nature, forests, marshlands, sites and landscapes, were now viewed as a legacy from past generations which was to be protected. Why were they 'sanctuarized' in this way? Apparently mainly because they were part and parcel of the collective cultural identity of the people, of their common history, symbols of a beautiful or glorious past, the memory of which had to be protected as a base of national unity. In any case, whatever the ideological content of the new conservationism, it was clearly directed *against* the local people, and especially against the peasants. Their customary rights of use and the depredations of their cattle were considered from then on as the major threat to the remaining forest areas.

It is no matter for surprise that these conservationist ideas were introduced in the nineteenth and early twentieth centuries in many areas of the tropical world in the wake of European colonial expansion, though generally with more exclusively utilitarian aims and at times considerable delays. The expansion of state control over nature was in fact much easier there because of the absolute character of colonial rule. However, one should not overlook the fact that official policies were only partially effective. There were frequent variations in official policy options. There were contradictory pressures from the non-official European settler communities. There was the chronic dearth of financial and human resources in a domain that was long considered of secondary importance. There was the lack of scientific and technical expertise. There were the numberless difficulties of policy implementation. And last but not least, there was the fear of social disorders. In spite of considerable variations in chronology and emphasis from colony to colony, the overall line of development was more or less the same everywhere. First, natural resources were exploited in a virtually uncontrolled fashion by the newcomers. Then, the colonial authorities would begin to protect them for their own use. Finally, the expanding modern state would increasingly take over the management and exploitation of these resources, while conservationist imperatives began to find a place in official policies.

The protection of nature in the colonies appears to have been mostly limited to the minimum required for the satisfaction of the states' needs for biomass. Early prohibitions on felling were made partly under pressure from the navies, for which the colonial forests were precious suppliers of timber for ship-building. Such was the case in the Netherlands Indies in the eighteenth century, as well as in British India at the beginning of the nineteenth century (after American independence had stopped the timber supply from North America), in New Zealand a little later, and again in French Indochina in the 1860s. South Africa's 'Forest and Herbage Preservation Act' dates from 1859. It was one of the earliest of its kind. Dutch action in Indonesia was unusually early, with the first forest regulations appearing in Java as early as the seventeenth century and the first attempts at sylviculture in 1730. But these were only sporadic localized efforts, not an overall policy. Forest regulations in Indonesia kept changing at short intervals up to the end of the nineteenth century, and they aimed only at ensuring a steady supply of teak. In British India there is evidence of governmental interest in environmental questions at least from the 1840s. But here also the main motivation was the necessity to meet state timber requirements (especially for ship-building and later for railway construction), and this was the single main consideration behind the famous Indian Forest Act of 1878.[25] In Ceylon, on the other hand, the planters' lobby managed to block any serious conservationist attempt on the part of the government until the twentieth century. This was more the case in New Zealand, where although a forest law had been passed as early as 1874, the public authorities shared, in a more or less unacknowledged fashion, the basic objective of the settlers, which was to extend agriculture through forest clearance. In the French colonies, where forest management seems to have been much less strict and systematic than in the British ones, no serious conservationist measure appears to have been taken before the twentieth century. The earliest forest reserves in Indochina date from after 1903. They only began to be created in French Africa from the 1920s onwards (although the first reports pointing out that they were needed date from 1900).

These matters often aroused the interest of public opinion in the colonized countries (mostly in European circles, at least to start with) from the end of the nineteenth century onwards. Colonial associations for the protection of nature appeared, which exerted pressure on the local authorities. The nationalist movements, it must be noted, were often suspicious of these bodies, and saw conservation as another ruse of the colonizers to alienate the local populations from their traditional natural resource bases. Official recognition of the gravity of the problem, in any case, sometimes took much longer to manifest. While in India the first effective measures of forest protection were taken towards the middle of the nineteenth century, in New Zealand nothing of the kind was done until after the First World War, and in French Indochina (where foresters had, however, been giving warning reports on the topic since the end of the previous century) before 1930.

One of the major problems of forest policy everywhere was lack of funds. Forest services were for very long periods a mere extension of departments of agriculture or revenue, and only gained independent departmental status much later. The forest department of British India, created in 1864, seems to have been the first of its kind, although Dutch initiatives in the same direction, but not followed up, had shown the way in Java. Before and even after the creation of these departments, the responsibility for the exploitation of the forests was often left to private enterprise, since the governments did not have the means or even the desire to take it up themselves. The French forest services in Africa and Indochina all date from the twentieth century, and that of New Zealand from 1920. One of the conditions imposed on these services was that they should be self-supporting and provide surplus revenue to the state. In India, for example, it is well known that the principle of British imperial policy was that the country had to pay for its own management. When the creation of the forest department was under discussion in the 1860s, one of the main objections that was raised against Brandis, the then inspector general of forests, was that a forest department was bound to be unprofitable and would be a burden on the colony's exchequer. After the creation of the forest department the suspicion remained, and the department always had to prove conclusively that it was making profits. Thus the forest departments had to put their main emphasis on commercial exploitation of the forests rather than on maintenance and improvement. The number of professional foresters was everywhere very limited. Both the administrative staff and the subordinate forest staff (especially forest guards) were too few in number and for a long time training was inadequate. To cite an Indian example: in Coorg, around 1890, there was only one qualified forester for 850 square miles of reserved and protected forests. In north Kanara district, in 1882, there was one forest guard for every 60 square miles of reserved and protected forests. The foresters, as a rule, rarely had time and money to spend on research, and they complained bitterly of this. For both forest conservation and sylviculture, they mostly proceeded empirically, by imitation or by trial and error, with frequent failures. The conservator of forests for Madras Central Circle, in the evidence which he laid before the Indian Industrial Commission of 1917, declared that 'the forest department in the Madras presidency is so seriously undermanned that it is quite impossible for any of its officers to engage in serious research work', that 'the government is content to keep it in a constant state of struggling inefficiency', and that 'there seems to be a deeply rooted objection on the part of government to permit the growth of the forest organization in this country to keep pace with the times'.[26]

The protection of animal life followed far behind forest conservation. Hunting regulations in the nineteenth century were only arrangements to maintain monopolies, similar to those imposed on their lands by the local rulers before the colonial era. In British India these regulations weighed mainly on tribal groups who hunted for subsistence, while the *shikar*, a European pastime, was allowed to thrive (as it did in the princely states). These game laws, it must be added, were widely evaded by the local people. It is, however, the Forest Act of 1878 which instituted closed hunting seasons and which made hunting permits compulsory. The first truly conservationist acts passed for the protection of endangered species date from the 1920s in Indonesia and the French African colonies. Overall, in actual official practice, the protection of nature, in the strong sense of maintaining sanctuaries, is a recent phenomenon. The first wildlife sanctuary and the first national park were created in India during the last twenty years of colonial rule (while there are today some 70 national parks and more than 400 sanctuaries covering 4.5 per cent of the total geographical area of the country). Throughout the larger part of the colonial period, conservation of the natural heritage everywhere aimed primarily at ensuring a permanent supply of forest products to governments and commerce.

Rationalization

Wherever state control over colonial natural resources expanded for the purpose of organized exploitation, it did so at the expense of local societies whose mode of subsistence was closely dependent on the natural resources in question and only marginally on the market. From the productivist point of view of modern management, the indigenous cultivator with his customary rights of usage, his manifold uses of biodiversity, his small-scale, erratic clearings, as well as the nomadic pastoralist with his destructive herds, represented a hindrance which had to be done away with somehow or other. The European colonizer had been brought up in an old foodgrain civilization and was ill-prepared to understand the modes of subsistence prevalent in tropical rainforest environments. He carried with him the archetypal opposition of the Latin agronomists between *ager* and *saltus*, which was deeply ingrained in the European mind. In his view, civilized order was not a climax forest with humans living in symbiosis with it, no matter how knowledgeable and sophisticated this interaction might be, but the domestic order of cultivated fields, or a plantation of selected species, where yields are carefully monitored and the return of spontaneous vegetation efficiently prevented. The representation of space which accompanied the expansion of the colonial state was the modern conception of the administered space, where the central authority carries the same weight everywhere within fixed territorial boundaries, where rights of occupation and usage are clearly defined, where limits are clearly drawn. This vision of things cannot easily accommodate collective and unwritten customary rights, the uncontrolled complementarity between agriculture and open forest, the migratory habits of shifting cultivators and nomadic herdsmen. Last, states cannot function without revenues. Accordingly, productive activities must be taxed, and the exercise of individual rights over public resources such as the forest ought to be licensed, a practice which discourages wastage while producing income. Thus colonial states everywhere created from scratch vast domains of public forests, by declaring all wood-covered areas without a certified owner to be government property. The social groups who derived all or part of their living from those forests on a customary basis were brought under strict control or displaced. In such cases, of course, the recourse to legal concepts such as 'general interest' or 'public good' was particularly convenient.

Nothing typifies this attitude better than the frequent repression of shifting cultivation. This activity, more than any other, felt the brunt of the ethnocentric ecological prejudices of the colonizers, because it combined all the features which the modern ideology condemns. The shifting cultivators felled and burned substantial areas of forest for the sake, it seemed, of a few poor crops of low yield and nutritive value. They had no established rights in the land they cultivated. They led an unsettled and mobile mode of life and paid little or no taxes. And their activity seemed incompatible with any organized policy of forest conservation. Nomadic pastoralism was criticized along similar lines. It was usually the alleged destructiveness of nomadic herding, its low profitability, and the mobility and indiscipline of the social groups practising it, which were incriminated. The policy of the colonial administrations, where they were bent on suppressing shifting cultivation or restricting it, consisted in limiting the forest areas where the clearings were allowed, in reserving the activity to strictly defined social categories, in subjecting the grant of permits to the performance of labour prestations for the forest departments, and finally, in encouraging the populations concerned to adopt sedentary ways of life as settled cultivators or agricultural labourers.

It is, however, important not to oversimplify colonial attitudes. In fact, they were neither uniform nor unchanging. By and large, the dominant trends were more or less similar all over the colonial world. But the timing, the thoroughness, the modalities of the policies, varied considerably. These policies were rarely adopted without discussions, which at times developed into vehement and protracted controversies, as was the case in India. In addition, the rules were often imprecise, the policy options varied, the latitude of evaluation and initiative left to the local administrators often considerable. In India, the discouragement of shifting cultivation often began at the initiative of the district authorities, before the question, when it assumed importance, was submitted to the provincial authorities and by them to the central government. At that level, it gave rise to some heated debate during the last third of the nineteenth century. There were, among the officials, many severe critics of the forest department, who indicted the ignorant and unsympathetic forest officers for the sufferings of the dispossessed hill people. But they were eventually defeated by the advocates of the 'civilizing mission' of the colonial state (implicitly defined, according to liberal conception, as the guardian of the general interest —which in the colonial context is not, to say the least, self-evident).

On a more general level, the question of whether management of the forests of India should be taken over entirely by the state or carried out through community forestry and joint management between the state and villagers, was subject to wide debate. Brandis, the first inspector general of forests, consistently (but eventually unsuccessfully) advocated the constitution of village forests of the kind that existed in his native country, Germany. The government of the Madras presidency, which was also in favour of community forest management, had similarly to give in for the sake of the superior interests of the imperial government (thus the Madras Forest Act of 1882 followed the Indian Forest Act of 1878 in all essentials).[27] The same debate was going on in France at about the same time between a small school of nonconformist foresters around Frederic Le Play, who refused the exclusion of the local communities from forest management, and the dominant tendency in favour of state monopoly over forest management. One authorized spokesman of state forestry (Berger) summed up in these terms the official thinking in 1865: 'The state alone, which does not die, can be concerned about the future of society and assume the task of raising for it these great plants which take centuries to grow.'[28] The terms of this old debate have of course become very relevant again in India today, thanks to the rise of social ecology, to the work of NGOs in this direction all over the country, and to the ongoing experiments in participatory forest management conducted first in West Bengal and then in various other states with the active support of the forest departments. But in the colonized world, the state always had the last word.

Holding Out

There was one limitation, however, which the colonial administrations could not totally ignore, which was the level of tolerance of the local populations. The social classes most affected by the regulations concerning the environment were often the poorest, the most vulnerable, the least able to pose a threat to the colonial governments: hunters–gatherers, shifting cultivators, nomadic pastoralists, poor peasants to whom the supplementary resources provided by the forest were indispensable. In the remote areas where the forest reserves were established, these regulations could represent the first truly disruptive intrusion of the modern state and of capitalism in the subsistence economy of the local people. Their apparent initial resignation, the overwhelming inequality in the balance of power between them and the state, the lack of structured channels through which they could express their anger or distress, could often create at first in the minds of the colonizers the illusion that they were indifferent to the changes. But forest regulations provided a superlative field for 'everyday forms of peasant resistance'[29] in the shape of myriads of petty offences which often passed undetected and which the forest establishments were incapable of preventing or punishing with any efficacy. Localized flare-ups of violence, especially against the underlings of the forest administrations, were not infrequent, however, depending on the circumstances. Tribal rebellions and peasant uprisings have punctuated the history of the colonial period everywhere. The ecological element that was often present in these movements has mostly been eclipsed in the eyes of historians by more obvious economic, political or religious motives. But premodern resistance movements can never be explained simply by the initiating incident which sparks them off. They are the outcome of complex combinations of social and cultural tensions connected in various ways with the life and values of the social groups involved, in which the disturbance of their relationship with nature often played an important part. To the colonial administrations, however, these crises fell under the category of agrarian or social disorders, the repression of which was part of the maintenance of public order. They were not considered as a serious danger so long as they were not taken up and organized by the educated elites able to widen their range by using modern forms of mobilization and political agitation.

The balance of forces, from this point of view, varied widely from one colony to another. In French West Africa, where the classification of forests was extremely unpopular, the government was nevertheless strong enough to proceed with the reservation of forests in the Senegal valley, despite the violence of the protests.[30] In Sri Lanka, the effects of the development of plantation economy on Kandyan agriculture played a role in the 1848 rebellion, and the repression of shifting agriculture was occasionally slowed down by collective resistance, particularly from the end of the nineteenth century, when it became a pretext or a tool in the conflicts which opposed local lawyers and speculators to the colonial administration.[31] The political effectiveness of these acts of resistance was greatest when there was a conjunction of popular discontent with agitation organized by nationalist elites, as was the case in some regions in India at the time of the non-cooperation movement (1920–22), and on a much larger scale during the civil disobedience movement of 1930–31, when movements which were labelled, in Congress parlance, as 'forest *satyagrahas*' (collective nonviolent violations of forest regulations), erupted all over the country.[32] The spread of state control over the environment encountered, in this case, a real obstacle. But in a context like this, it was in fact the colonial situation itself which was being challenged, with ecological dispossession figuring as one of many aspects of a domination which was globally called into question. India, whose national liberation movement was the earliest in the colonized world, was a precursor in this respect.[33]

Conclusion

Before winding up, let me first restate my initial point. Strictly speaking, it would be inaccurate to characterize colonial periods uniformly as the most dramatic phases of ecological devastation for the countries concerned. The first official measures for protecting nature, whatever their motives and effectiveness, arose in these countries on the initiative of colonial governments. And independence has not put a stop anywhere to the destructive processes that were underway. On the contrary, they have accelerated. But it is nevertheless true that it was colonization which in most cases initiated the processes from which all later developments originated. The newly independent states took over from the colonial states. The economic and political pressures from the developed world persisted everywhere after independence was acquired. Legislation, policies and administrative structures relating to the exploitation and management of natural resources were for the most part maintained. The disruption of the relationship between local societies and their natural resource bases has continued in the worldwide movement towards modernization, which goes together practically everywhere with an unprecedented increase in the industrial demand for biomass arising from higher rates of industrial growth, and of demographic pressure on the environment due to the population explosion. In post-independence India, the new ruling elite, supported by the business class, was committed to a resource-intensive, state-subsidized pattern of industrialization, the ecological cost of which was bound to be heavy. But at the time, this ecological trap in post-war growth policies went largely unnoticed.

Thus, the colonial phase of the history of tropical nature has to be set against the general background of the human history of nature. This is a history of continuous alterations and traumas, and of continuous human responsiveness to those changing conditions. Human societies have shown, and still show, an almost limitless capability for situational adjustment. It would be erroneous to present the precolonial relationship between societies and their environment as a golden age of 'equilibrium' which colonial conquest disturbed or destroyed. Such a view, like the now obsolete 'tradition vs modernity' paradigm, assumes the normative operation in precolonial times of a system which in reality probably never existed, and which is in fact a culturalist construct, an ideal type meant to provide a baseline for the assessment (and indictment) of colonial change. We cannot concur in the mythology of the unspoilt, primeval, sacred wilderness with which indigenous societies supposedly lived in perfect balance from the dawn of history until the advent of Europe. This is one of the myths which lies at the base of that green fundamentalism which is known nowadays as 'deep ecology'. What we need, on the contrary, is a radical critique with regard to this aspect of capitalist expansionism, of which the colonization of nature on a world scale has been one of the major objectives, and whose essential dynamics remain in operation, in a multipolar and greatly diversified context, throughout the formerly colonized world today.

Notes and References

1 R. Bechmann, *Des arbres et des hommes: La foret au Moyen Age*, Flammarion, Paris, 1984, pp. 25–26.

2 M. Godelier, 'Anthropology and Biology: Towards a New Co-operation', *International Social Science Journal*, Vol. 26, 1974.

3 O. Lattimore, *Nomads and Commissars: Mongolia Revisited*, Oxford University Press, New York, 1962, pp. 34–37.

4 See D.E. Dumond, 'Swidden Agriculure and the Rise of Maya Civilization', *Southwestern Journal of Anthropology*, Vol. 17, 1961; U.M. Cowgill, 'An

Agricultural Study of the Southern Maya Lowlands', *American Anthropologist*, Vol. 64, 1962.

5 See S. Sinha and R. Herring, 'Common Property, Collective Action and Ecology', *Economic and Political Weekly*, Nos. 27–28, 3–10 July 1993.

6 This thesis has been convincingly criticized by R. Attfield, 'Christian Attitudes to Nature', *Journal of the History of Ideas*, No. 14, July–September 1983.

7 H.E. Falk, 'Wilderness and Kingship in Ancient South Asia', *History of Religions*, Vol. 13, 1973.

8 For instance, J. Le Goff, 'Le desert-foret dans l'Occident medieval', in J. Le Goff, *L'imaginaire medieval*, Gallimard, Paris, 1985.

9 See, for instance, the studies collected in D. Bourg (ed.), *Les sentiments de la nature*, La Decouverte, Paris, 1993.

10 I borrow this phrase from the Canadian ethnobotanist J. Rousseau, 'Des colons qui apportent avex eux leur ecologie', in J.M.C. Thomas and L. Bernot (eds), *Langues et techniques, nature et societe*, Vol. 2, Klincksieck, Paris, 1972. See also J. Barrau, 'Les hommes dans la nature', in J. Poirier (ed.), *Histoire des moeurs*, Vol. 1, Gallimard, Paris, 1991.

11 R. Mukherjee, *Awadh in Revolt 1857–1858*, Oxford University Press, Delhi, 1984, Appendix, pp. 175–83. For similar systems in Tipu Sultan's Mysore, see J. Deloche, 'Les monts fortifies du Maisure meridional', *Bulletin de l'Ecole Francaise d' Extreme-Orient*, Vol. 79, No. 2, 1992.

12 J. Barrau, 'Indigenous and Colonial Land-Use Systems in Indo-Oceanian Savannas: The Case of New-Caledonia', in D.R. Harris (ed.), *Human Ecology in Savanna Environment*, Academic Press, London, 1980. See also J. Barrau, *L'agriculture vivriere autochtone de la Nouvelle Caledonie*, Commission du Pacifique Sud, Noumea, 1956, pp. 112–14; J. Dauphine, *Les spoliations foncieres an Nouvelle Caledonie, 1853–1913*, L. 'Harmattan, Paris, 1989, pp. 157–58, 162–63, 290–91.

13 R.P. Tucker, 'The British Colonial System and the Forests of the Western Himalayas, 1815–1914', in R.P. Tucker and J.F. Richards (eds), *Global Deforestation and the 19th-Century World Economy*, Duke University Press, Durham, N.C., 1983, pp. 162–63.

14 See R.P. Tucker, 'The British Colonial System', pp. 158–61; M. Gadgil and Ramachandra Guha, *This Fissured Land: An Ecological History of India*, Oxford University Press, Delhi, 1992, pp. 119–22.

15 E. Meyer, 'Les forets, les cultures sur brulis, les plantations et l'Etat colonial a Sri Lanka (1840–1930)', *Revue Francaise d'Histoire d'Outre-Mer*, Vol. 80, No. 2, 1993.

16 W. Beinart, 'The Night of the Jackal: Sheep, Pastures and Predators in South Africa 1900–1930', paper presented at the African Seminar, SOAS, London University, 1992; J. Barrau, 'Indigenous and Colonial Land-Use Systems'.

17 National Archives of India, India, Home (Public) Department, 6 June 1868, part B n° 153; B.L. Rice (ed.), *Imperial Gazetteer of India, Provincial Series—Mysore and Coorg*, Calcutta, 1908, p. 306.

18 E. Meyer, 'Les forets'.

19 Ibid.

20 See R.H. Grove, 'Colonial Conservation, Ecological Hegemony and Popular Resistance: Towards Global Synthesis', in J.M. MacKenzie (ed.), *Imperialism and the Natural World,* Manchester University Press, Manchester, 1990; 'Conservation and Colonialism: The Evolution of Environment Attitudes and Conservation Policies on St. Helena, Mauritius and in Western India 1660–1854', in Dargave, Dizon and Semple (eds), *Changing Tropical Forests: Historical Perspective on Today's Challenges in Asia, Australia and Oceania,* Centre for Resource and Environment Studies, Canberra, 1988.

21 M.M. Osako, 'Forest Preservation in Tokugawa Japan', in R.P. Tucker and J.F. Richards (eds), *Global Deforestation*; C. Totman, *The Green Archipelago,* University of California Press, Berkeley, 1989.

22 S.A. Ashead, 'An Energy Crisis in Early Modern China', *Ching-shih Wen-t'i,* Vol. 3, 1974.

23 Besides the articles already cited, see, R. Grove, 'Surgeons, Forests and Famine: The Emergence of the Conservation Debate in India, 1788–1860', *Indian Economic and Social History Review,* Vol. 27, 1990; and 'Conserving Eden: The (European) East India Companies and their Environmental Policies on St. Helena, Mauritius and Western India, 1660 to 1854', *Comparative Studies in Society and History,* 1993.

24 E. Choay, *L'allegorie du patrimoine,* Seuil, Paris 1992.

25 Ramachandra Guha, 'An Early Environmental Debate: The Making of the 1878 Forest Act', *Indian Economic and Social History Review,* Vol. 27, 1990.

26 Government of India, Indian Industrial Commission, *Minutes of Evidence, 1916–17, Volume 3, Madras and Bangalore,* Calcutta, 1918, pp. 242–44.

27 Ramachandra Guha, 'An Early Environmental Debate'.

28 B. Kalaora and A. Savoye, *La foret pacifice: les forestiers de Ecole de Le Play, experts des societes pastorales,* L 'Harmattan, Paris, 1986.

29 J.C. Scott, *Weapons of the Weak: Everyday Forms of Peasant Resistance,* Yale University Press, New Haven (Conn.), 1985.

30 A. Bergeret, 'Discours et politiques forestiers coloniales en Afrique et a Madagascar', *Revue Francaise d'Histoire d'Outre-Mer,* Vol. 80, No. 1, 1993; C. Bernard, 'Les debuts de la politique de reboisement dans la vallee du fleuve Senegal (1920–1945)', ibid.

31 E. Meyer, 'Les forets'.

32 On forest *satyagrahas,* see S. Sarkar, 'Primitive Rebellion and Modern Nationalism: A Note on Forest Satyagraha in the Non-Cooperation and Civil Disobedience Movements', in K.N. Panikkar (ed.), *National and Left Movements in India,* Vikas, New Delhi, 1980; D.E.U. Baker, '"A Serious Time": Forest Satyagraha in Madhya Pradesh 1930', *Indian Economic and Social History Review,* Vol. 21, 1984; Ramachandra Guha, 'Forestry and Social Protest in British Kumaun, c.1893–1921', in Ranajit Guha (ed.), *Subaltern Studies IV,* Oxford University Press, Delhi, 1985.

33 For an overview of the confluence of ecological movements and emergent nationalism in anglophone Africa in the twentieth century, see R. Grove, 'Colonial Conservation', pp. 37–40.

Human Rights and International Solidarity

Nandita Haksar

It was almost a year ago that I received a letter from Alice Thorner inviting me to deliver the Sixth Daniel Thorner Memorial Lecture. She said that the idea of making an endowment with the Indian Statistical Institute was born from a desire to 'connect India and Daniel'. She also wrote that since I knew Daniel personally it was an added reason for asking me to give the lecture. What would I speak on?

Reading the letter, I remembered Dan Chacha (as we called him). The first memory I have of him is of a very warm human being advising my mother on how to handle a difficult child—me. The Haksar–Thorner friendship began in 1939 and continues till today. It is a friendship that spans several decades and embraces the families and friends of the Thorners and Haksars.

Yet, when I suggested that I speak on 'Human Rights and International Solidarity', both Alice Thorner and my father were surprised. They had never seen their friendship as an expression of international solidarity. Perhaps they were not entirely comfortable with the idea of human rights. But it would not have occurred to them to dissuade me. A reflection of their liberalism, in the best sense of the word.

When I look back I realize that my first awareness of human rights is also linked to the Thorners. As a child I was aware that they were Americans but living in France. When I asked my mother why the Thorners did not live in their own country, she explained to me

This is the text of the Sixth Daniel Thorner Memorial Lecture, delivered at the Indian Statistical Institute, Bangalore, on 17 June 1995. It was first published in *Man and Development*, September 1995.

that they were communists and how communists were being hunted in the USA. She told me of the horrors of the McCarthy era. She gave me *Silas Timberman* by Howard Fast and that was the first political novel I read. I read about how Alger Hiss was falsely accused and imprisoned. I read the Testament of Ethel and Julius Rosenberg. The photograph of their lawyer Emanuel Bloch holding their two young sons just before the execution has haunted me all these years. My mother told me of the agony on Jawaharlal Nehru's face when he was asked to intervene on their behalf.

I think this is a good occasion to remember some facts and figures of that era, which has not gone by. During the first three-and-a-half months of its existence in 1919, the General Intelligence Division (predecessor to J. Edgar Hoover's FBI) compiled personal histories of some 60,000 individuals thought to be radicals; before long the special indices grew to include more than 200,000 names. The Division's translators also perused some 500 foreign-language newspapers in order to keep up with 'radical propaganda'.[1]

The FBI had engaged in some 6.6 million security investigations between March 1947 and December 1952. The Thorners were subjects of investigation. I would like to read out some extracts from the FBI file: 'Confidential Informant, T-I of known reliability, advised information was received from [word blacked out] in August 1942 that Daniel and Alice Thorner spent 1939 and 1940 in Great Britain and that while there, they were known to be in sympathy with Indian extremists and were active in Freedom for India Movement.' These extremists with whom the Thorners sympathized included V.K. Krishna Menon, K.S. Shelvankar, P.N. Haksar, K.T. Chandy, Feroze Gandhi. . . .

Further on, the FBI file states that Daniel Thorner helped Indian friends by supplying information for a book entitled *American Shadow over India*, and that 'a perusal of that book would prove without doubt that it was written with intent to do harm to American interests in India and stated that it had been extremely successful in this regard'.[2]

Daniel Thorner had to surrender his passport to the Consulate General in Bombay in July 1953.

It never occurred to the Thorners or the Haksars to look upon all this as human rights violations. For them it was repression of communism and communists. In fact Alice Thorner once said to me that she often wondered why the communists did not admit that they were communists and then claim the protection of the First Amendment. It was certainly not lack of courage. It was simply because communists did not take human rights seriously and rejected it as a tool of imperialist propaganda. And so, after the Second World War, when the independent nation-states met at the United Nations to pass the Universal Declaration of Human Rights, the Soviet Union and the Eastern Bloc abstained.

Right to Food Not a Human Right

It was true that the Universal Declaration of Human Rights sought to make the ideals of a capitalist society, based on the right to private property and the rule of law, universal values. The right against colonialism and the right against apartheid were not included in the Universal Bill. Communists had good reasons for rejecting the liberal democratic model of universality which did not recognize basic economic rights, such as the right to food, as human rights.

The communist vision of a universal order was founded on a vision of a society free from the economic exploitation based on private property and political repression by the capitalist state. William Morris articulated that dream thus: 'The bond of Communistic Society will be voluntary in the sense that all people will agree in its broad principles when it is fairly well established, and will trust to it as affording mankind the best kind of life possible. . . . And what is this common bond but authority—that is, the conscience of the association voluntarily accepted in the first instance.'[3]

Communist universalism was based on humanism. It rejected racism, oppression of women, national chauvinism and all narrow identities based on religion, caste or community. The slogan 'Workers of the World Unite' reflected this humanistic universalism. It was a vision which emphasized the similarities in the worldwide struggle to survive. May I give one personal example? In 1985, I had an opportunity to visit Central America. It was around Christmas time and I was sitting in a house in Panama, owned by a Venezuelan woman, given to political exiles from Nicaragua and El Salvador.

I was invited to a party. A 72-year-old woman, who was a political refugee from El Salvador, asked me to write a poem in my language and then translate it into English. I wrote these few lines from an Urdu poem born in the Indian freedom struggle:

> *Hukm hakim ka tha faryaade zaban ruk jaya*
> *Dil ki behati hui Ganga ki rawani ruk jaye*
> *Kom kahati hai hawa band ho*
> *Pani ruk jai*
> *Lekin yeh mumkin nahi ke desh ki*
> *Josh aur jawani ruk jaye*
> *Hoin khabardar! Jinhon ne yeh aziyat di hai*
> *Kom ne karvat li hai.*

> (The rulers ordered that the people shall remain silent, the river of life flowing from their hearts must stop. The people say, the winds may become still, the waters may stop flowing, it is not possible to stop the country's youth and fervour. Beware! Those who dare pass such orders! The people have taken a turn.)

I gave the poem to the woman, a total stranger to me. She asked a friend to translate it into Spanish. She read it quietly, with intensity, in a corner. Then she came up to me with tears in her eyes and said, 'We are all the same people.'

The Communist Dream

The communists dreamt of doing away with all differences—of race, sex (they did not speak of gender), nationalities and of class. They dreamt of speaking Esperanto, sang the *International*, named their children after revolutionaries in other parts of the world. One writer writing in the 1960s paid this tribute to the communists of Daniel Thorner's generation:

> In their excavations of the radical past, the historians have dug up little but fragments and ruins. Yet surely a movement which involved so many intelligent and generous men and women cannot be barren of significance. The strong impact of communism's programme, even upon those writers who opposed it, must be reckoned with. So must the vitalizing influence of the left-wing intellectuals, who stirred up controversies, discovered new novelists and playwrights, opened up hitherto neglected areas of American life and broke down barriers that had isolated many writers from the great

> issues of their times. . . . We who precariously survive in the sixties can regret their inadequacies and failures, their romanticism, their capacity for self-deception, their shrillness, their self-righteousness. It is less easy to scorn their efforts, however, blundering and ineffective, to change the world.[4]

Speaking for myself and for the children of communists of the generation of the Thorners and Haksars, I can say that this deeply humane and universalistic vision is my most precious inheritance and I value it above all else. I have spent time in emphasizing this so that the critique I will now present of the inadequacies of that old universalism may be seen in a historical context. I want to try and show why the universalist vision of the communists has been most inadequate in dealing with the questions that have arisen in the contemporary debates on human rights and international solidarity. I believe these comments are true for communists in India and perhaps for other communists as well.

There is no doubt that 'human rights' has been a slogan of western imperialists, especially the United States. As a student of Columbia University pointed out in an article written in a journal of the American Bar Association:

> . . . we should consider the discourse of human rights as the most evolved form of western imperialism. Indeed, human rights can be viewed as the latest masquerade of the west—particularly America, the torch-bearers since the end of World War II of western values—to appear to the world as the epitome of civilization and as the only legitimate arbiter of human values.[5]

Eduardo Galeano, a Latin American writer, has said this in more powerful language in his essay, *In Defense of the World*:

> Freedom in my country is the name of a jail for political prisoners, and 'democracy' forms part of the title of various regimes of terror; the word 'love' defines relationships of a man with his automobile; and 'revolution' is understood to describe what a new detergent can do in your kitchen; 'glory' is something that a certain smooth soap produces in its user; and 'happiness' is a sensation experienced while eating hot dogs. 'A peaceful country' means, in many countries of Latin America, 'a well-kept cemetery' and sometimes 'healthy man' must read as 'impotent man'.[6]

A Repressive Society and State

Many of us in India do not realize how repressive society and state are in the US. McCarthy may be dead, but the witch-hunting of all genuinely democratic forces continues with a ruthlessness that strikes terror in the hearts of all those who try to resist. In the 1990s, the FBI launched its Cointelpro Operations (counter-insurgency operations) which were modelled on the successful programmes of earlier years undertaken to disrupt the American Communist Party. The FBI did eavesdropping, sent bogus mail to spread disinformation and sow suspicion among activists, undertook 'black' propaganda by fabricating leaflets, infiltrated targeted organizations, used snitch-jacketing or bad-jacketing through spread of rumour, manufactured evidence and undertook large-scale arrests and repeated arrests of targeted individuals. When all else failed they were involved in outright physical elimination or assassination of selected political leaders.[7]

These operations started in the 1960s, mainly against the Black Panther Party and the American Indian Movement, but continues till this day against even solidarity groups and left-wing organizations. The FBI and the CIA justify such surveillance in the name of national security. A report of the USA intelligence services concludes: 'It is axiomatic that individual liberties are secondary to the requirements of internal security and internal civil order.' The CIA counter-intelligence staff chief, Angleton, said he found it 'inconceivable that a secret intelligence arm of the government has to comply with all the overt orders of the government'.[8]

The background in which human rights was promoted by the United Nations in the period since 1947 includes

> an unparalleled, worldwide economic expansion by the United States, its establishment of a global military presence with a peak of over 3,000 foreign military bases virtually surrounding both the Soviet Union and China and interventions in the affairs of other states that are unmatched in number, scale, violence and global reach.[9]

Communists in India, therefore, could never look at the human rights movement from any other point of view than as a tool of imperialism. Their only reply was rational analysis and exposure of western hypocrisy and cynicism. They emphasized the fact that the most basic of all human rights are the rights to food, clothing, shelter, education and health. This led them to emphasize the primacy of social and economic rights over civil and political rights and thus accept the western division of human rights into three generalizations. It also led them to overemphasize the welfare functions of the Indian state, and the failure to recognize the increasing state violence and repression. A large section of communists even supported the national emergency declared in 1975.

The human rights movement which came up in the post-emergency period was inspired by the Marxist–Leninist parties and the original purpose was the release of a large number of political prisoners. However, over the years these groups made a systematic documentation of human rights violations and exposed the growing authoritarian nature of the Indian state. They visited nearly every part of the country, often at the risk of their lives, to expose the false encounters carried out by the police, the murder of poor people in the lock-ups, police firing on protesting landless labourers and attacks on intellectuals who dared expose the violence of the Indian state.

Not Concerned with Questions of Democratic Theory

However, even the human rights movement was not really concerned with questions of democratic theory. In fact, implicit in the movement was the idea that rights are totally illusory. There was no attempt to build a theory of human rights. The human rights movement grew along with but separate from the feminist and ecological movements in India, which owed their origin to the post-emergency period. The only serious debate that has been raging is the controversy over whether human rights groups should also take up the human rights violations committed by armed opposition groups. But most of the debate is in terms of expediency rather than the need for a perspective on human rights violations within civil society, whether it is violation of the rights of minorities or women or caste violence.

This lack of theory and our inability to generate informed debates and discussions on a variety of questions arising out of the movement has left the human rights groups in India feeling rather isolated and ineffective. This is especially true in the context of the imposition of the structural adjustment programme by the World Bank–International Monetary Fund, the entry of multinational companies and the disintegration of the Soviet Union. The World Bank, Ford

Foundation and other funding agencies are pouring in thousands of dollars for promotion of human rights education and promoting NGOs to do the task.

The Indian state has set up the National Commission for Human Rights; it has started training teachers for human rights and universities have started offering courses on human rights. Overnight, human rights has become a lucrative business. We have taken a back seat and largely a rejectionist stand—against the Indian Human Rights Commission, against the NGOs, and more recently, against the linking of human rights standards with international trade sanctions.

The debate over the social clause has sharply brought out the need for a theory and more complex understanding of the issues relating to human rights. The human rights movement took a rejectionist stand against the Indian state and did not support its Human Rights Commission; the trade union movement took a rejectionist stand on the social clause and identified completely with the Indian state—the main violator of labour standards. Is there any alternative?

I believe that while human rights is a powerful tool in the hands of imperialists, it is an equally powerful tool in the hands of those fighting imperialism. We need to evolve much more sophisticated political strategies to intervene in the human rights discourse, or, to put it in other words, we need to 'radically engage' with human rights discourse. Radical engagement has been defined as

> an attitude of practical contestation towards perceived sources of danger. Those taking a stance of radical engagement hold that, although we are beset by major problems, we can and should mobilize either to reduce their impact or to transcend them. This is an optimistic outlook but one bound up with contestatory action rather than a faith in rational analysis and discussion.[10]

Radical Engagement at the UN

In a sense, international human rights law has grown as a result of a radical engagement between the states of the western world on the one hand and the erstwhile Soviet Union, Eastern Bloc along with the Group of 77 on the other hand, especially at the Untied Nations. The international community which passed the Universal Declaration of Human Rights included the right to private property as a universal right. It refused to accept the right against foreign domination as a universal right.

Within two decades the right to private property was dropped and has not appeared in any of the international declarations or covenants on human rights. In 1974, the developed states had to accept the Charter of Economic Rights and Duties of the States and the Declaration on the Establishment of a New International Economic Order. In 1986 the United Nations General Assembly passed the Declaration on the Right to Development. Even more important was the establishment of the UN Centre on Transnational Corporations, which was in the process of drafting a code of conduct for transnational companies.

All these developments were supported by the traditional communist parties in India. On all international matters these parties supported the Indian state and saw no contradiction between their support for the release of Nelson Mandela and their deafening silence on human rights violations by the Indian state in Nagaland, Jammu and Kashmir or the Punjab. Sectarianism prevented them from raising their voice against the false encounter deaths in which hundreds of Naxalites were murdered in Andhra Pradesh and Bihar.

Communists in the traditional parties have accepted the arguments of the Indian state on the danger to Indian sovereignty and threat to national security as justifications for the large-scale violation of human rights. They also do not have a critique of the development model and so they implicitly accept the argument that a certain amount of repression is inevitable for national development. Thus, they endorse the argument that there is a contradiction between human rights violations and development.

The universalist vision of the communists, and this includes both the traditional parties and the M–L parties, has no place for differences. Thus, the social movements that have arisen in the past twenty years or so have rejected the communist vision. There have been movements for self-determination of tribal peoples in Jharkhand, in the Northeast and in other parts of the country; there are language movements; and there have been struggles against specific aspects of development, such as those against big dams; there have been intense movements against caste oppression and there have been the autonomous feminist movement and various struggles of women. These movements are born in India but are a reflection of worldwide trends. Like their counterparts in other parts of the world, many of these new social movements have been influenced by postmodern politics with its emphasis on subversion of the dominant discourse. These struggles 'seek to demonstrate the inherent instability of seemingly hegemonic structures, that power is diffused throughout society, and that there are multiple possibilities for resistance by oppressed people'.[11]

Cutting across Traditional Class Lines

The new social movements (which are not so new and perhaps a more appropriate description would be post-ideological) include the environmental, anti-nuclear, peace, gay and lesbian movements. These movements are 'anti-materialistic, anti-bureaucratic, anti-statist', and seek to 'cross traditional class lines in favour of humanistic, interpersonal and communitarian values'. The goal of this politics is 'extensive citizen participation in free, democratic egalitarian societies'.

These social movements are based on a politics without a unifying world vision of a future, in fact postmodern politics celebrates its lack of global vision. For the postmodernist

> to recognize such historical character is to acknowledge that any attempt at radical transcendence of norms and perspectives given by historical circumstances is implausible. They characteristically refuse any attempted privileging of world-views and endorse a democratic pluralism as the only possible value. Postmodernism holds that the standardization of any particular perspective or value is to be definitely avoided. It affirms a pluralism of values and outlooks which are considered reducible to a mere plurality of styles and genres. . . . It is this easy acceptance of a relativist outlook and suspension of a search for any perspective from which the present can be evaluated[12]

which is criticized by leftists.

The international human rights discourse is taking place largely within the postmodernist framework and many assumptions that are made show how deeply this has permeated the human rights movement. A comparison of the Universal Declaration of Human Rights of 1948 with the Vienna Declaration of 1993 would bring out this point. The latter includes a much wider range of human rights, including rights against illicit dumping of toxic and dangerous substances, right against external debt, women's rights, right to culture, the right of indigenous peoples to their own way of life, rights of disabled people. However, what is missing is a vision of a future society. The human rights declarations and covenants in the past invariably contained a vision of the future and this vision informed the Articles. In the Vienna Declaration there is no vision and there is no connection between the various rights which often conflict with each other.

The logic of postmodern politics is the rejection of all political parties, mass organizations or institutions as representatives of the people. Western imperialists have been promoting the idea that third world states cannot represent the people, since they are the greatest violators of human rights. The Reagan Doctrine rejected the inviolability of sovereignty—the basis of international law. And postmodern politics fits in well with these. Thus, the only representatives of 'the people' are deemed to be the NGOs. And that is what the Vienna Declaration does when it recognizes these NGOs as virtually the only legitimate guardians of human rights.

NGOs Accountable to Funding Agencies

Indian communists have always rejected NGOs and have no theoretical understanding of their postmodernist politics. It is true that NGOs seldom have any mandate to represent the people; they are not accountable to them or to their own members who are mere employees. These NGOs are mostly funded by foreign funding agencies who set their agenda and the NGOs are accountable to them alone. Most of these agencies are funded by the western states.

However, it is also true that at many places these NGOs are the only groups organizing the people and taking up vital issues—which the political parties or their mass organizations have neglected. In some cases, NGOs have been able to set their own terms and conditions on their donor agencies. Many of the funding agencies themselves have realized how the model of development, sought to be imposed on the third world by the World Bank and IMF, has resulted in large-scale human rights violations. For instance, Oxfam and Christian Aid produced reports condemning the Bretton Woods institutions. Christian Aid's booklet, *Who Run the World*, is an indictment of the World Bank in no uncertain terms.

Communists have long ignored many vital aspects of cultural

politics, and the contribution of postmodernism to our understanding of the repressed political dimensions of cultural activity of all kinds has to be acknowledged. Postmodernism holds out many possibilities for the revival and widening of cultural politics.

The importance of the ideas of cultural relativism and democratic pluralism were brought home to me while I was working on a human rights case in the Northeast. These concepts are very important in our struggle against the ethical ethnocentrism of western imperialism. Let me give two examples. The first is from an anthropologist's report on Africa. The brightest boy in class, in reply to a question by his teacher on whether he had attempted all the questions in a school exam, said, no, he had not. The teacher expressed surprise and said, 'You should have known the answer.' The boy replied: 'Yes I knew the answer, but I knew the others did not. It would not have been right to have answered.'

I was asking a headman from a Naga village about the atrocities committed by the armed forces. He gave a detailed account of how the villagers had been grouped in the playground and beaten. Since it was raining they were made to go into the village church. They were not allowed to go to the toilet and had to 'do it' in the church. They spent days there. I had rehearsed this story several times and it was only on the last occasion that he told me that his own baby had died in the church. He had not forgotten to mention it. As a village elder how could he speak of his own sufferings? It was for the others to tell me.

I give these examples of values which are a direct challenge to possessive individualism and competition in capitalist societies. Can we evolve a politics which does not fall into the trap of romanticizing the marginal but of deepening a cultural politics which is linked to a wider vision? These values are a living challenge to the cynicism and pragmatism which permeate the dominant culture.

Critical Role of NGOs

So far the major solidarity which has been expressed towards indigenous peoples' movements or women's movements, has been through a network of NGOs, in an increasingly depoliticized atmosphere. These NGOs cannot mobilize on a large scale and thus can never challenge imperialism by mass resistance. Yet, when these NGOs have come together on particular issues they have been able to play a critical role. For instance, they were able to make the international community take up the issue of women's rights at the Vienna Conference.

The potential and possibilities for international solidarity are even greater in an era of globalization, because it creates a world that can be increasingly experienced as one. However, we need to build a new basis for this solidarity which cuts across different cultural groups, without denying the reality of class or class struggle. It will have to be a different sort of internationalism from the old one which was either based on party or on state.

The older international solidarity within the human rights movement has already been substantially undermined by the reorganization of the United Nations. The reorganization has virtually wiped out the achievements of the past five decades. We now face the very real danger of a lowering of international human rights standards. The UN Secretary-General has abolished several posts and departments in the social and economic sectors, including the post of Director-General for International Economic Co-operation and Development and the Untied Nations Centre for Transnational Corporations. These posts and departments were created by special resolutions of the General Assembly. And yet the Group of 77 has remained silent.

A radical engagement with the international human rights discourse requires that we evolve a new politics based on a new universalism, a new vision. A vision which embraces a myriad groups, organizations, beliefs and values. A vision which looks upon differences as a potential asset to be converted into a positive political force, without trying to integrate them into a 'national mainstream'. A vision which does not allow these movements to remain isolated because our rejectionist politics has no place for them.

We need a new philosophy or political morality to fight what William Morris called the 'grievous flood of utilitarianism which the full development of the society of contract has cursed us with'. We need a politics which unites the personal with the local, the national and the international, by fighting the twin violators of human rights—the Indian state and the WTO which is backed by transnational companies. We need a theory of socialist human rights, a political economy of human rights and a socialist jurisprudence.

New Movement Based on Shared Values

We need to build new political alliances based on shared values and principles, not expediency—alliances based on a much deeper understanding of culture in the age of the technological revolution. What kind of movements am I referring to?

- The worldwide feminist movement, especially the socialist feminists whose critique of Marxism, of social sciences and theory of knowledge is as critical as their critique of the principles of organization or institution-building and their emphasis on the link between the personal and the political
- The indigenous peoples movements for self-determination which are carrying on a life-and-death battle against privatization of natural resources and theft of the bio-diversity which has been preserved by them for centuries
- The movements of racial minorities in the west, especially the blacks in the USA, who have had the longest and most bitter experience of imperialism and who have found the most innovative cultural and religious forms of protest from the blues to rap music
- The migrant workers in the west who have no rights at all, not even the right to citizenship, forced to leave their homes because of World Bank and IMF-imposed economic policies
- Those Islamic movements which are a reflection of protest against the hypocrisy and cynicism of the west and are engaged in fighting both the forces of imperialism and fundamentalism, like the Sufis in Malaysia or the 'Women Living under Islam' movement influenced by Islamic liberation theology
- Those Christian movements which are engaged in fighting the Christian right, the official church and neo-colonialism, especially in the Philippines and in Latin America
- The anti-caste movements including the Dalit movement which has been facing the most brutal state violence and violence of a caste-based society
- The ecological movements which have exposed the violence committed on our natural surroundings and also many social, economic, cultural and scientific assumptions which had gone unquestioned for the last two centuries.

I do not wish to deny or undermine the reality of class divisions or class conflicts even for one moment, but without an understanding of how class exploitation is linked with racism, patriarchy, caste and ethnicity, we cannot even hope to understand the world around us, let alone take up the challenge of changing it. We need to take up the 'Rainbow Challenge' and build a 'Rainbow Coalition'[13] as a basis for global solidarity.

Notes and References

[1] Ward Churchill and Jim Vander Wall, *Agents of Repression*, South End Press, Boston, 1990.

[2] *Economic and Political Weekly*, 22 May 1995.

[3] A.L. Morton (ed.), *Political Writings of William Morris*, Seven Seas Books, Berlin, 1973.

[4] Jack Conroy, *The Carleton Miscellany*, Winter 1965; quoted in Joseph North (ed.), *New Masses, An Anthology of the Rebel Thirties*, International Publishers, New York, 1992.

[5] Vinay Lal, 'The Imperialism of Human Rights', in *Focus on Law Studies*, American Bar Association, Fall 1992.

[6] Eduardo Galeano, *Days and Nights of Love and War*, Monthly Review Press, 1983.

[7] Churchill and Vander Wall, *Agents of Repression.*

[8] Frank J. Donner, *The Age of Surveillance*, Vintage Books, New York, 1981.

[9] Noam Chomsky and Edward S. Herman, *Political Economy of Human Rights*, Vol. 1, Spokesman, Nottingham, 1979.

[10] Peter Waterman, 'Globalization, Civil Society and Solidarity' (Part 1), in *Transnational Associations*, 2/94, Brussels.

[11] Joel F. Handler, 'Postmodernism, Protest and the New Social Movements, The Presidential Address, 1992', *Law and Society Review*, Vol. 26, No. 4, 1992.

[12] Sean Sayer and Peter Osborne (eds), *Socialism, Feminism and Philosophy*, Routledge, London, 1990.

[13] See 'Rainbow and Class: An Exchange by Vicente Navarro and Sheila Collins', in *Monthly Review*, July 1987. The idea of a 'Rainbow Coalition' was also written about by the late trade union leader of Chhatisgarh Mukti Morcha, Shaheed Shankar Guha Neogi.

Disinherited Peasants, Disadvantaged Workers

A Gender Perspective on Land and Livelihood

Bina Agarwal

My first acquaintance with Daniel Thorner's writings was as an undergraduate studying Economics when I read the little classic *Land and Labour in India* (1962), a book of essays by him and Alice Thorner. I was struck then and once again on rereading the volume recently, by the challenge their arguments posed to many aspects of received wisdom on the subject. Today I will focus on the themes of land and labour which were the subject matter of that book and of Daniel Thorner's *The Agrarian Prospect in India* (1956)—themes which have also been of long-standing concern in my own research. But I will examine these themes through the lens of gender.

Daniel Thorner passed away in 1974—a year before the International Decade for Women began, but had he lived longer he would no doubt have gendered his analysis, as Alice Thorner did subsequently. In any case, I believe he would have agreed with the challenge this perspective poses to conventional economics.

Challenges

A gender perspective poses at least three types of challenge to conventional economics. First, and most importantly, it challenges the assumption that the household is an undifferentiated unit in which members pool incomes and resources, and share common preferences and interests, and intra-household allocations are guided mainly or solely by altruism. These assumptions are implicit in much of standard

This essay is an expanded version of the Seventh Daniel Thorner Memorial Lecture, delivered at the Nehru Memorial Museum and Library, New Delhi, on 21 February 1997. It was published in a version close to this one in *Economic and Political Weekly*, March 1998.

economic theory and embodied in the unitary household model. A unitary approach to the household has also been central to development policies, which (until recently) have directed economic resources mainly to male household heads, assuming that the resources will be shared equitably within the family. Growing evidence over the past twenty-five years on intra-household gender inequalities indicates otherwise. In India, these inequalities are revealed most starkly in the allocation of basic necessities such as health care, education, and in several regions also food; in access to property and assets; and in the gender division of labour.[1]

Similarly, there is substantial evidence of gender differences in preferences, as revealed in income-spending patterns as well as in the use of productive resources. In terms of consumption expenditure, for instance, women in poor rural households are found to spend the income they control mostly on the family's, especially children's, basic needs, while men spend a significant proportion of their incomes on personal goods. This is found to be so not only in India, but in many other countries as well.[2] It is difficult to establish whether women's concern with family needs arises out of a greater proclivity toward altruism than men, or from self-interest, given women's greater dependence on family members.[3] But it does suggest that enhanced income in women's hands could benefit the whole family to a greater extent than enhanced income solely in men's hands.

Second, a gender perspective challenges the assumption that women's class can be derived simply from their family's property status and class position. Undoubtedly women of propertied households gain from their father's or husband's class positions in terms of their living standards. But to the extent that women, even of propertied households, do not own property themselves, their class position remains vicarious: a well-placed marriage can raise it, divorce or widowhood can lower it. The risk of marital breakdown leaves even women who are married into rich households economically vulnerable.[4]

The third challenge is posed by the need to understand the *process* of intra-household dynamics and allocations. Anthropological and sociological descriptions of families reveal highly complex processes of interaction and negotiation. A number of economists are today trying to grapple with such complexities and seeking to develop alternatives to the unitary household model (for details see Agarwal, 1997a). Most characterize household decision-making as some form of 'bargaining', and use the game theoretic approach to incorporate the complexity of family decision-making, variously allowing for individual differences in preferences, control over resources use, etc. They also recognize individual self-interest as a central component of family interactions.

Within the bargaining framework, intra-household interaction is characterized as containing elements of both cooperation and conflict. Household members cooperate in so far as cooperative arrangements make each of them better-off than non-cooperation. However, many different cooperative outcomes are possible in relation to who does what, who gets what goods and services, and how each member is treated. These outcomes are beneficial to the negotiating parties relative to non-cooperation. But among the set of cooperative outcomes, some are more favourable to each party than others—that is, one person's gain is another person's loss—hence the underlying conflict between those cooperating. Which outcome emerges in terms of the allocation of resources, tasks, and so on, depends on the relative bargaining power of the household members (see also Agarwal, 1997a). It needs emphasis, though, that bargaining need not be an explicit process; outcomes which favour, say, men over women could also be a result of men's implicit bargaining power.

While much of the discussion on bargaining has been in terms of formalized models, these have limitations especially in their ability to accommodate qualitative factors that affect bargaining outcomes. Bargaining power, for instance, is dependent not only on economic parameters, but also on social norms and on social perceptions about a person's contributions and deservedness. To improve women's bargaining position would need both strengthening their economic situation, and changing gendered norms and perceptions. Hence, as I have elaborated elsewhere, I favour the use of a bargaining 'approach', rather than a formal model, to talk about these issues. A bargaining approach, while based on the cooperation–conflict framework and the notion of bargaining power, is not pre-constrained by the structure that formal modelling imposes (see also, Agarwal, 1997a; Seiz, 1991).

Admitting the possibility of gender-specific differences in interests and preferences within a bargaining framework of analysis, opens up the space for recognizing that resources in women's hands could promote not only gender justice, but also welfare and efficiency. Recognizing that women as a gender could have common interests which, in particular contexts, could outweigh divisive class/caste interests, opens up the possibilities of broad-based collective action by women for changing existing gendered structures.

These challenges, and the avenues of inquiry they open up in relation to the question of land and livelihood, provide the starting point of this paper. As will be shown in the discussion which follows, not only has the pace of agrarian transformation in India left the vast majority of the population still dependent on land-based livelihoods, but the form it has taken has created significant gender disparities in non-farm livelihood options. As a result, although access to land remains important for the bulk of rural households, it is critically so for women. It affects not just a few women but a majority of them. This is a feature of agrarian change which has been obscured by the absence of a gender perspective in most analysis and policy formulation.

At the same time, there is need to view the issue of women's independent access to land and livelihood as linked not just to welfare improvement and poverty alleviation, but also in important ways to productive efficiency. Prevailing male bias in access to land and in infrastructural support to farmers is undercutting the very real potential that exists for enhancing production through a more gender-egalitarian approach. To fully realize this potential, however, will need looking beyond the conventional approach of family-based farming, to experimenting with and promoting a range of alternative institutional arrangements, involving various degrees of jointness in investment and management by groups of women.

To push for such alternatives, as also for the complex set of measures needed to reduce existing biases in women's access to land and livelihood, the paper emphasizes the critical importance of collective action by women. In this context, although recognizing that class and caste differences between women could pose difficulties, it is argued here that there are significant gender-linked commonalities of interests that would make cooperation among a broad spectrum of women possible on many counts.

Consider these aspects in detail below.

Disadvantaged Workers

What are rural women's and men's sources of livelihood? It is typically assumed that agrarian transformation will involve a shift of labour from agriculture to non-agriculture. At the aggregate level this holds for India, although the pace is slow. The percentage of all rural workers in agriculture declined from 84 in 1972–73 to 78 in 1993–94. However, this decline is due largely to male workers moving to non-agriculture, while women have remained very substantially in agriculture; indeed their dependence on agriculture has increased in recent years, and the gender gap is growing (Table 1 and Figure 1). Today 58 per cent of all male workers but 78 per cent of all female workers, and 86 per cent of all *rural* female workers, are in agriculture.

Although the absorption of both men and women into the non-agricultural sector has slowed down since 1987–88, for women the slowing down has been dramatic: the compound growth rate of

TABLE 1: ***Percentage of Work Force of Given Category in Agriculture (usual status)***

Year	*All Workers*			*Rural Workers*		
	Females	*Males*	*Difference*	*Females*	*Males*	*Difference*
1972–73	84.3	68.8	15.5	89.7	83.3	6.9
1977–78	81.8	65.6	16.2	88.2	80.7	7.5
1983	81.2	62.6	18.6	87.8	77.8	10.0
1987–88	77.7	58.7	19.0	84.8	74.6	10.2
1993–94	78.0	58.3	19.7	86.1	74.0	12.1

Source: Computed from Visaria (1996: 731–32).

FIGURE 1: ***Per Cent of Rural Labour Force in Agriculture***

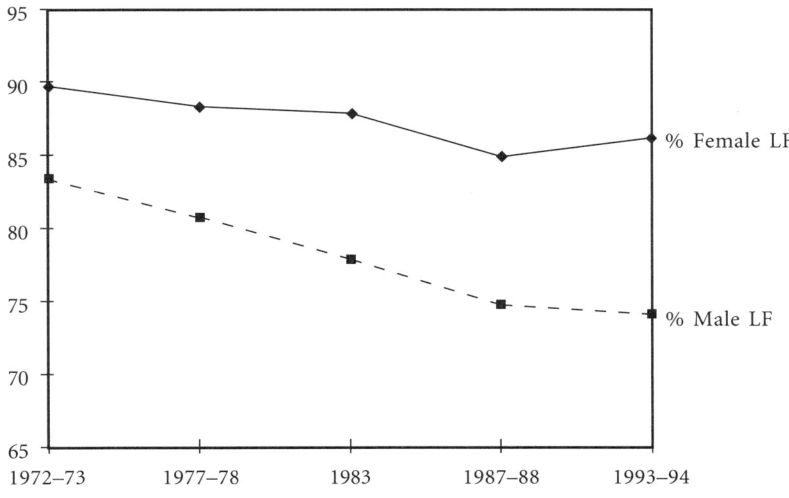

female non-agricultural employment fell from 5.2 per cent over 1978–88 to 0.2 per cent over 1988–94 (Chadha, 1996). Over this latter period, while 29 per cent of rural male additions to the labour force in the over-14 age group were absorbed into non-agriculture, less than 1 per cent of the additional female workers were so absorbed (GoI, 1990a, 1996a). This low absorption of women has been compounded by the general stagnation of rural non-farm employment in the post-reform period.

Moreover the non-farm sector is very heterogeneous, containing both high-return/high-wage activities and low-return/low-wage ones. These variations are apparent both regionally and by gender. The countrywide survey undertaken in 1987 by the National Commission on Self-Employed Women and Women in the Informal Sector (*Shramshakti*, 1988), and micro-studies of women workers in individual occupations,[5] suggest that women are largely concentrated in the low-and-insecure-earnings end of the non-farm occupational spectrum. Women's domestic work burden, lower mobility, lesser education and fewer investable assets, not only limit their general entry into non-agriculture in relation to men, they also severely limit the range of women's non-farm options. Today, even though male workers still constitute some 60 per cent of the total agricultural work force, this percentage has shown a decline and that of female workers a parallel increase in recent years.

All said, what we appear to be observing is a feminization of agriculture. It is not dissimilar to what happened in several Southeast Asian countries in the early 1970s. In Malaysia, for instance, as more men moved to non-agriculture, women began to undertake tasks such as land preparation which were traditionally done by men (Ng, 1994).[6] But subsequently most of Southeast Asia saw a substantial absorption of women outside agriculture, not their confinement within agriculture, as in India.[7]

Moreover, a large percentage of rural households in India are *de facto* female-headed, from widowhood, marital breakdown or male outmigration, estimates ranging from 20 per cent (Buvinic and Yossef, 1978) to 35 per cent (GoI, 1988). And we can expect female-headedness to grow over time. Marriages are less stable today, kinship support systems less reliable, and rural to urban migrants are still largely men.

At the same time, the nature of work women do in agriculture is to a greater extent than for men casual in nature.[8] And while casualization has been increasing for both sexes, the increase since 1987–88 has been more for women. Moreover, the rise in real agricultural wage rates for both sexes and the decline in the gender wage gap, apparent between the mid-1970s and mid-1980s, has not sustained into the 1990s. Compared with men, women continue to have lower real wage rates in most states, and lower average real wage earnings in both agriculture and non-agriculture in all states (Unni, 1996).

In other words, we can expect a growing gender divergence in dependence on agriculture. As more men shift to urban or rural non-farm livelihoods, an increasing number of households will become dependent on women managing farms and bearing the significant burden of family subsistence and reproduction. The future face of the peasant may thus be increasingly female. Are our policies within agriculture geared to take this into account?

As matters stand today, women in agriculture operate as disadvantaged workers, whether as casual labourers or as self-employed workers. Unlike self-employed men, self-employed rural women are mostly unwaged workers on male-owned family farms. I therefore come to the next part of my story: the disinherited female peasant.

Disinherited Peasants

In 1979, a group of poor women from West Bengal made the following demand to their village panchayat (Vina Mazumdar, 1992, personal communication): 'Please go and ask the *sarkar* [government] why, when it distributes land, we don't get a title? Are we not peasants? If my husband throws me out, what is my security?' There are many cases of women from well-off households being deprived of their rightful property shares by prosperous relatives, and being left destitute on desertion or widowhood (Omvedt, 1981; Agarwal, 1994). In most regions of India, women would also constitute a disproportionate number of the poor and especially of the chronically poor. And in *de facto* female-headed households, women are managing both family subsistence and cultivation, with little male assistance, and without possessing a field of their own. As elaborated below, the question of women's rights in land is central to both welfare and efficiency (apart from considerations of equality and empowerment which I will not detail here).[9]

Welfare

First, take welfare. As noted earlier, there are systematic gender inequalities in access to basic necessities within households. There are also notable gender differences in income-spending patterns. Women's and children's risk of poverty would thus depend crucially on women's direct access to income and resources, and not just access mediated through husbands or male relatives.

But access to land is especially important. The negative relationship between the risk of rural poverty and land access is well established.[10] Apart from direct production advantages through growing crops, fodder or trees, land titles increase access to credit, enhance bargaining power with employers, help push up aggregate real wage rates, and serve as mortgageable or saleable assets during crisis.[11] In addition, owning land would enhance women's self-confidence and ability to demand their due in government programmes, such as for health care, education, etc.

For widows and the elderly, owning land also improves support from kin. As old people are found to observe: 'Without property children don't look after their parents well.'[12] In other words, owning land can improve welfare not just directly, but also by enhancing a person's entitlement to family welfare. Moreover, recent research in Bangladesh on mortality rates among widows living in different household arrangements shows that those living with male relatives, other than adult sons, face much greater health risks than widows who are heads of households (Rahman and Menken, 1990), and who presumably have some independent means of income.

It needs emphasis here that access to land is important, even if it cannot serve as the sole basis of livelihood. Indeed, a large proportion of rural households do not own enough land for all family members to subsist on that basis alone. *But even a small plot can be a critical element in a diversified livelihood system and can significantly reduce the risk of poverty.* As a number of studies show, having some land is usually necessary even for viable rural non-farm activity; and it considerably expands the range of non-farm options for poor rural households.[13] Thus, a plot which is not large enough for subsistence through crop cultivation can still enhance other means of earnings. A detailed survey of three states (Bihar, Andhra Pradesh and Uttar Pradesh) by Chadha (1992), showed that in all three states small farmer households earned substantially more than landless labour households in terms of daily household earnings from self-employment in the rural off-farm sector; and in Andhra Pradesh the former's earnings from this source were eight times those of the latter. Hence, even for ensuring rural women's entry into the higher-earning segments of the non-farm sector, an initial strengthening of land rights for women might prove to be necessary in many regions.

Efficiency

Improved welfare is only one part of the argument. As agriculture gets feminized, an increasing number of women will be faced with the prime responsibility for farming, but without titles to the land they cultivate. Production inefficiency associated with insecurity of tenure has been one of the important rationales for land reform. But the rationale has typically not been extended to women. In fact in many contexts, entitling women would increase overall production, especially but not only in female-headed households.

First, there is the *incentive effect.* Secure rights in land and control over its produce would motivate women farmers (especially in cases where they are the main cultivators) to adopt improved agricultural technology, put in greater effort in cultivation and make longer-term investments in the land. This important effect, which has received substantial emphasis in land reform literature, especially in terms of giving tenants more secure rights to enhance their motivation to invest in the land, has been paid little attention in relation to family members. This is presumably on the assumption that family members will put in their best effort even if the land is owned by the male household head, due to family loyalty and/or because the benefits would be distributed equitably. Some recent studies suggest, however, that disincentives can exist equally within the family. Evidence from some African countries, where men and women typically cultivate both separate and joint plots, dramatically highlights this. In Kenya, for example, the introduction of weeding technology in maize production raised yields on women's plots by 56 per cent where women controlled the output, and only by 15 per cent on the men's plots where too women weeded but men obtained the proceeds (Ongaro, 1988, cited in Elson, 1995). The crop yield and overall productivity implications of a gender-specific incentive effect need to be examined in the Indian context as well.

Second, there is what can be termed the *credit and input access effect.* Titles would enhance women's ability to raise production by improving their access to agricultural credit, as well as by increasing women's independent access to output, savings and cash flows for re-investment.

Third, there is the *efficiency of resource use effect.* Evidence suggests that women might use resources more efficiently than men in given contexts. For instance, in terms of credit, poor women taking Grameen Bank loans in Bangladesh were found to have a better repayment record than the men. Poor women themselves often emphasize that they would make more productive use of loans than men. In a discussion on land access and government credit in Bihar, women peasants insisted: 'If the land is in women's names, the loan money cannot be spent on drink or frittered away' (Alaka and Chetna, 1987: 26).

In terms of land use again, research in Africa suggests considerable potential for productivity gains through a more gender-equal approach to input allocation. A study in Burkina Faso found, for example, that because of their choice of cropping patterns, women achieved much higher values of output per hectare than did their husbands on the plots the latter controlled (Udry *et al.*, 1995: 411). However women's yields for given crops were lower than men's because women had less access to inputs, especially fertilizers, which were concentrated on the men's plots. The study estimated that output could be increased by as much as 10–20 per cent if factors of production (such as manure and fertilizers) were reallocated from plots controlled by men to those controlled by women in the same household (Udry, 1995: 418). That is, we might improve allocative efficiency with better intra-household gender distribution of inputs. Systematic research examining resource use efficiency by gender is clearly warranted in the Indian context as well.

Quisumbing's (1996) review of studies from several countries in Africa and Southeast Asia also throws light on the relative efficiency of male and female farmers. She notes unequivocally that 'male and female farmers are equally efficient farm managers, controlling for levels of inputs and human capital' (p. 1579). *Output could, however, be increased if women farmers had the same access to inputs and education as male farmers.* In other words, there is a potential productivity loss because of constraints to women's access to inputs and information. In the South Asian context, constraints would include male bias in the delivery of technical information, credit and inputs, tenure insecurity, and social norms which restrict women's mobility, literacy and infrastructural access. These constraints would need to be removed for realizing the potential efficiency benefits.

Fourth, there is the *gender-specific knowledge and talent pool effect.* Including women as farm managers would make for a more talented and better-informed pool, than one consisting solely of men. In many South Asian communities, for example, women are often better informed than men about traditional crop varieties, and especially in the hill and tribal areas, women are usually the main seed selectors (Acharya and Bennett, 1981; Burling, 1963; Merry, 1983). In so far as titles increase women's direct participation in farm decision-making, their specific knowledge could have positive output effects, in addition to preserving or enhancing biodiversity in cultivation. A more diverse system of cultivation could also arise due to gender differences in crop preferences: in the earlier mentioned Burkina Faso study, for instance, men's and women's plots had different cropping patterns (Udry *et al.*, 1995).

Fifth, and especially important, is the enhanced *bargaining power and empowerment effect* of possessing land titles. This is illustrated most graphically from the experience of the Bodhgaya movement in Bihar in the late 1970s. In this movement, when women received land in two villages, they responded: 'Now that we have the land we have the strength to speak and walk' (Manimala, 1983). This sense of empowerment accompanying improved land rights would critically enhance women's ability not only to assert themselves better within the home, but also to demand and negotiate their due in various government schemes, and in infrastructure and services. It would also help them to be more assertive with agencies that provide inputs and extension information.

Many oppose women's inheritance on the grounds that it will reduce output by reducing farm size and increasing fragmentation (what could be termed the *farm size and fragmentation effects*). However, as I have elaborated in Agarwal (1994), existing evidence from South Asia gives no reason to fear an adverse size effect: the negative relationship between size and productivity is found to still hold after the green revolution.[14] And fragmentation can arise equally with male inheritance. Also, where necessary, farmers have dealt with fragmentation in various ways. Land-leasing arrangements help consolidate cultivation units, even where the ownership units are fragmented.

The post green-revolution period has also seen a spurt in farmer-initiated consolidation in India (Ray, 1996). Probably due both to this and to government consolidation efforts, there has been a notable decline at the all-India level in the number of fragments per holding, from 5.7 in 1960–61 to 2.7 in 1991–92 (GoI, 1997a: 17). In addition, as I discuss further on, we need to think of new institutional arrangements for joint investment and cultivation by groups of women. As Daniel Thorner (1956) also recognized, the unit of ownership need not define the unit of cultivation. While arguments for women's land rights have received some policy attention, this has been mainly in terms of welfare improvement in the context of poverty, and sometimes in terms of gender justice. There is yet little recognition of the potential efficiency implications. If an increasing number of future farmers are likely to be female, then women need to be central, not marginal, figures in policies for increasing agricultural production and improving food security.

Source of Land

But where is the land going to come from? Since this is a common question, it needs to be addressed directly. In most part the land has to come from private sources. The availability of public land for distribution is very limited. A stricter implementation of ceilings could increase the amount, but not dramatically. According to mid-1996 figures (GoI, 1996b), the area declared surplus (above the ceiling) to date, for all-India, came to only 3 million hectares or 1.6 per cent of arable land, and just 0.2 per cent of arable land is still available for distribution. In addition there is some limited availability of common land—about 13 per cent of India's arable land. Even in West Bengal, a state which had the largest amount of area declared surplus to date, and the largest number of scheduled caste/scheduled tribe beneficiaries, total ceiling surplus land came to only 8.7 per cent of the state's arable land, and today virtually none is left for distribution. For women to get a share of land, therefore, it is critical that they stake a claim in privatized land.

In India today, about 86 per cent of arable land is private[15] and 89 per cent of rural households own some land,[16] even though most hold very small plots. These figures belie the popular misconception that access to privatized land is an issue of importance to only a small percentage of rural women. Even if this figure were assessed on the most conservative side, we would still get about 78 per cent of rural households owning some land, giving a very large percentage of rural

TABLE 2: ***Rural Widows Who Inherited Land as Daughters and Widows***

Region/State	*Total sample*[1]	*Father-owned land*[2]	*Women who inherited as daughters*		*Husband-owned land*	*Women who inherited as widows*	
	No.	*No.*	*No.*	*%*	*No.*	*No.*	*%*
Northern India	262	229	18	8	193	98	51
Bihar	71	70	2	3	57	16	28
Rajasthan	49	42	2	5	39	27	69
Uttar Pradesh (hills)	50	50	1	2	45	23	51
West Bengal	92	67	13	19	52	32	62
Southern India	283	241	43	18	87	45	52
Andhra Pradesh	79	77	12	16	37	18	49
Kerala	104	65	28	43	15	10	67
Tamil Nadu	100	99	3	3	35	17	49
All regions	545[3]	470	61	13	280	143	51

Notes: [1] For all states, other than Kerala, the sample contains only Hindu widows. In Kerala, it also includes some Muslim Mappila households, who in north Kerala traditionally followed matrilineal inheritance practices.

[2] To take account of matrilineal inheritance, the Kerala sample also includes cases where the mother owned land.

[3] This is a sub-sample consisting of currently-widowed women. The original sample consisted of 562 ever-widowed women spread over fourteen villages, two each in the seven states listed above.

Source: Marty Chen (personal communication of results from her 1991 survey).

women a stake in family land.[17] Access to this land is mainly through inheritance (and limitedly through the market).

Where are women placed in terms of land inheritance? Unfortunately no large-scale rural surveys collect gender-disaggregated data on land ownership and use. But from numerous village studies, and a 1991 survey on widows by development sociologist Marty Chen, it is clear that few women inherit land; even fewer effectively control any. In Chen's sample of rural widows across seven states, only 13 per cent of 470 women with landowning fathers inherited any land as daughters (Table 2). The figure was slightly higher for south India (18 per cent) than for north India, where only 8 per cent inherited as daughters. This means that 87 per cent of the surveyed women did not receive their due as daughters.[18] The percentage of women inheriting as widows was greater. Of the 280 widows whose deceased husbands owned land, 51 per cent inherited some, but this still means that half the widows with claims did not inherit anything. And of those that did, typically their shares were not recorded formally in the village land records. Other studies show that where the land is so recorded, the widow's name is invariably entered jointly with adult sons, who effectively control the land.[19] The popular perception is that the widow's share is for her maintenance and not for her direct control or use. Widows without sons rarely inherit. Moreover, widows constitute only about 11 per cent of rural women, 75 per cent of whom are over fifty years old, many of them too old to effectively work the land. A recognition of widows' rights alone is thus inadequate for women to reap the efficiency or welfare benefits that they could reap if they also inherited as daughters (see also Agarwal, 1998).

Obstacles to Women Inheriting and Managing Land

What obstructs women from realizing their land claims? The obstacles are partly legal and in large part social and administrative. These are described in detail in Agarwal (1994) but need a brief reiteration here, to set the discussion in context.

Unequal Laws[20]

Legally, although women enjoy much greater inheritance rights today than they did, say, at the turn of the century, substantial inequalities remain. To begin with, the inheritance laws of both Hindus and Muslims treat agricultural land differently from other property. For instance, the Hindu Succession Act (HSA) of 1956 exempted tenancy rights in agricultural land from its purview. Women's inheritance rights in tenancy land thus depend on state-level tenurial laws. In the southern states, since the tenurial laws are silent on devolution, it can be presumed that for Hindus the HSA will also apply to tenancy land. In most northwestern states, however, tenurial laws do specify an order of devolution. This order strongly favours inheritance by male agnatic heirs, women coming very low in the order of heirs, as was the case under centuries-old customs. Moreover, in Uttar Pradesh and Delhi, the definition of tenants in the land reform laws is so broad as to include under that category interests arising from *all* agricultural land. Hence in these two states, of which Uttar Pradesh contains one-sixth of

India's population, women's inheritance rights in most agricultural land stand severely curtailed. And these inequalities cannot be challenged on constitutional grounds because land reform laws come under the Ninth Schedule of the Constitution. This constitutional provision was meant to protect these laws from being challenged by entrenched class interests, but in the process (albeit unwittingly), it also entrenched gender inequality.

A second source of inequality in Hindu law lies in the continued recognition in the HSA of *Mitakshara* joint family property, in which sons but not daughters have rights by birth. Again, while three of the southern states (Andhra Pradesh, Tamil Nadu, Karnataka) and Maharashtra have amended this by including daughters as coparceners, and Kerala has abolished joint family property altogether, all other states remain highly unequal. In addition, even in the three southern states and Maharashtra, an anomaly has been introduced through the amendments: by including as coparceners only daughters and not other Class I female heirs, such as the widow and mother, the amendments have increased the shares of daughters but reduced those of other Class I female heirs (see Agarwal, 1995, for elaboration).

Likewise, the Shariat Act of 1937, still applicable to Muslims in India, excluded all agricultural land (both tenanted and owned) from its purview. Subsequently, some of the southern states extended the provisions of this Act to also cover agricultural land. Legislation to this effect in 1949 covered Tamil Nadu, parts of Karnataka that fell in former Madras Province, and the Andhra area of Andhra Pradesh. In 1963 Kerala followed suit. In all other regions, however, the treatment of agricultural land, unlike other property, continues to devolve variously on customs, tenurial laws or pre-existing other laws. Such laws and customs give women's property rights very low priority in most of northwestern India. In addition, there is the inherent inequality of daughters being allowed only half the share of sons under Islamic law.

The regional contrast is striking in both Hindu and Muslim law. If we map Hindu law, for instance, gender inequality increases as we move from south India northwards. In the four southern states women can inherit agricultural land, whether owned or under tenancy. Also, in these states, due to amendments in the HSA, at least daughters have shares on par with sons in relation to joint family landed property. In the northwestern states, however, women are still seriously disadvantaged in relation both to agricultural land and joint family property.

Middle India comes in-between. The map of women's legal rights under Muslim law looks very similar in terms of the contrast between northwestern India and the rest of the country.

Unequal laws, however, cannot explain the enormity of women's disinheritance such as that noted in Chen's survey, with only 13 per cent of daughters inheriting. Rather, among the critical factors underlying both unequal laws and the vast gap between law and practice, are social and administrative biases.

Social and Administrative Bias[21]

To begin with, consider the gap between legal rights and actual ownership. In most communities which were traditionally patrilineal (i.e. where inheritance was through the male line), there is strong male resistance to endowing daughters with land. Quite apart from the reluctance to admit more contenders to the most valuable form of rural property, one of the important factors underlying such resistance is a structural mismatch between contemporary inheritance laws and traditional marriage practices. Traditionally, among matrilineal communities where daughters had strong claims in land (as in Kerala and Meghalaya), post-marital residence was in or near the natal home. This kept the land under the overall purview of the natal family, as did close-kin marriage. In contrast, in traditionally patrilineal communities, post-marital residence was patrilocal (the woman joined the husband in his natal home) and often in another village. In many such communities in northern India close-kin marriage was also forbidden, and there were social taboos against parents drawing upon the help of married daughters during economic crises.

However, today's laws recognize a daughter's claims among all groups, including patrilineal ones, while marriage practices continue to follow traditional norms, thus creating a structural mismatch between inheritance laws and marriage systems. Today this mismatch is greatest among upper-caste Hindus of the northwest who forbid marriages within the village or with close-kin typically marry daughters into distant villages, and among whom taboos against parents seeking help from married daughters also largely persist (even if changing at the margins). These are conditions under which endowing a daughter with land would be seen by the natal family as bringing virtually no reciprocal benefit, and any land inherited by her would be viewed as lost to the family. Here daughters face the greatest opposition to their claims.

Opposition is less in south and northeast India, where in-village and close-kin marriages are allowed, and parents can seek economic support from married daughters during crises.

Many women also forego their shares in parental land in favour of brothers. In the absence of an effective state social security system brothers are seen as an important source of social security, especially in case of marital break-up. Cultural constructions of gender, including how a 'good sister' would behave, also discourage women from asserting their rights, as does the emphasis on female seclusion in many areas.

Where women do not 'voluntarily' forgo their claims, male relatives file court cases, forge wills, or resort to threats and even physical violence. In eastern India, most of the witch murders among tribal groups in recent decades are found to be of widows who typically have customary claims (mostly usufruct rights) to land (Kelkar and Nathan, 1993; Chaudhuri, 1987).

These constraints are compounded by the unhelpful approach of many government functionaries who typically share the prevalent social biases and often obstruct the implementation of laws in women's favour. The bias appears to be especially prevalent in the recording of daughters' inheritance shares by the village *patwari* in northern India.

The gap between legal rights and actual ownership is matched by that between ownership and effective control. Marriages in distant villages make direct cultivation by women difficult. This is compounded in many areas by high illiteracy, high fertility, and social restrictions on women's mobility and public interaction. In particular, the ideology of female seclusion (which operates in complex ways and is more widespread than the practice of veiling) restricts women's contact with men by gendering forms of behaviour and gendering public and private space. Indeed in many north Indian villages, there are identifiable spaces where men congregate which women are expected to avoid, such as the marketplace. This territorial gendering of space reduces a woman's mobility and participation in activities outside the home (be it work in the fields or market interaction), limits her knowledge of the physical environment, and disadvantages her in seeking information on new technologies and practices, purchasing inputs, and selling the product. *Purdah* practice is strongest in northwest India and virtually absent in the south and northeast. Of course, the cultural construction of gender, which defines appropriate female behaviour and roles, is not confined to northwestern India; it also restricts women in southern India. But the strong ideology of *purdah* in the northwest circumscribes women in particular ways.

This regional difference in social restrictions on women is reflected too in women's labour force participation in both agricultural and non-agricultural jobs: women's participation rates are among the lowest in the northwest. Although this does not imply lesser work input by women in aggregate terms, it does indicate lesser work mobility, lower economic visibility, and sometimes lesser exposure to the range of agricultural tasks.

Other difficulties facing women farmers include their limited control over cash and credit for purchasing inputs, gender biases in extension services, ritual taboos against women ploughing, and demands of advance cash payments by tractor or bullock owners for ploughing women's fields. (No such demand is usually made of male farmers who, even if they are small owners, are assumed to be more credit-worthy.) Taboos against ploughing increase women's dependence on male help, reduce yields if ploughing is not done in time, and disqualify women as claimants where the policy of 'land to the tiller' is applied literally.

However, the factors that constrain women in either claiming or cultivating land are not uniformly strong. There are four regional bands in terms of the degree of difficulty women are likely to face. South India is the region of least obstacles. Here legal rights are relatively more equal, in-village and close-kin marriage is allowed, there is virtually no *purdah*, and female labour force participation is medium to high. Northwest India is the area of most difficulty on all these fronts. Northeast and central India come in-between (see Agarwal, 1994, for this regional mapping).

Biases in Land Reform and Public Land Distribution

So far I have focused on private land. But gender bias is equally apparent in public land distribution. Although, as noted, the amount of arable land in government hands is limited, it is still important since it is land on which the state has direct control, and state policy can also influence social norms and attitudes in relation to women's claims in private land. Typically, however, the government replicates private biases and allots land to male household heads, be they in schemes of land reform, poverty alleviation or resettlement.

In particular, land reform programmes of all political parties have been strongly male-biased, not just in the 1950s and 1960s but even in the late-1970s, as in West Bengal's *Operation Barga* programme. This important land reform initiative for the registration of tenants essentially registered men. Although an exception was made, in principle, for single-women households—those divorced, deserted, etc., and without adult sons—few even among them received land in practice. A village in Midnapur district studied by Gupta (1993) is indicative: 98 per cent of the 107 *khas* holdings distributed there went to men. In nine out of ten female-headed households, the land went to the women's sons; and only eight of the eighteen single women received land. None of the married women received joint titles. While it is doubtful that anyone will call this gender-biased distribution a historical blunder, one could certainly say: what an opportunity lost!

What underlies this gender bias in land reform? To begin with, in classic land reform terms, the claimant is identified as the one who tills. As Daniel Thorner (1956: 79) elaborated: 'We may begin [land reform]. . . by putting forward one fundamental principle: lands and the fruits thereof are to belong to those who do the tilling, the tillers being defined as those who plough, harrow, sow, weed, and harvest.'

While this definition works fairly well if applied to the household, it does not work when applied to individuals, given the gender division of labour. Women get excluded, as they typically do not plough (indeed, are socially barred from doing so). But clearly the definition is not the main reason for excluding women and privileging men, since if applied literally, many men too would be excluded, as most men do not sow or weed. I believe there are at least four other factors underlying the gender bias.

One is the social perception that men are the breadwinners and women the dependents. The legitimate claimant of land is thus seen as the male head of household. Even under *Operation Barga* the possibility that poor widows who were leasing out their land might lose control over it, was set aside by some with the argument: '[T]he number of such widows left alone without any adult male relatives looking after them cannot be very large' (Dasgupta, 1984: A90). This view unquestioningly endorses women's dependency on male relatives, and assumes that they will be well looked after by such relatives. Evidence on mortality rates among widows, quoted earlier, indicates otherwise.

The second factor is the social perception (in many quarters) that women's roles are (or should be) largely limited to the domestic sphere, and that they have few capabilities in the public sphere. Here patrilineal biases have tended to influence even matrilineal communities. For instance, in Meghalaya, when I asked officials why even in a traditionally matrilineal society they did not allot plots to women, I was told: 'Women cannot come to our office to fill out papers.' Yet in nearby streets there were numerous women traders selling their wares.

The third factor is the assumption (mentioned earlier) of a unitary household, wherein transfers to men are assumed to benefit all family members.

The fourth is the notion of the household as a space of harmony ('the heart of a heartless world') that property considerations would shatter. For instance, in 1989, when I gave an invited presentation on gender and land, at a land reform seminar held by the Planning Commission, to a gathering which included two cabinet ministers, the then Minister of Agriculture who came from northwest India exclaimed: 'Are you suggesting that women should be given rights in land? What do women want? To break up the family?' Ironically, what this statement effectively implies is that family stability rests on gender inequity, which women, once they have property, may not be willing to tolerate!

The assumption of women's dependency also underlies the fixation of ceilings and land distribution in resettlement schemes. Typically, a family unit is defined as constituted of the cultivator, spouse and minor children. An adult son is usually counted as a separate unit and therefore entitled to additional land, but an adult daughter is not. The peculiar result is that in most states unmarried adult daughters get totally excluded. They are not counted as members of parental families and, being unmarried, have no marital families in which they have claims. This also leads to anomalies in resettlement schemes. When I visited the Narmada valley project in 1992, several tribals commented on the fact that families with adult sons were being allotted additional land but not those with adult daughters. They asked me: 'What about those of us who have only adult daughters?'

The assumption that households are units of dependent women and male earners, in fact, informs most public policy schemes. In the social security schemes of most states, for instance, widows with adult sons are not entitled to a widow's pension.[22]

Changes Needed and Institutional Alternatives

What kinds of changes are necessary to enhance gender equality in relation to land and livelihood? In overall terms, there is need for a shift in the approach to rural development programmes of both governmental and non-governmental bodies, such as to reflect the centrality of access to land in women's livelihood systems. In specific terms, changes appear necessary on at least five counts: conceptual, legal, social, institutional and infrastructural. Below, I will examine the first three aspects and the last one in brief, and dwell in some detail on the relatively neglected area of institutional arrangements.

Conceptual and Empirical

For a start, it appears necessary to dislodge from its position of primacy the conventional model of a harmonious male-headed family in both analysis and policy, and recognize the family for what it is: a unit of both cooperation and conflict, of both sharing and selfishness, where women and men can have different interests, preferences and motivations, where self-interest also enters, and where allocations are often unequal and affected by differential bargaining power. Despite the emerging consensus among gender-aware economists around the validity of the bargaining framework for understanding intra-household dynamics, ideologically, the unitary household model holds strong. If we are to think of radical and effective interventions, a shift to more realistic assumptions about intra-family behaviour and a gender perspective in planning are thus critical.

In this context it is also important to gather systematic gender-disaggregated information on land ownership and use, both for better understanding of the existing situation, and for planning and monitoring changes. The Agricultural Census of India and the National Sample Surveys (NSS), which both carry out periodic data collection on land ownership and use, only collect aggregated household-level information. There is a case here for incorporating, in the next NSS round, a special module of questions for obtaining gender-disaggregated intra-household information. If necessary, this could initially be tried on a pilot basis, and later extended to the full survey.[23] Researchers collecting land-related data in other projects could also be encouraged to collect gender-disaggregated information on land ownership and use.

Legal

These would need to include at least three elements.

(i) Changes in the law. Inheritance laws applicable to both Hindus and Muslims would need amending, to bring agricultural land on par with other forms of property. Equally, in the HSA, the *Mitakshara* joint family property provision would need to be abolished, as done in Kerala. In addition, in ceiling laws, sons and daughters need to be treated on par, both in assessing ceiling-surplus land and in land redistribution schemes. This may well require a scaling down of ceilings.

(ii) Legal literacy. This is essential to make laws effective. There is need here to reach both adults and those near adulthood. For the latter, legal literacy could perhaps be made a part of the curriculum in the senior years of school.

(iii) Recording of women's shares. Village women would need support to ensure that their land shares are correctly recorded by the village *patwari*, and might need legal advice and help on various counts, if they have to contest their claims either with the family or with the administration.

In all these efforts, gender-progressive groups could play a significant role.[24]

Social

Unless women's claims begin to be seen as socially legitimate, parents can and will use the right of testation to disinherit daughters, even if the laws are made fully gender-equal. Equally, a change is necessary in perceptions about women's appropriate roles and abilities, and in social norms that restrict their public mobility and interaction. For instance, the problem that village exogamy (marriage outside their natal village) poses for women arises only partly from the distances involved, and more substantially from social strictures on women's mobility and from social perceptions about their lesser abilities and deservedness. Men are seldom denied their property rights even if they migrate to distant parts. In fact the bulk of job-related migration from the village to the city is of young men (Bardhan, 1977, and Bora, 1996).

Changes in social attitudes, norms and perceptions are not easy to bring about, but there are certainly interventions that could further the process. For instance, initiatives by the government to transfer land titles and infrastructural support to women farmers could have a demonstration effect. More general interventions to strengthen extra-family economic support for women, including through a government social security scheme, would help reduce women's dependence on relatives, especially on brothers in whose favour they often forego their claims. Overall, economic support would also enhance women's ability to challenge inequalities in the family and community. In so far as the popular media is one of the arenas where gender roles and relations are both projected and constructed, media interventions in a gender-progressive direction would also have an impact on social attitudes.

Institutional

Most importantly, we need to experiment with alternative institutional arrangements for cultivation. There is a long-standing assumption in public policy that farms will be cultivated on a family basis. Interventions in the form of land distribution to the landless, or to those displaced by large irrigation schemes, also assume this. The same approach is replicated in the rare cases when land is given to women. For instance, in the limited recognition of women's claims to land under poverty alleviation schemes, the emphasis so far has been on giving poor women joint titles with husbands, and occasionally on giving women individual titles. The Eighth Five Year Plan recommended that 60 per cent of all land distributed to the landless should go to both spouses, and 40 per cent to women alone.

While having some land is better than having none, both joint and individual titles could present some problems for women. In the case of joint titles with husbands, for instance women often find it difficult to gain control over the produce, or to bequeath the land as they want, or to claim their shares in case of marital conflict. As some Bihari rural women told me: 'For retaining the land we would be tied to the man, even if he beats us.' Wives may also have different land use priorities from husbands which they would be less in a position to exercise with joint titles. Also, joint titles constrain women from exploring alternative institutional arrangements for cultivation and management.

Individual titles, in contrast, potentially provide women considerable flexibility in terms of control over the land, but here a different set of problems can arise. One is the inability to fully exploit the productive potential of the plot, since poor women seldom have the resources for investing in necessary equipment or inputs on an individual basis. In Bodhgaya (Bihar), for instance, several of the women received an acre each in their own names as a result of the land struggle in the late 1970s, but subsequently, I understand, a number of women (as also men) had to mortgage their holdings because of a lack of necessary investible funds for profitable cultivation.[25] Moreover, where holdings are very small, it can prove uneconomic to invest in capital equipment on an individual basis. Individual women also face considerable pressure from male relatives who want to control the land themselves. In addition, there remains the question of who would inherit the land from the women. In many cases, women end up bequeathing the land to sons on the grounds that daughters will leave the village on marriage.

Are there institutional solutions to these problems? I believe there are. They involve various forms of collective efforts by women, efforts that mostly embody attempts to define units of investment and cultivation larger than the unit of ownership. As Daniel Thorner (1956: 72) insightfully argued:

> It is often implicitly assumed or even stated that to set limits on the size of property units would be equivalent to limiting the size of units of cultivation. This need not be the case. There is no inherent reason why small units of ownership . . . could not make up much larger units of cultivation. . . . Many parts of India have a live tradition of mutual help, whether for irrigation, as in the *phads* of southern Bombay, or for the entire range of cultivation, as in the *metis* of eastern Hyderabad.

In Agarwal (1994) I had suggested group rights in land for landless women, and collective management by them as an alternative to family-based farming. Since then, looking at the issue more systematically, I find many cases of women investing and managing land in groups, which serve as examples of alternatives (Table 3). Consider the following.

One alternative could be for women who own individual holdings (whether obtained through inheritance, purchase, or from the government) to invest in capital inputs jointly with other women, while managing production individually. Male farmers have done this in a number of regions, for instance, jointly invested in a tubewell where they have contiguous plots. This reduces the individual cost of lumpy investments. Women owners of plots could be encouraged to do the same. In fact, when land was distributed to poor peasants as a result of the Bodhgaya struggle in Bihar, to deal with the shortage of investable

TABLE 3: ***Women Managing Cropland under Various Institutional Arrangements***

Form of Control	*Source of Land*	*Investment*	*Cultivation*	*Use*	*Examples of Actual Practice*
		Conventional Approach			
Individual women	Inherited or purchased	Individual	Individual	Crops	Typical
		Alternatives			
Individual women	Inherited, purchased, or government transfer	Joint (with other women)	Individual	Crops	Bodhgaya (Bihar) (government promoted)
Individual ownership, group management by women	Group purchase of private land by women, divided into individually owned plots	Joint (with other women)	Joint	Crops	Deccan Development Society (DDS) in Andhra Pradesh
Group of women	Group lease of private land	Joint	Joint	Crops, vegetables	DDS (AP) Kerala, BRAC (Bangladesh)
Group of women	Male owners; cultivation overseen by women's groups	Individual	Individual	Crops	DDS's Community Grain Fund Scheme
Group of women	Village commons, or male-owned private land, or government-owned degraded forest land	Joint	Joint	Trees	Many, including Bankura (West Bengal), SEWA (Gujarat)
Group of women	Government transfer to women's groups	Joint	Joint	Crops	Untried so far

resources faced by the beneficiary farmers, I understand the government initiated a scheme of providing funds to groups of five farmers each to invest in pumpsets. Two such groups are constituted only of women farmers (personal communication from former Chhatra Yuva Sangharsh Vahini activists). Although there are no subsequent reports on how well the scheme has functioned, it is a step in the right direction. (Group investment, however, would only solve one problem facing individual women farmers; other problems, such as family pressure to give up the land and the issue of who would inherit it, would still remain.)

A second type of institutional arrangement could be for women to enter the private land market, purchasing land jointly, owning it individually and farming it collectively. There are several examples of this. One of the most interesting to my knowledge is that of the Deccan Development Society (DDS), an NGO working with poor women's collectives in some seventy-five villages in Medak district—a drought-prone tract of Andhra Pradesh. DDS has helped women from landless families establish claims on land through purchase and lease, using a variety of government schemes.[26]

For instance, the Scheduled Caste Development Corporation of Andhra Pradesh gives subsidized loans to landless scheduled caste women for buying agricultural land. Catalyzed by DDS, women form a group and apply for the loan after identifying the land they want to buy. Land records are scrutinized to ensure that the title is litigation-free, and an endorsement is obtained from the *patwari* and the Mandal revenue officer that the women applicants are indeed landless. The purchased land is then divided among the group members. Each woman is registered as the owner of a plot. Today, women's groups in eighteen villages are said to be cultivating 350 acres of purchased land, each woman owning about one acre but cultivating it jointly. The size of a group cultivating jointly can range from six or seven women to as many as twenty in some cases, veering to an average of about ten.[27] In the process of working together, the women have learnt to survey and measure land, hire tractors, travel to distant towns to meet government officials, obtain inputs and market the produce. Moreover, DDS has been actively promoting organic farming in all its cultivation schemes.

This approach of joint purchase of land and joint cultivation could be followed in other states as well, on the basis of other government schemes. For instance, since 1995–96 loans can be obtained by the poor for land purchase through the central government's Integrated Rural Development Programme directed to alleviate poverty (GoI, 1996c). Women's groups could also take advantage of this scheme.

A third type of institutional arrangement could be for women to lease in land as a group and cultivate it jointly. DDS again provides an illustrative example. Under one of its programmes, women in Andhra Pradesh are leasing in fallow land from large owners. Women contribute part of the rent and DDS provides the rest as seed money. Initiated in 1989, the programme is now said to cover 800 acres across fifty-six villages. Under another of its efforts, DDS successfully lobbied the state government to allow women's groups to use the loan money available via the government's poverty alleviation scheme, DWACRA (Development of Women and Children in Rural Areas), for leasing in land, rather than for activities such as tailoring, milch cattle, handicrafts, etc., for which such funds are conventionally disbursed. Committees of women examine the lease proposals put forward by the women's groups, assess the land quality, keep records of each woman's work input, and ensure equitable distribution of wages and produce. Fifteen women's groups have used the revolving fund provided under this scheme to collectively lease in and cultivate land. In 1995 each woman participant received enough cereal and pulses to feed the whole family for a month, in addition to receiving harvest wages.

DDS is not the only NGO encouraging land leasing by women. Michael Tharakan (1996, and personal communication) describes a village in Kerala's Kannur district, where three women's groups are leasing in land from farmers in the off-season for vegetable cultivation.[28] In Bangladesh, the Bangladesh Rural Advancement Committee (BRAC), an NGO which provides credit and technical support to poor rural men and women, also helps women to lease and cultivate land collectively. In a number of cases they have been able to do so successfully, despite opposition from orthodox villagers (Chen, 1983).

A fourth type of institutional arrangement is again one that has been tried by DDS, where women are jointly overseeing the cultivation of undercultivated or fallow land by private male owners. They have also set up a Community Grain Fund in the process. They are focusing on cultivable fallows and marginal land, most of which is ceiling surplus land distributed by the government to landless men. The land was of very poor quality and remained substantially uncultivated, while the families depended heavily on the public distribution system (PDS). Menon (1996) and Satheesh (1996, 1997a) describe how DDS persuaded the state government to provide one-eighth of the money it spent on subsidizing PDS to help poor farmers over three years to cultivate their fallow or underused land. Over the next five years, the farmer pays a specified amount of the grain he harvests to the Community Grain Fund, in repayment for the support. Committees of women manage the whole programme, identifying the land to be so used, ensuring that the farmers use the loans for cultivation, supervising the operations, ensuring use of organic manure and mixed cropping, and collecting the harvest share for the Community Grain Fund. Each of the villages under this scheme typically has a committee of five women, and each woman in the committee personally oversees about twenty acres. The women's committee also identifies the poorest households in each village to whom this grain is sold at a low price (to offset costs). The Community Grain Fund thus serves as a form of alternative PDS. This project is now said to be working in thirty-two villages, covering some 2,675 acres and 1,720 marginal and small farmers, and is estimated to have produced about 687,500 kilograms of extra grain (Satheesh, 1997b).[29]

A fifth type of arrangement could be the one earlier suggested by me in Agarwal (1994), but for which so far I have not found a ground example. Under this arrangement, poor rural women would hold group rights over land distributed by the government or otherwise acquired by women. Each woman in the group would have use rights but not the right to dispose of the land. The daughters-in-law and daughters of such households who are resident in the village would share these use rights. Daughters leaving the village on marriage would lose such rights, but could establish them in their marital village if a similar arrangement were operating there. Also, they could re-establish their rights in their parental village should they need to return, say on divorce or widowhood, by rejoining the production efforts. In other words, land access would be linked formally with residence and working on the land, as was the case under some tribal systems when land was held collectively by a clan.

There are four important ingredients in these success stories. Three of these—the presence of a gender-progressive NGO, the use of a group approach, a focus on landless women—are found in many stories of poor women's economic betterment in India. What is uncommon is the fourth ingredient, namely, the focus on land for women, as opposed to the typical and usually less sustainable income-generating activities promoted by the government and most NGOs. In fact, by focusing on land, the organizations are upholding many poor women's own priorities. As some landless women in Andhra Pradesh said to Maria Mies and her co-researchers in 1979, when asked if they wanted better housing: 'We want land, all the rest is humbug' (Mies *et al.*, 1986).

In the institutional alternatives I have described (summarized in Table 3), women have direct control over crop production and distribution, and are not just adjunct workers on family farms. Cooperation is not between households but between women with shared interests. And these arrangements help resolve several of the difficulties women face in obtaining and cultivating land. Here women can gain access to land not only via inheritance but also through the market or through the community—access which women operating as individuals rarely have. And, where linked with land pooling, joint investment and collective management, these arrangements can help overcome any problems of small size and fragmentation. In this way, they could also help undercut the oft-stated resistance to women's land claims on the grounds that it will increase fragmentation and so reduce output. Indeed, given that by the latest 1992 NSS survey on landholdings some 72 per cent of landowning households own under one hectare (GoI, 1995: 22), it appears important to promote various forms of collective investment/management even for holdings owned by men.

For women, a collective approach to land management would also help them mobilize funds for capital investment, take advantage of economies of scale, and cooperate in labour sharing and product marketing.[30] If, in addition, the land is under a system of group rights (as in the fifth alternative), this would strengthen women's ability to withstand pressure from male relatives and retain control over the land; and it would by-pass the problem of inheritance, since the women's group would have use rights but not rights of alienation. It would also bypass the problem of outside-village marriages, since women's rights would be established only by residence.

A number of women elected to panchayats in Madhya Pradesh whom I met in 1995 and asked about their perceptions of the advantages and disadvantages of individual titles, joint titles with husbands, and group rights with other women, strongly supported the idea of group rights. They, as well as some of us invited in an advisory capacity, were asked to comment on the draft Madhya Pradesh Policy on Women that the state government was framing; and my recommendation of group rights was subsequently incorporated in a modified form, in the final version of the policy, as follows: 'All land distribution and redistribution undertaken by the government will be made in future in women's names. Wherever possible, preference will be given in such allotments to groups of poor rural women which will have full rights of use and control over the land' (Govt. of Madhya Pradesh, 1996: 11). Some other recommendations in Agarwal (1994) were also incorporated in the Madhya Pradesh policy, such as placing unmarried adult daughters on par with adult sons and treating them as separate units in land distributed in resettlement schemes. It remains to be seen how all this is implemented in practice, but such policy directives are themselves a notable step forward.

Several elements in the institutional arrangements described above can be found in traditional agrarian institutions, or have been discussed in the literature on agrarian transformation, but the focus has been on households as units. For instance, reciprocal labour-sharing arrangements have been a common feature of agricultural cultivation in rural, especially tribal, communities, but the terms of reciprocity are typically established between households.[31] Similarly, in the 1950s and early 1960s, land reform and cooperative farming were the buzz-words of rural development. Here again the focus was on households and on male heads as representatives of households. At that time, not only did gender receive no mention but inadequate attention was paid also to socio-economic inequalities between households. As a result, cooperatives often (albeit not uniformly) tended to be large-farmer dominated (Frankel, 1978). Today, we need to recognize not only that households can be arenas of gender-based conflict of interests, but also that communities are spaces that are often both class/caste-differentiated and highly gendered. This impinges on the kind of institutional forms that would be effective. In the forms discussed here, factors such as class and gender are centrally recognized, in that the groups are constituted of women from poor rural households. Often the groups are also homogenous in their social composition, being composed only of the scheduled castes or tribes. To a fair extent this is also true of women's groups that are today successfully planting and protecting trees collectively, some on village commons, others on fallow land donated by male owners, yet others on degraded government forest land.[32] Overall, these examples suggest an important window of opportunity to revive land reform, community cooperation and joint farming in a radically new form, by centering them on poor women.

A window of opportunity is also provided by the growing attention being given to watershed development and localized irrigation schemes by a number of NGOs and some government agencies, in several parts of the country today. Experiments in semi-arid parts of

Maharashtra, such as that of Anna Hazare in the village of Ralegaon Siddhi and its environs, and that of Vilasrao Salunke in what are termed the Pani Panchayat villages, have made both private and common land more productive.[33] But once land value rises with the availability of water for irrigation, women's rights in the land are seldom recognized. The opportune time to establish women's claims is prior to developing the watershed or irrigation facility, not afterwards.

More generally, for improving the implementation of women's inheritance claims and for trying out some of the alternative institutional arrangements for land management, the southern and western states could be starting points, since here both laws and the social context are relatively more favourable to women.

Infrastructure

Critically linked to the success of women's farming efforts, whether as individuals or groups, is access to infrastructural support. As noted earlier, there are significant gender (in addition to class) inequalities associated with access to credit, labour, other production inputs (including hired equipment) and information on new agricultural technologies. Poor women cultivating very small plots have the most difficult time in this regard. More generally, the cultural constructions of gender roles and behaviour also reduce women's ability to function effectively in factor and product markets, as well as in the marketplace in general.

There is clearly a need here for a systematic effort to remove prevailing biases in the delivery mechanisms of government infrastructure. A greater female presence in agricultural input and information delivery systems (women extension agents are often recommended for the latter) would no doubt be helpful in reducing some of the gender bias, but it appears equally necessary to reorient these systems so that even male functionaries recognize the importance of contacting and assisting women farmers.

Also, dependence on the state alone would not be enough, or probably have as much potential for success in reaching women as non-governmental initiatives. Certainly in the delivery of credit to poor women, NGOs such as the Grameen Bank in Bangladesh and the Self Employed Women's Association (SEWA) in India have been markedly more successful than have government agencies. The role of NGOs could similarly be important in providing technical information, production inputs and marketing facilities to groups of women farmers. BRAC in Bangladesh is a case in point: although it does not focus specifically on women farmers, as noted earlier, it provides a range of relevant informational, technical and market support services to its members. A systematic promotion of women's cooperatives for production inputs and marketing would also be important.

Thorner and Thorner titled one chapter of their book *Land and Labour in India* as 'Ploughing the Plan Under'. It is indeed time to plough gender-biased plans under, and sow a new gender-equal one.

Collective Action

For the mentioned legal, social, infrastructural and institutional changes to be initiated and sustained, the committed involvement of many actors will be needed, including the government, political parties and NGOs. But such an involvement is unlikely to emerge automatically in most cases. To bring it about, concerted efforts will be needed, especially through various forms of collective action by women at many levels: the state, the market, the community and the household.

After over two decades of the women's movement in India, the importance of collective action is well recognized. But much of the effort in relation to women's economic empowerment has been for demands other than land, such as for better wages, or for closing the gender gaps in wage rates and earnings, or for setting up group credit schemes especially in the urban context. Attention now needs to focus on group action for gaining access to land, in recognition of the central importance of land in most rural women's livelihoods, whether as the primary or a significant supplementary source of income.

The local bureaucracy would be more likely to accurately register individual women's claims in family land if there were collective pressure from gender-progressive groups. Such organizations could also provide women with vital information about the laws and contact with legal experts, if necessary. In fact, a woman's group in the Santal Parganas is doing just that, even providing monetary support to help women who wish to contest their claims.[34] Similarly, SEWA in Gujarat is providing women loans to help them register their names as joint owners in their husbands' land (personal communication, Renana Jhabvala, 1997).

Gender-progressive organizations could similarly strengthen

women's fall-back position through economic and social support structures which reduce women's dependence on male relatives, especially their brothers, in whose favour women often forfeit their claims. As a woman member of BRAC tellingly asserted: 'Well the organization is [now] my "brother"' (Hunt, 1983: 38).

Equally, a collective challenge by women can facilitate change in social norms which, as noted, restrict women's ability to obtain their due. In Bangladesh, for instance, women members of BRAC are beginning to question the legitimacy of *purdah*. Economic exigency created the need to challenge *purdah*, but group solidarity has strengthened women's ability to sustain the challenge. As some BRAC women noted (cited in Chen, 1983: 177, 165):

> They said . . . [w]e are ruining the prestige of the village and breaking purdah. . . . Now nobody talks ill of us. They say: 'They have formed a group and now they earn money. It is good.'
>
> Before the village elders . . . abused . . . us for joining the group, now they are silent. . . . Before we did not know our rights, now we . . . exert pressure to receive our due. . . . Before we did not go outside our homes, but now we work in the field and go to the town. . . . Before our minds were rusty, now they shine.

In fact, challenging restrictive social norms may emerge as a by-product of forming groups for the more effective delivery of economic programmes. The experiences of the Grameen Bank, BRAC, SEWA and of many other groups support this conclusion.

Building group support among and for women, both locally and nationally, is crucial for empowering women both as wage workers and as peasants. Such support can come both from separately constituted groups which provide specialized help to village women and from organizations comprised of village women themselves. A significant female presence in the village panchayats, resulting from the one-third reservation for women provided for by the 73rd Constitutional Amendment in 1992, also has potential for strengthening rural women's hands. Although women's presence in such bodies need not *guarantee* more gender-progressive programmes, the record of elected all-women panels in village panchayats in parts of India (such as Maharashtra and Madhya Pradesh), leaves room for optimism: women in these bodies are found to be more sensitive to women's concerns and to give priority to local women's needs in ways that male panchayat members typically do not (Gala, 1990; Gandhi and Shah, 1991). The presence of women in decision-making roles and positions of authority also has a wider impact on social attitudes; and women, especially but not only in *purdah*-practising communities, are more likely to take their grievances to women representatives than to all-male bodies.

However, support for women's land claims on a large scale and beyond localized experiments will need much more broad-based collective action by women. There are some who insist that class differences between women would prevent the emergence of such cooperation among them. While undoubtedly there would be contexts in which divisive class/caste interests would outweigh cohesive gender interests, I believe that this cannot be generalized. As noted at the beginning of this paper, women's class position, if derived from the property position of male relatives, is much more vicarious than that of men. Moreover, there are significant areas of mutual benefit that cut across class lines, which could serve as starting points. One is legal reform. Women of both large and small peasant households with a stake in family land stand to gain from gender-equal inheritance laws. (And, as noted, the percentage of such women is very substantial, despite the highly skewed distribution of land.) Rural women across a wide socio-economic spectrum would also gain from the amendment of ceiling laws that bring adult daughters on par with sons. Equally, challenging restrictive social norms holds benefits for women of both well-off and poor households.

The experience of the women's movement in India also indicates that women with varied socio-economic backgrounds can cooperate strategically for legal reform, as borne out by campaigns to amend dowry and rape laws, for which women's groups successfully formed a common front despite significant differences in ideologies, agendas and social compositions. Moreover, many urban middle-class women activists have played and continue to play important roles in promoting poor rural women's economic and social concerns. The role of such activists was critical in catalyzing a focus on poor women's independent rights in agricultural land within the Bodhgaya movement in Bihar, the Shetkari Sanghatana in Maharashtra, and in NGOs such as DDS in Andhra Pradesh. There are numerous other examples of such middle-class activism supporting poor women's efforts to improve their livelihoods, such as through wasteland management and forest protection, higher wages, better returns from informal sector enterprises, and so on. These experiences again indicate that cross-class action is possible in many contexts.

More generally, in recent years, an expanding empirical and theoretical literature suggests that collective action can arise in a range of contexts, including those where socio-economic inequality might prevail.[35] In other words, socio-economic equality may be neither a necessary nor a sufficient condition for cooperation in many cases.

All said, I believe there is a favourable climate now for raising the question of women's independent claims to land and livelihood. Although most women's groups have not focused on land rights and many have not focused even on women's livelihoods from other sources, they have spread general awareness of gender concerns. This has created an environment within which women's independent claims for land and livelihood can be placed more centrally in the arena of public concerns—something that was not easy to do two decades ago.

In 1961 Daniel and Alice Thorner noted that in north India's villages: 'A man's *haisiyat* [social standing] is his land'[36] (Thorner and Thorner, 1962: 201). Perhaps it is now time we judge a man's *haisiyat* by whether or not his wife and daughters too command shares in land and livelihood. Certainly it appears time to heed the demand posed by poor women in West Bengal twenty years ago, and by many others since: 'Why don't we get a title? Are we not peasants?'

I am grateful to Abhijit Sen, Kumkum Sangari, Patricia Oberoi and S. M. Agarwal, for their useful comments on an earlier draft.

Notes

1 On health care and food see, among others, Harriss (1990), Dreze and Sen (1995), and Agarwal (1986); on education see Dreze and Sen (1995); on property see Agarwal (1994); and on the gender division of labour see Dasgupta and Maiti (1986).

2 See e.g. Mencher (1988) for India; Roldan (1988) for Mexico; and Blumberg (1991) for several other countries.

3 For elaboration, see Agarwal (1997a).

4 See also Omvedt (1981), Agarwal (1994) and Barrett (1980).

5 See, various case studies in Singh and Kelles-Vitanen (eds, 1987).

6 The same is noted among tribal communities in parts of India where, with male outmigration, women now often do many of the agricultural tasks that mostly men did earlier (Fernandes and Menon, 1987).

7 In Malaysia and the Republic of Korea today, less than 20 per cent of total

female workers are in agriculture, and even in Sri Lanka, the percentage is under 50 (ILO, 1995), compared with India's 78 per cent.

[8] In 1993–94, 38 per cent of rural female workers and 33.8 per cent of rural male workers were casual labourers (GoI, 1996a).

[9] For a detailed spelling out of arguments around all four considerations, see Agarwal (1994).

[10] See especially Gaiha and Kazmi (1981), Ali *et al.* (1981), Sundaram and Tendulkar (1983), and Lipton (1985).

[11] See Agarwal (1994) for elaboration.

[12] See Caldwell *et al.* (1988: 191); also personal communication to this effect during my interviews with elderly widows in Rajasthan.

[13] See e.g. Islam (1986); Papola (1987); Saith (1991), and Chadha (1992).

[14] See, Boyce (1987), Agarwal (1983), and Berry and Cline (1979).

[15] Computed from the latest available land use statistics for India. Total arable land is the aggregate of new sown area, fallow land (current and other fallows), cultivable wasteland, and miscellaneous tree crops and groves. Of this, net sown area, current fallows and miscellaneous tree crops and groves can broadly be assumed to be in private hands.

[16] This is based on the latest 1992 National Sample Survey (48th round) figures on land ownership patterns (GoI, 1995).

[17] The figure of 89 per cent of land-owning households in the NSS includes both households owning agricultural land and those owning only homestead land. Hence 11 per cent own neither agricultural nor homestead land. The figure of landless households would be higher if we took as 'landless' those households which own no agricultural land but do own some homestead land. No direct information on this is available, but one indirect indicator would be the percentage of rural households not cultivating any land, which comes to 21.8 per cent in 1992 (GoI, 1997b: 17). However, this figure would include not just households owning no agricultural land but also those which have leased out all their owned agricultural land. The actual percentage of those owning no agricultural land would thus be less than 21.8.

[18] On the positive side, in some parts of the country, attitudes toward daughters' claims appear to be changing. A *patwari* I interviewed in 1996 in a village in Maharashtra near Pune, said that over the past three to four years there had been an improvement in the recording of daughters' shares, and fewer women were willing to sign away their shares in favour of brothers. He himself felt that all children, irrespective of gender, had a right to parental property. In answer to the question: 'what if daughters get a dowry?' he said: 'Giving a dowry is parental duty; inheritance is a right.' He added: 'Where a daughter gets a dowry she should get only one-fourth of her inheritance share. If there is no dowry she should get the full share.'

[19] Nandwana and Nandwana (1996) and my own survey in some villages of Rajasthan and Maharashtra.

[20] For details, see Agarwal (1994, 1995).

[21] See Agarwal (1994) for a detailed discussion of these biases.

[22] The only exception to this assumption of dependency in pension provisioning appears to be Tamil Nadu, where there is some provision for pensions for deserted and destitute wives (GoI, 1990b).

[23] The idea of adding a special section has in fact been successfully tried out earlier by the NSS in its 32nd round, in relation to women's work participation which is under-reported in several states. This involved adding a set of probing questions to the regular questionnaire, to be put to women normally categorized as engaged in 'domestic work', in order to distinguish between those who were engaged in 'domestic duties only' from those also engaged in economically gainful work such as free collection of goods (firewood, fish, wild fruits, etc.) for home consumption, maintaining a kitchen garden, sewing, tailoring, tending cattle and poultry, and so on. See Sen and Sen (1985) for further details of this special survey.

[24] The term 'gender-progressive', as used here and subsequently, relates to those laws, practices, policies, etc., which reduce or eliminate the inequities (economic, social, political) that women face in relation to men. Individuals and organizations that work toward removing gender inequities are also so described. 'Gender-retrogressive' has the opposite meaning.

[25] Personal communication in 1993 from some activists of the Chhatra Yuva Sangharsh Vahini (CYSV) which helped catalyse the struggle. See Agarwal (1994) for a detailed discussion on the Bodhgaya struggle.

[26] See Menon, 1996; Satheesh, 1996, 1997a, 1997b; DDS, 1994–95. Also personal communications from Rukmini Rao, chairperson, DDS, during 1997–98.

[27] Personal communication, Rukmini Rao, DDS, January 1998.

[28] I understand that twenty-three groups were constituted, each consisting of ten to twenty unemployed youth. Of these, three groups were of women alone (personal communication, Michael Tharakan, 1997).

[29] I understand from Rukmini Rao, in a recent communication (December 1997), that despite its highly innovative nature this particular project has lately been facing some problems at the district administration level, in terms of delays in the release of loan instalments. If such new institutional efforts are to succeed, it is clearly important that both local and central government administrations are committed to support them.

[30] The one problem which could arise in joint cultivation is that of ensuring that each woman puts in an equal work effort for equal benefit-sharing. However, this problem is not insurmountable. In the DDS groups, for instance, the problem was minimized by the fact that the groups were small, the women constituting them all knew each other, and any slackness was reported, explanations asked for, and appropriate action taken, in the weekly meetings of the groups.

[31] See e.g. Kar (1982), Agarwal (1990).

[32] Examples include the Bankura project in West Bengal (Mazumdar, 1989) and several groups in Rajasthan (Sarin and Sharma, 1991), Gujarat, the Uttar Pradesh hills, Andhra Pradesh, and elsewhere (Singh and Burra, 1993; Agarwal, 1997b).

[33] Personal observation on field visits to both sites in 1997. Also see Pangare

and Pangare (1992) on Ralegaon Siddhi, and Pangare and Lokur (1996) on the Pani Panchayats.

[34] Personal communication from social activist Nitya Rao, Bombay, 1997.

[35] For a useful review of some of this literature, see especially Baland and Platteau (1994).

[36] *Haisiyat*: also 'capacity'.

References

Acharya, M. and L. Bennett (1981). *An Aggregate Analysis and Summary of Village Studies, The Status of Women in Nepal*, II, Part 9, CEDA, Tribhuvan University, Kathmandu.

Agarwal, B. (1983). *Mechanization in Indian Agriculture: An Analytical Study of the Indian Punjab*, Delhi, Allied Publishers; reprinted in 1986.

——— (1986). 'Women, Poverty and Agricultural Growth in India', *The Journal of Peasant Studies*, 14 (4), July.

——— (1990). 'Tribal Matriliny in Transition: Changing Gender, Production and Property Relations in North-East India', World Employment Programme Research Working Paper, WEP 10/WP 50, International Labour Office, Geneva.

——— (1994). *A Field of One's Own: Gender and Land Rights in South Asia*, Cambridge University Press, Cambridge.

——— (1995). 'Women's Legal Rights in Agricultural Land in India', *Economic and Political Weekly*, Review of Agriculture, March.

——— (1997a). ' "Bargaining" and Gender Relations: Within and Beyond the Household', *Feminist Economics*, 3 (1), pp. 1–50. Also published as FCND Discussion Paper No. 27, International Food Policy Research Institute, Washington DC.

——— (1997b). 'Environmental Action, Gender Equity and Women's Participation', *Development and Change*, 28 (1), pp. 1–44.

——— (1998). 'Widows versus Daughters or Widows as Daughters: Property, Land and Economic Security in Rural India', *Modern Asian Studies*, Vol. 1 (Part 1), pp. 1–48.

Alaka and Chetna (1987). 'When Women Get Land: A Report from Bodhgaya', *Manushi*, No. 40, pp. 25–26.

Ali, I., B.M. Desai, R. Radhakrishna and V.S. Vyas (1981). 'Indian Agriculture at 2000: Strategies for Equality', *Economic and Political Weekly*, Annual Number, 16 (10–12), pp. 409–24.

Baland, J.M. and J.P. Platteau (1994). 'Should Common Property Resources be Privatized? A Re-examination of the Tragedy of the Commons', Discussion Paper, Centre for Research in Economic Development, Namur University, Belgium.

Bardhan, K. (1977). 'Rural Employment, Wages and Labour Markets in India: A Survey of Research', *Economic and Political Weekly*, 12 (26), 25 June, pp. A–34 to A–48; 12 (27), 2 July, pp. 1062–74; and 12 (28), 9 July, pp. 1101–18.

Barrett, M. (1980). *Women's Oppression Today: Problems with Marxist Feminism*, Verso, London.

Berry, R.A. and W.R. Cline (1979). *Agrarian Structure and Productivity in Developing Countries*, Johns Hopkins University Press, Baltimore and London.

Bora, R.S. (1996). *Himalayan Migration: A Study of the Hill Region of Uttar Pradesh*, Sage Publications, Delhi.

Boyce, J. (1987). *Agrarian Impasse in Bengal: Institutional Constraints to Technological Change*, Oxford University Press, Oxford.

Blumberg, R.L. (1991). 'Income Under Female vs. Male Control: Hypotheses from a Theory of Gender Stratification and Data from the Third World', in R.L. Blumberg (ed.), *Gender, Family and Economy: The Triple Overlap*, Sage Publications, Newbury Park, pp. 97–127.

Burling, R. (1963). *Rengsanggri: Family and Kinship in a Garo Village*, University of Pennsylvania Press, Philadelphia.

Buvinic, M. and N.H. Youssef (1978). 'Women-Headed Households: The Ignored Factor in Development Planning', Report submitted to AID/WID, International Centre for Research on Women, Washington DC.

Caldwell, J.C., P.H. Reddy and P. Caldwell (1988). *The Causes of Demographic Change: Experimental Research in South India*, University of Wisconsin Press, Wisconsin, 1988).

Chadha, G.K. (1992). 'Non-farm Sector in India's Rural Economy: Policy, Performance and Growth Prospects', mimeo, Centre for Regional Development, Jawaharlal Nehru University, Delhi.

———— (1996): 'Gender Differences in Some Aspects of Non-farm Employment in Rural India', paper presented at the IEG–ISLE Seminar on 'Gender and Employment in India: Trends, Patterns and Policy Implications', Institute of Economic Growth, Delhi, December.

Chaudhuri, A.B. (1987). *The Santals: Religion and Rituals*, Ashish Publishing House, New Delhi.

Chen, M.A. (1983). *A Quiet Revolution: Women in Transition in Rural Bangladesh*, Schenkman Publishing, Cambridge.

Dasgupta, B. (1984). 'Sharecropping in West Bengal: From Independence to Operation Barga', *Economic and Political Weekly*, June, pp. A85–A96.

Dasgupta, S. and A.K. Maiti (1986). 'The Rural Energy Crisis, Poverty and Women's Roles in Five Indian Villages', World Employment Programme Technical Cooperation Report, International Labour Office, Geneva.

DDS (1994–95). *Deccan Development Society Report 1994–95*, Hyderabad.

Dreze, J. and A.K. Sen (1995). *India: Economic Development and Social Opportunity*, Oxford University Press, Delhi.

Elson, D. (1995). 'Gender Awareness in Modelling Structural Adjustment', *World Development*, 23 (11), pp. 1851–68.

Fernandes, W. and G. Menon (1987). *Tribal Women and Forest Economy: Deforestation, Exploitation and Status Change* , Indian Social Institute, Delhi.

Frankel, F. (1978). *India's Political Economy, 1947–1977: The Gradual Revolution*, Princeton University Press, New Jersey.

Gaiha, R. and N.A. Kazmi (1981). 'Aspects of Rural Poverty in India', *Economics of Planning*, 17 (2–3), pp.74–112.

Gala, C. (1990). 'Trying to Give Women their Due: The Story of Vitner Village', *Manushi*, 59, pp. 29–32.

Gandhi, N. and N. Shah (1991). *The Issues at Stake: Theory and Practice in the Contemporary Women's Movement in India*, Kali for Women, Delhi.

Government of India (GoI) (1988). *National Perspective Plan for Women: Report of the Core Group set up by the Department of Women and Child Development*, Ministry of Human Resource Development, Government of India, New Delhi.

——— (1990a). *Sarvekshana*, September, pp. S188–89.

——— (1990b). *Report of the Study Group on Economic and Social Security*, National Commission on Rural Labour, Ministry of Labour, Government of India, New Delhi.

——— (1995). *Report on Some Aspects of Household Ownership Holdings, 48th Round, 1992*, National Sample Survey Report No. 399, Department of Statistics, Ministry of Planning and Programme Development, Government of India, New Delhi.

——— (1996a). *Key Results on Employment and Unemployment, Fifth Quinquennial Survey, NSS 50th Round (July 1993–June 1994)*, NSS Report No. 406, Department of Statistics, Government of India, New Delhi.

——— (1996b). 'Quarterly Progress Report (Cumulative) on Implementation of Land Ceiling Laws for the quarter ending September 1996 (2nd quarter)', mimeo, Planning Commission of India, New Delhi.

——— (1996c). 'Draft Report of Steering Group on Poverty Alleviation and Area Development in Rural India for the Ninth Five Year Plan', Planning Commission, Delhi, November.

——— (1997a). *Livestock and Agricultural Implements in Household Operational Holdings, 1991–92*, Land and Livestock Holdings Survey, NSS Forty-Eighth Round, National Sample Survey Report No. 408, Department of Statistics, Ministry of Planning and Programme Development, Government of India, New Delhi.

——— (1997b). *Some Aspects of Operational Holdings, 48th Round, 1992*, Land and Livestock Holdings Survey, National Sample Survey Report No. 407, Department of Statistics, Ministry of Planning and Programme Development, Government of India, New Delhi.

Government of Madhya Pradesh (1996). *The Madhya Pradesh Policy for Women*, final draft, Department of Women and Child Welfare, Government of Madhya Pradesh, Bhopal.

Gupta, J. (1993). 'Land, Dowry, Labour: Women in the Changing Economy of Midnapur', *Social Scientist*, 21 (9–11), pp. 74–90.

Harriss, B. (1990). 'The Intrafamily Distribution of Hunger in South Asia', in J. Dreze and A.K. Sen (eds), *The Political Economy of Hunger*, Clarendon Press, Oxford, 1990, pp. 351–424.

Hunt, H.I. (1983). 'Intervention and Change in the Lives of Rural Poor Women in Bangladesh: A Discussion Paper', Bangladesh Rural Advancement Committee (Dhaka), December.

International Labour Organization (ILO) (1995). *Yearbook of Labour Statistics*, International Labour Organization, Geneva.

Islam, R. (1986). 'Non-Farm Employment in Rural Asia: Issues and Evidence' in R.T. Shand (ed.), *Off-Farm Employment in the Development of Rural Asia*, Australian National University, Canberra, pp. 153–73.

Kar, P.C. (1982). *The Garos in Transition*, Cosmo Publications, New Delhi.

Kelkar, G. and D. Nathan (1993). *Gender and Tribe: Women, Land and Forests in Jharkhand*, Zed Books, London; Kali for Women, Delhi.

Lipton, M. (1985). 'Land Assets and Rural Poverty', World Bank Staff Working Paper No. 744, Washington DC.

Manimala (1983). 'Zameen Kenkar? Jote Onkar! Women's Participation in the Bodhgaya Land Struggle', *Manushi*, 14, Jan–Feb, pp. 2–16.

Mazumdar, V. (1989). 'Peasant Women Organize for Empowerment: The Bankura Experiment', Occasional Paper No. 13, Centre for Women's Development Studies, Delhi.

Merry, D.J. (1983). 'Irrigation, Poverty and Social Change in a Village of Pakistani Punjab: A Historical and Cultural Ecological Analysis', unpublished PhD dissertation, Department of Anthropology, University of Pennsylvania.

Mies, M., K. Lalita and K. Kumari (1986). *Indian Women in Subsistence and Agricultural Labour*, International Labour Organization, Geneva.

Mencher, J. (1989). 'Women's Work and Poverty: Women's Contribution to Household Maintenance in Two Regions of South India', in D. Dwyer and J. Bruce (eds), *A Home Divided: Women and Income Control in the Third World*, Stanford University Press, Stanford.

Menon, G. (1996). 'Re-negotiating Gender: Enabling Women to Claim their Right to Land Resources', paper presented at the NGO Forum of the UN Conference on Human Settlements: Habitat II, Istanbul, June.

Nandwana, R. and S. Nandwana (1994). 'Land Rights of Widows', paper presented at a conference on 'Widows in India', Bangalore, March; forthcoming in M. Chen (ed.), *Widows in Rural India*, Sage Publications, Delhi.

Ng, C. (1994). 'Land Tenure and Female Subordination in Semanggol, Perak, and Pulau Tawar, Pahang', in M. Stivens, C. Ng, K.S. Jomo and J. Bee (eds), *Malay Peasant Women and the Land*, Zed Books, London and New Jersey.

Omvedt, G. (1981). 'Effects of Agricultural Development on the Status of Women', paper prepared for the International Labour Office Tripartite Asian Regional Seminar on Rural Development and Women, Mahabaleshwar, India, 6–11 April.

Ongaro, W.A. (1988). 'Adoption of New Farming Technology: A Case Study of Maize Production in Western Kenya', PhD Dissertation, University of Gothenberg, Gothenberg.

Pangare, G. and V. Pangare (1992). *From Poverty to Plenty: The Story of Ralegaon Siddhi*, Indian National Trust for Art and Cultural Heritage (INTACH), Delhi.

Pangare, G. and V. Lokur (1996). *The Good Society: The Pani Panchayat Model of Sustainable Water Management*, INTACH, Delhi.

Papola, T.S. (1987). 'Rural Industrialization and Agricultural Growth: A Case Study in India', in R. Islam (ed.), *Rural Industrialisation and Employment in Asia*

International Labour Organization, Asian Employment Programme, New Delhi, pp. 59–106.

Quisumbing, A. (1996). 'Male–Female Differences in Agricultural Productivity: Methodological Issues and Empirical Evidence', *World Development*, 24 (10), pp. 1579–95.

Rahman, O.M. and J. Menken (1990). 'The Impact of Marital Status and Living Arrangements on Old Age Female Mortality in Rural Bangladesh', paper no. 1, Department of Epidemiology, Harvard School of Public Health, and Population Studies Centre, University of Pennsylvania.

Roldan, M. (1988). 'Renegotiating the Marital Contract: Intrahousehold Patterns of Money Allocation and Women's Subordination among Domestic Outworkers in Mexico City', in D. Dwyer and J. Bruce (eds), *A Home Divided: Women and Income in the Third World*, Stanford University Press, Stanford, pp. 229–47.

Saith, A. (1991). 'Asian Rural Industrialization: Context, Features, Strategies', in J. Breman and S. Mundle (eds), *Rural Transformation in Asia*, Oxford University Press, Delhi, pp. 458–89.

Sarin, M. and C. Sharma (1991). 'Women's Involvement in Rehabilitation of Common Lands in Bicchiwara Block of Dungarpur District, Rajasthan', paper prepared at the ILO workshop on 'Women and Wasteland Development', International Labour Organization, Delhi, January.

Satheesh, P. V. (1997a). 'History in the Making: Women Design and Manage an Alternative Public Distribution System', 'Forests, Trees and People', Newsletter No. 34, September.

———— (1997b). 'A Background Note on the Alternative Public Distribution System and the Current Controversy', mimeo, Deccan Development Society, Hyderabad, 18 September.

Seiz, J. (1991). 'The Bargaining Approach and Feminist Methodology', *Review of Radical Political Economics*, Spring.

Sen, G. and C. Sen (1985). 'Women's Domestic Work and Economic Activity: Results from National Sample Survey', *Economic and Political Weekly*, 20 (17), Review of Women's Studies, 27 April, pp. WS–49 to WS–56.

Shramashakti (1988). *Report of the National Commission on Self-Employed Women and Women in the Informal Sector*, New Delhi.

Singh, A.M. and A. Kelles-Vitannen (eds) (1987). *Invisible Hands: Women in Home-based Production*, Sage Publications, Delhi.

Singh, A. and N. Burra (eds.) (1993). *Women and Wasteland Development in India*, Sage Publications, Delhi.

Sundaram, K. and S. Tendulkar (1983). 'Towards an Explanation of Inter-regional Variation in Poverty and Unemployment in Rural India', Working Paper No. 237, Delhi School of Economics.

Tharakan, M. (1997). 'Towards a Humane Community: Local Efforts and Economic Liberalization', in K.A. Manikumar (ed.). *History and Society: Essays in Honour of Professor S. Kadhirvel*, Madras (published privately by the felicitation group), pp. 249–64.

Thorner, D. (1956). *The Agrarian Prospect in India* (Five Lectures on Land Reform delivered in 1955 at the Delhi School of Economics), Delhi School of Economics, University of Delhi, Delhi.

Thorner, D. and A. Thorner (1962). *Land and Labour in India*, Asia Publishing Hous, Bombay.

Udry, C., J. Hoddinott, H. Alderman, and L. Haddad (1995). 'Gender Differentials in Farm Productivity: Implications for Household Efficiency and Agricultural Policy', *Food Policy*, 20 (5), pp. 407–23.

Unni, J. (1996). 'Women Workers in Agriculture: Some Recent Trends', paper presented at the IEG–ISLE Seminar on 'Gender and Employment in India: Trends, Patterns and Policy Implications', Institute of Economic Growth, Delhi, December.

Visaria, P. (1996). 'Structure of the Indian Labour Force: 1961–1994', *Indian Journal of Labour Economics*, 39 (4), October–December, pp. 725–40.

Land Reforms and the Question of Food in Kerala

Pulapre Balakrishnan

I am honoured by the invitation to deliver the Eighth Daniel Thorner Memorial Lecture here at the Centre for Development Studies, Thiruvananthapuram. The invitation had come to me along with a suggestion of some themes on which I may wish to speak, without of course precluding others. When from among these I chose the theme 'Land Reforms and the Question of Food in Kerala', I did so essentially out of an immediate recognition of both land reforms and the question of food being central to the concerns of the late Daniel Thorner. I believe also that for this very reason it would be a fit topic for an occasion chosen to commemorate his life and work. So my intention here is to explore a link between the two elements in the theme. I do not begin from a position that there exists a relationship between land reforms and the question of food in Kerala.

To economists of my generation Daniel Thorner is a somewhat distant figure, a name from Indian economics of the fifties. As students we had known of his lectures on land reforms at the Delhi School of Economics and of his perhaps more widely quoted work with his wife Alice. Over two decades later, when I was invited to deliver this lecture, I had the opportunity of reading not only a large part of his professional corpus, but also about him. The latter has proved to be equally interesting. My main source has been the article by Alice Thorner (1982) entitled 'Excerpts from an FBI File', published in the *Economic and Political Weekly*. The article mostly comprises raw clippings from FBI files now available in the public domain after the lapse of the period for which the dictates of official secrecy require of the American state no

This is the text of the Eighth Daniel Thorner Memorial Lecture, delivered at the Centre for Development Studies, Thiruvananthapuram, on 25 February 1999.

such disclosure. These clippings make fascinating reading and help one imagine both the life that Daniel Thorner had attempted to lead and the political circumstances that had crowded him in as a free-thinking individual. However, one can always read into them a lighter side. For instance, in 1953 the United States Department of State had requested the American Consul in what was then Bombay to have Thorner sign an affidavit whether or not he was or had ever been a member of the Communist Party, and whether or not he had had any part in the making of the book *American Shadow over India* then recently published. What appeared to bother the State Department was that the Indian author of the book—in their view calculated to do harm to American interests in India—had expressed his debt to an American friend who had furnished material, time and energy for this book but who wished to remain anonymous. While it may not have been entirely unsound of the authorities to have imagined that the 'American friend' in question may have been Daniel Thorner, then actually travelling through India, it is the reason given that is noteworthy. The memo item, believed by the State Department to clinch the issue, was that the 'meticulous indexing, use of footnotes and heavy economic approach to the subject' (Thorner, 1982: 882) was characteristic of Thorner. It is encouraging to note that not even the secret service can resist the seductions of scholarship.

Daniel Thorner, however, was not content with scholarship. He went on to do some important work on Indian agriculture which, what is more, was based on considerable field work. And as a free thinker he appears to have been not content with having invited the attention of the infamous Committee on Un-American Activities, itself a thinly veiled front for authoritarianism. In India he mentions having disappointed what he affectionately terms the *panchayat* of Indian economists. This time it was that in Delhi in the early seventies he had dared to revise his earlier, somewhat pessimistic view of the prospects for Indian agriculture, now actually being optimistic about it. Daniel Thorner appears to have led somewhat of a full life!

In perhaps his best-known work on India, Daniel Thorner had taken on as his subject of investigation the agrarian prospect in India as forecast in the mid-fifties. Such an attempt cannot be a task for the fainthearted since for over half a century by then per capita foodgrain production had remained stagnant. While half a century may not appear an overly long period for those used to thinking in terms of millennia, it must have appeared a heck of a long time for an American economic historian. However, Daniel Thorner's concern for the stagnation of Indian agriculture can hardly be put down to any culturally driven impatience with India's slow rate of progress. From his writings we are able to sense that this concern springs from an appreciation of the central importance of foodgrain production to any serious project of raising out of poverty numbers as large as in India. To Daniel Thorner land reform was a large part of the solution, even as he was not oblivious to the role of vested interests in watering down even the most radical proposals. Early on, commenting on the provisions of the U.P. Zamindari Abolition Act which left plenty of room for the persistence of non-tilling absentee cultivators, he had noted that:

> The real questions at issue were much larger than that of the feelings of particular castes or sub-castes in certain areas of the U.P. For no state in India—not even the recent communist regime in Kerala—has passed a land reform or agrarian relations act requiring the cultivators to till. The fact is that there is in India an age-old feeling that manual labour, physical work, is degrading. . . . In the villages there is one sure sign by which successful cultivators show that their economic condition is improving and that they now wish to raise their social standing: they and the members of their families, stop doing the field work. . . . (Thorner, 1961: 6).

Later in my talk today I shall have occasion to refer to this observation made to the 25th International Congress of Orientalists held in Moscow in 1960. Daniel Thorner, it seems, had a clear idea of what land reforms mean. Legislation which absolved the so-called cultivator from tilling did not quite add up to reform in his scheme of thought. This takes us to the idea most closely associated with Thorner and to what has been seen as the role of land reforms in general and in India in particular.

Thorner saw the agrarian structure in India as unique, combining remnants of the pre-British economic order which included above all a layered set of rights, including that of the state, to draw income from the soil in the form of rents, and the modern western concept of private property. He claimed that this complex of legal, economic and social relations served to produce a built-in effect stifling agricultural growth, and this effect he had termed 'the depressor'. Stagnant agricultural production restricted the home market for the developing manufacturing sector and thereby the depressor cast a pall on the entire Indian economy. There seems to have been little doubt in Thorner's mind that India's plans for economic development could not get very far without a concerted effort to remove the depressor, and land reforms were the route.

Of course, even as Daniel Thorner was propounding his view of the constraints on Indian agricultural growth, the Indian state had adopted a certain position vis-à-vis land reform. A version of this is presented in the Third Five Year Plan document, from which I quote:

> Land reform programmes, which were given a place of special significance both in the first and second plan, have two specific objects. The first is to remove such impediments to increase in agricultural production as arise from the agrarian structure inherited from the past. This should help to create conditions for evolving as speedily as possible an agricultural economy with high levels of efficiency and productivity. The second object which is closely related to the first is to eliminate all elements of exploitation and social injustice within the agrarian system, to provide security for the tiller of the soil and assure equality of status and opportunity to all sections of the rural population. ('The Third Five Year Plan': 220).

We see that even as its implementing arm was weak the Indian state armed itself with reasoned ambition.

Finally, continuing with the question of what was expected of land reforms, I turn to an entirely different segment of opinion-makers set in a different period. A study on agrarian reforms in developing economies under the auspices of the International Labour Organization in the 1980s has the following to say:

> Some economists take the view that the only valid criterion for judging agrarian reforms is provided by the imperatives of industrialization, i.e., the possible movements of the marketed surplus as a consequence of agrarian reforms. At the other end of the spectrum of opinions, there are those who insist that the welfare of agricultural producers should receive priority over the imperative of rapid industrialization.

Observing that the marketed surplus can increase even in a situation of widespread starvation the study concludes that:

> For buoyant growth, growth of marketed surplus, and hence the

> growth of the industrial sector, must depend on the growth of agricultural output and not on growth of deprivation. By the same reasoning, agricultural growth must be one of the basic objectives of any agrarian reform programme, for rapid industrialization is a necessary condition for development in the long run. To view agrarian reform as primarily a distributive mechanism is to ignore the lessons of history. (Ghose, 1980: 123).

From the views expressed here which comprise those of an independent researcher, the Indian state and an international development agency, we see that for the over three decades during which these views were expressed there had existed a broad consensus on the likely consequences for growth of land reforms.

For close to fifteen years following the formation of Kerala state in November 1956, we witnessed a range of initiatives pertaining to the reform of agrarian relations, most of this conforming to the widely-used term, land reforms. These initiatives have received wide attention not only in India but also internationally. K.N. Raj and Michael Tharakan (1983: 31) have provided a reason for why this may have been so. They observe that 'Agrarian reform in Kerala over the last quarter of a century is generally believed to have been more far-reaching and effective than elsewhere in India, though carried out within the same administrative and political framework as in the rest of the country.' While the question of what exactly the political leadership of the state had envisaged as the outcome when embarking upon the reforms remains, from the economist's point of view there might be expected a certain interest regarding performance of agricultural production in the state since land reforms.

In keeping with the theme of this lecture I confine attention solely to the production of rice. Historically pulses have not figured much in Kerala's production structure as they do elsewhere in the country. On the other hand, the output of tapioca, which was not only historically a staple of sorts here but was also widely cultivated, has more or less behaved akin to rice. In Table 1, then, are presented data on the area and output of rice production in Kerala since 1956. To start with, I focus on the behaviour of output. While there are many interesting observations that may be made, I make only one. By the agricultural year 1996–97 the output of rice is lower than it was estimated to have been in 1956–57. However, it is not as if rice production in Kerala has

TABLE 1: *Rice Acreage and Output*

Year	*Area (1000 hectares)*	*Output (1000 tonnes)*
1955–57	762.0	887.2
1957–58	766.8	925.5
1958–59	768.4	954.4
1959–60	759.0	1038.0
1960–61	779.0	1068.0
1961–62	753.0	1004.0
1962–63	803.0	1093.2
1963–64	805.1	1128.0
1964–65	801.1	1121.4
1965–66	802.3	997.5
1966–67	779.4	1084.1
1967–68	809.5	1124.0
1968–69	873.9	1251.4
1969–70	874.4	1225.4
1970–71	875.0	1292.0
1971–72	875.2	1351.7
1972–73	874.0	1376.4
1973–74	874.7	1257.7
1974–75	881.5	1333.0
1975–76	876.0	1331.2
1976–77	854.4	1254.0
1977–78	840.4	1294.6
1978–79	799.2	1272.7
1979–80	793.3	1299.7
1980–81	801.7	1272.0
1981–82	807.0	1339.9
1982–83	798.0	1308.0
1983–84	740.4	1207.9
1984–85	730.4	1255.9
1985–86	678.3	1173.1
1986–87	663.1	1133.8
1987–88	577.6	1002.3
1989–90	583.4	1141.2
1990–91	559.5	1086.6
1991–92	541.3	1060.4
1992–93	537.6	1084.9
1993–94	507.8	1003.4
1994–95	503.3	975.1
1995–96	471.2	953.9
1996–97	431.0	871.0

Source: Kerala State Planning Board

CHART 1: ***Rice acreage and output***

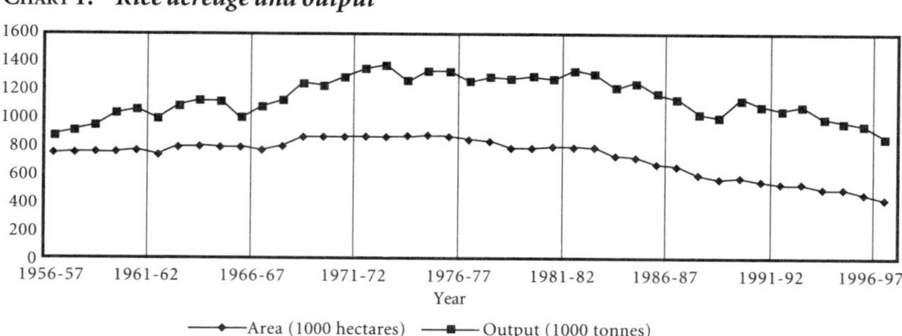

declined steadily from the very beginning of this period. Indeed the period breaks down more or less into two halves, each of a rising and a declining trend in production. The year of the turnaround in the rice economy may be put down to 1974–75, when acreage under rice peaks. Since that date the trajectory of rice acreage in the state is inexorably downwards, and output follows with a lag. The key events associated with the implementation of land reforms in Kerala may be put down to span the period 1959—the date of the passing of the Kerala Agrarian Relations Bill—and 1 January 1970—the date as of which tenancy legally ceased to exist in the state. Essentially, this intervening period was the occasion of the implementation, piecemeal, of various land reform legislations. The sixties were a period of continuous growth of output, and this dynamic appears to have carried over into the first third of the seventies. While this does not by itself establish a benign role for land reforms in the subsequent history of the growth of rice production in Kerala—a history of unmitigated decline—it does provide reason to believe that the principal cause for the outcome needs be sought elsewhere. Indeed, I shall argue that such an explanation can be provided, and proceed to do so.

You may notice that I do not present data on the behaviour of rice yield. Actually yields have grown more or less without faltering right through the four decades since 1956. However, I do not consider increasing yield in the context of declining production, and very likely employment, a significant achievement at all. In any case, I find[1] that the increase in yield over the twenty-five years starting from the agricultural year 1971–72 was only marginally higher than the increase in yield over the fifteen-year period ending 1970–71. So while there might even be a *prima facie* case for arguing that land reforms have contributed to a decline in agricultural production, there is not even a *prima facie* case for these having contributed to any increase in yield. For the remainder of my lecture I do not discuss yields.

The experience with rice production in Kerala is easily seen as the outcome of developments in a small open economy. While openness as an idea is easily understood, the reference to size is in the sense in which it is used in trade theory, whereby the country's external terms of trade are given so that its producers are price-takers. I consider the latter a point worth stressing in the context of Kerala. Equally, while openness may be understood as a concept, its implications in determining the trajectory of Kerala's economy has mostly been overlooked. This has led on the one level to a focus on the wrong variable, and on the other encouraged the belief that the policy-maker has been in control.

The decline of food production in Kerala may be seen as similar to the case of a traded goods sector in a small open economy being constricted by a boom elsewhere in the economy. Referred to as the 'Dutch Disease', so called to describe the decline of manufacturing in the Netherlands after natural gas was discovered there, this phenomenon has now come to be recognized as a distinct case in open economy macroeconomics, with a sizeable literature devoted to it. Since I consider this a worthwhile line of enquiry I shall spend some time on expositing the theme, and subsequently presenting a model due to Max Corden and Peter Neary (1982).

The Dutch Disease, a phenomenon common to the developed and the developing economies, essentially refers to the coexistence within the traded goods sector of booming and lagging, or progressing and declining, sub-sectors. In many cases, the booming sector has been of an extractive kind—such as minerals in Australia, natural gas in the Netherlands and North Sea oil in the UK—and the sector that is placed under pressure is the traditional manufacturing sector. For this reason the resulting condition has been referred to as de-industrialization. However, the sequence of events is generic and are applicable to situations where the booming sector is not extractive, such as the displacement of older industry by technologically more advanced ones, and even to the case of a boom that is occurring offshore so to speak. Indeed the results from the analysis of the Dutch Disease may be profitably applied to the study of the effects of booms arising from a variety of exogenous shocks in a small open economy. To run ahead a little, it is these latter cases that are particularly relevant to Kerala.

An analysis of the Dutch Disease best proceeds by a decomposition of the effects of a boom on the functional distribution of income and the size and profitability of the manufacturing sector. Consider a small open economy producing two goods traded at exogenously given world prices, and a third non-traded good, the price of which adjusts to clear the market. Label the two traded goods 'energy' and 'manufactures' and the non-traded good 'services', even though a range of possibilities exists. Equally, while there may be many sources of a boom in the traded goods sector, consider the specific case of a one-shot Hicks-neutral improvement in technology. The model is made to work by recognizing two effects of the boom, namely, the *resource movement* effect and the *spending* effect. The boom in the energy sector leads first of all to an increase in the marginal products of the mobile factors employed there. This draws resources from other sectors. This in turn gives rise to adjustments in the rest of the economy. It is this drawing of resources into the booming sector that is described as the resource movement effect. If the booming sector uses relatively few resources that can be drawn from elsewhere in the economy, this effect must naturally be small and the main impact of the boom must be due to the spending effect. Within this model the spending effect works via the higher real income resulting from the boom leading to extra spending on services, raising their price and leading to further adjustments. Naturally, the impact of the spending effect depends upon the marginal propensity to consume services. Note that while some of the spending from increased real income would automatically fall on the traded goods also, notably manufactures, in this model, their price cannot rise since these are set in world markets. This has a major impact on the realignment of production in the economy.

The Pre-Boom Equilibrium

Figures 1 and 2 depict the effects of the boom on the labour market and the commodity market, respectively. In the former, the wage rate (in terms of manufactures) is measured on the vertical axis and the economy's total labour supply is given by the horizontal axis OsOt. Employment in services is measured by the distance from Os, while the distance from Ot measures employment in the two traded goods sectors together. It is assumed that the demand for labour in each sector is a decreasing function of the wage rate relative to the price of that sector's output. Thus, Lm is the labour demand schedule for the

FIGURE 1: *Effect of the boom on the labour market*

FIGURE 2: *Effect of the boom on the commodity market*

manufacturing sector and by laterally adding to this the labour demand schedule for the energy sector we obtain Lt, the pre-boom labour demand schedule for the entire traded goods sector. Similarly, Ls is the labour demand schedule for services drawn for a given price of services. Pre-book equilibrium is at point A where the Lt intersects with Ls, yielding an initial wage rate of wO. Figure 1, however, cannot by itself provide a complete story. Note that the location of the Ls, schedule depends upon the initial price of services and this, unlike the price of the traded goods, is not exogenous but determined as part of the complete general equilibrium of the model.

The determination of the initial equilibrium price of services may be illustrated via the Salter diagram with traded goods on the vertical axis and services on the horizontal one. Fixed terms of trade allow the aggregation of manufacturing and energy into a single Hicksian composite traded good. The pre-boom production possibility curve is TS. If indifference curves may be used to summarize aggregate demand in the economy the initial equilibrium is at point *a* and the price of services is given by the slope of the common tangent to the two curves at this point.

Effects of the Boom on Outputs

Consider the occurrence of a boom in the form of Hicks-neutral technical progress in the energy sector. To highlight the two distinct effects of the boom described earlier, we analyse their consequences separately and in turn. Further, in the case of the resource movement effect we conduct the analysis in two stages. First, the relative price of services is held constant, and then it is allowed to vary to clear the market. In terms of the two diagrams here, at the first stage, the labour demand schedule Ls in Figure 1 and the price ratio in Figure 2 are held constant.

Beginning with the resource movement effect, the labour demand in the energy sector increases. Note that the effect of the technological progress is to increase profitability at a given wage rate akin to an increase in the price of energy. Now, in Figure 1, the composite labour demand schedule Lt shifts out to L't yielding the new equilibrium B. This has associated with it a higher wage rate and lower employment in both the services and the manufacturing sectors. Concentrating on the manufacturing sector, we note that with employment having fallen from OtM to OtM' the resource movement effect has given rise to direct de-industrialization. Turning to Figure 2, the boom raises the economy's maximum output of traded goods but not that of services. The production possibility curve shifts out asymmetrically to T'S, with OT' representing the new maximum in the traded goods sector. The resource movement effect may be represented by a movement of production from *a* to *b*. The point *b* lies to the left of the point *a* since the shifting out of labour causes a decline in output in the services sector.

Since we are isolating the resource movement effect we assume that the income elasticity of demand for services is zero ignoring the spending effect. This assumption implies an income consumption curve that is vertical through *a*, intersecting the production possibility curve at *j*. We note that at the original relative price there is excess demand for services. The relative price now increases switching demand away from the good and dampening, but not reversing, the fall in the output of services. The equilibrium point must lie somewhere between *b* and *j* on TS' implying that the output of services is reduced due to the resource movement effect.

Turn now to consider the spending effect on its own. To isolate the resource movement effect assume that the booming sector, energy, uses no labour. This translates into the coinciding of curves Lt and Lm in Figure 1 and no effect of the boom may be discerned here at the original relative price. In Figure 2 the boom displaces the production possibility curve vertically upward with point *b* now lying directly above point *a*. Provided that services are a normal good in the aggregate, at the original relative price the demand may be expected to grow along an income consumption curve such as O*n* implying point *c* as indicative of demand. Once again, given the original relative price, there is excess demand for services and the price of services increases. In the new equilibrium, which must lie somewhere between *j* and *c*, the output of services is higher when compared to the original situation.

We see that while both the resource movement effect and the spending effects on their own cause an increase in the relative price of services, their impact on the output of services is asymmetrical. The former tends to reduce output while the latter tends to raise it, and there is no presumption as to which will dominate.

The entire point of this exercise, as far as my present concerns go, is to bring out that while there may be some ambiguity regarding output response in the services sector there is none of this whatsoever in the case of the manufacturing sector. We can see this from Figure 1 directly. Allowing for the rise in the price of services, the labour demand schedule for that sector must shift outwards. At the new equilibrium G we find the wage rate still higher at w2 and the employment in manufacturing still lower at OtM". At the end of the analysis we see that the boom gives rise to direct de-industrialization reflected in the further lowering of output from OtM to OtM' and indirect de-industrialization reflected in the further lowering of output from OtM' to OtM". The former is caused by the resource movement effect alone while the latter is caused by the rise in the price of services resulting from a lower output due to the resource movement effect and the higher demand from the spending effect. Since the manufacturing sector's employment unambiguously falls the same must be true of output within that sector.

Effects of the Boom on Factor Incomes

We start with a consideration of the effect of the boom on the real wage. The resource movement effect taken on its own leads to a decline in output in the services sector. This must be associated with a rise in the wage measured in terms of services. From Figure 1 we see that the same effect raises the wage in terms of traded goods. Thus the real wage—which takes into account the prices of all goods consumed by the workers—must rise due to the resource movement effect. Now turn to the spending effect. On its own it leads to a fall in the wage measured in terms of services since the output of services has increased. On the other hand the wage in terms of traded goods rises because of the spending effect. All told, and combining the two effects, therefore, the effect of the boom on the real wage is uncertain. However, it is easy to see that a fall in the real wage is more likely the stronger the spending effect relative to the resource movement effect and the greater the share of services in the wage basket.

The changes in the returns to the specific factors in the three sectors may be interpreted as measures of the impact of the boom on the profitability of each sector. To keep things focussed we may confine ourselves to the manufacturing sector. It is clear that profitability in the manufacturing sector must unambiguously fall because of the rise in the wage relative to the price of traded goods brought about due to both the resource movement and the spending effects.

We are now in a position to summarize the essential results of the literature on the Dutch Disease as they pertain to the manufacturing sector. When de-industrialization is defined as a fall in output and employment in manufacturing, there must be de-industrialization in this model provided there is any spending or resource movement effect. Profitability in manufacturing must fall when measured in terms of traded goods and, when there is a rise in the price of services, even more when measured in terms of services. Furthermore the balance of trade in manufacturing must deteriorate since domestic spending increases (so long as manufactures are a normal good) due to the boom while output in this sector has fallen.

Thus far in the analysis only labour has been considered to be mobile. Once we allow for the mobility of capital across sectors—depending upon the relative factor intensities of the traded and non-traded goods—several alternative outcomes are possible including so-called pro-industrialization or the expansion of the manufacturing sector. I do not pursue this line of analysis because I do not find capital mobility particularly relevant to the context. Instead, I now propose an explanation of the decline in rice production in Kerala.

The standard version of the Dutch Disease has concentrated on the case of a booming natural resource sector exerting a squeeze on the manufacturing sector, the boom itself having been caused by a fresh discovery of the good or technological progress in the production of it. However, as I have already indicated, the formal structure of the model is consistent with many alternative interpretations concerning both the structure of the economy and the source of the boom. This I exploit to provide an explanation of the decline of agriculture in general and food production in particular in Kerala.

The decline of rice production in Kerala since the early seventies may easily be explained within the framework of open economy macro models developed to account for the Dutch Disease. Within the specific version that we have just looked at this only requires that 'manufacturing' is replaced by 'agriculture' and that the boom in the domestic energy sector be replaced by a boom offshore. In the very same Figure 1, then, the labour demand for the energy sector may be replaced by demand for domestic labour to service this offshore boom, you may call it labour exports. Indeed the specific reality of Kerala was that, starting the early seventies, there has been an expansion in the demand for migrant labour following the rise in real income in the Arabian Gulf region being the bounty of the four-fold hike in oil prices in 1973. So it has even been an energy sector that has boomed, though not the domestic one. I find this application of the standard model quite persuasive. Neither the assumption of full employment equilibrium in the original version nor the feature of a single economy-wide wage rate need lead to our baulking at its use. The role of full employment in the original model is to ensure that the resource movement effect always bites in that every outflow of labour from a line of production or sector in the language of the model leads to a decline in output. The observation in an economy of unemployment *per se* does not guarantee the free flow of labour between lines of production within an economy. If the hubris that allows for the appeal to the idea that 'nature abhors a vacuum' is foolhardy in the context of the industrial economies, we ignore the highly segmented labour markets of traditional agricultural labour markets only at our own peril. In particular, I refer to a long-term feature of the labour market in Kerala, prevalent into the seventies, that not all occupational boundaries disappeared fast enough as wages altered. Thus any outflow of labour traditionally engaged in agriculture does not necessarily lead to this being filled by labour inflow from among the unemployed within the economy.

Coming to wages, it is not necessary to insist on interpreting the model as predicting a wage rate common to all sectors of the economy and therefore being irrelevant for a situation with market segmentation. Where historic wage relativities tend to be preserved, the change in the wage rate within the model may be seen as indicating, correctly, the direction of change of the entire wage structure.

Finally, while the standard model of the Dutch Disease is a static general equilibrium model with all its limitations, when used to analyse developments occurring in an economy over a twenty-five-year period it does score in providing an economy-wide angle with certain distinct advantages which I shall return to. However, the model's alleged strengths are its weakness too. It is economistic, so to speak, and has no room for sociological factors which can be as important. For instance we cannot escape from a serious consideration of traditional social attitudes towards manual labour referred to by Daniel Thorner, which alone can account for the decline in the once steady supply of female agricultural labour so vital to the cultivation of paddy. However, even here the primary role is that of the boom and this is captured sufficiently well by the model.

Two pieces of evidence with respect to the evolution of Kerala's rice economy give me reason to believe in the validity of the explanation that I have proposed, this explanation, let me emphasize, being that the origin of the agricultural decline lies in the exit of labour from the sector. The first of these is that area under cultivation peaks in the very first year after the quadrupling of the price of oil in the winter of 1973. It has not escaped my attention, though, that this is altogether too neat! Therefore, I prefer to highlight the second piece of evidence that I refer to. That the behaviour of real wages—of male and female agricultural workers—and the output of paddy in Kerala since 1973 is in line with the predictions in the model of the Dutch Disease. That is, the real wage has risen as the output has fallen. This would not have been worth mentioning for even a moment if the very same relationship had not puzzled some earlier researchers. Thus in the well-known compilation of a real wage series for agricultural workers by A.V. Jose the author remarks on the egregious behaviour of these variables in Kerala which singles it out from the rest of the country. In most Indian states, agricultural production and real wages were found to have moved together. However, it was found that in Kerala the real wages of male and female agricultural labour have increased while agricultural production has declined. Since Jose's study is largely empirical in its approach it is not clear from what perspective the surprise need be expressed. However, I might make one comment in passing. This is that from Jose's data I am now surprised to find that the extent of increase in the real wage for male agricultural workers over the period 1971–85 is actually lower than the extent of its increase over 1956–71. Of course, *I* am surprised only to the extent that this goes against the requirements of an explanation based on a faster growth of wages. However, while it may pose some problems to those who attempt to explain the decline of production in terms of high wages, it poses no particular problems to the explanation of the same phenomenon as a case of the Dutch Disease. For, in that story the wage is endogenous, *ergo* it can have no explanatory power *per se*. A pointer from the model is that the wage rate is determined by economy-wide factors, something that is missed when the focus is on the relation between wages and employment in the agricultural sector alone. Studies in the latter mode exist of course and routinely claim to have provided an explanation of declining production by pointing out that real wage growth has exceeded the growth of yield (a proxy for labour productivity when fixed proportions are assumed in the technology). Observe that this cannot by itself be considered an explanation. At best, it only succeeds in pointing out that the relationship between output and some key variables is in line with a version of the neo-classical model of profit maximization. By contrast, an application of the model of the Dutch Disease does succeed in providing an account of the origins of the decline of agriculture in Kerala and in predicting accurately some of the subsequent sequences. In conclusion, I wish to add the caveat that the real wage data of A.V. Jose, upon which many commentators including I have relied on, is in terms of a basket of commodities, while most theoretical explanations of the trajectory of output are based on the product wage. Perhaps some young graduate student in this audience would be sufficiently enthused to check whether that which has been claimed for the behaviour of wage rates in terms of a basket of commodities also holds for the wage rate in terms of the price of paddy, the so-called product wage.

I presume that I have been able to make a reasonable case for the view that the decline of rice production in Kerala has little to do with the land reforms that have preceded it. I have argued that it has instead to do with the flight of labour from this sector consequent upon the boom in the Arabian Gulf. However, I am yet to get rid of two potential arguments that link land reforms with the decline. Both these are of a mould which suggests that the nature of land reforms in Kerala and the manner of their implementation may have created the preconditions for migration.

It may be argued that one of the consequences of land reforms in Kerala is to have created a labour market where one did not exist. While to those familiar with the situation this would be of no surprise, the creation due to land reforms of a labour market is not an obvious consequence and the very possibility needs to be explained. What I refer to is the destruction of an institution peculiar to Kerala, an institution which, curiously, is best recognized in terms of the nomenclature of the rights accorded to one set of participants. I refer to the arrangement whereby families were permitted to set up a *kudil* or hutment on landed property upon the understanding that they participated in the agricultural activity of the *janmi* and even of his or her *kudiyaan*, in return for the right to habitation. This institution is to be seen as a timeless arrangement central to feudalism in Kerala, and its principal role was to ensure a supply of labour. In the context of agricultural production, especially where commercialization was less than complete, the guarantee of labour supply was of far greater importance to the functioning of the system than the fact that it was cheap, an observation which has been made even as it is of dubious significance while referring to a situation where a labour market did not exist, which in turn renders comparison with the market wage entirely hypothetical. I digress here to state that in perhaps the only case of a somewhat hasty overgeneralization that I encountered in Thorner's work was his view, based on some work on Rajasthan by European historians, that feudalism as a category does not apply to India. For Kerala, where this term has entered common parlance when speaking of the past and where the claim has even been made of the evidence of agrestic slavery, this seems particularly off the mark. Be that as it may, Thorner's comment that it may be unsound to conceive of agrarian India in terms of an evolutionary sequence from feudalism to capitalism to socialism has not only proved to be prescient, it evokes our admiration in that it was made as early as 1960. We were still over a decade away from the full flowering of the 'mode of production' debate in India!

In a provision unique to the legislation in Kerala, land reforms here left the members of each hutment entitled to ten cents of land surrounding the *kudil* on grounds of *kudikidappu avakasham*. This had the immediate effect of alienating the beneficiary from the existing labouring arrangement, leaving him and his family free agents, so to speak. It is in this sense that we may speak of land reforms having created a labour market where it did not exist hitherto. However, by the seventies this arrangement is likely to have been largely confined to the erstwhile Malabar district while the decline in rice production has been pretty much uniformly spread across the state. As for migration to the Gulf, the districts recording the largest migration are Malappuram, Thrissur and Thiruvananthapuram.

The second of the two arguments linking land reforms to the decline of agriculture in Kerala is perhaps a more roundabout one. It might be initiated by asserting that the very fact of migration from agriculture lets us infer that land reforms had not succeeded in vesting ownership of land in the hands of the tiller, succeeding only in transferring it to the intermediary. If established, this would be a serious indictment of a programme led by a political party committed to the ending of landlordism. However, this would yet leave the argument to deal with the counterfactual of how tillers of the soil, had they been beneficiaries of land reforms, would have responded to an increase, in this instance quite phenomenal, in the ex-farm wage rate. There is of course no reason whatsoever to presume that the peasantry—being used here without the slightest normative associations given to this term by both the Marxists and the Chayanovians, but only in the descriptive sense, meaning household producers—would not shift out of agriculture as ex-farm wages and the probability of finding employment increases. This was indeed the presumption underlying the standard problematic in the conventional formalization of dualism and the associated phenomenon of migration out of the family farm. To recognize that not even the peasant household is impervious to a rising off-farm income opportunity alerts us to the folly of accounting for the decline of agriculture in Kerala by focussing on intra-farm variables. I have already referred to studies that point out the differential rates of growth of real wages and productivity as the factor accounting for the phenomenon. It is easy to see, at least by now, that this line of reasoning leaves out altogether the opportunity cost of engaging in agriculture. For it is not only the hypothetical peasant of our consideration but also cultivators using hired labour who could be motivated by a higher alternative rate of return. Indeed for many an agriculturist in Kerala this has not even required migration, for the conventional multiplier effect has brought the offshore boom to their doorstep. The price of land has been bid-up, partly also by speculation, to levels far exceeding the capitalized value of ground rent. The paddy field had become real estate.

In the prototype model of the Dutch Disease presented here the spending effect of the boom is on 'services'. Note that the characteristics of the good are not particularly relevant here. The idea meant to be conveyed is that of a good, the price of which is set on the domestic as opposed to the world market, and the price of which varies according to market conditions. It is easy to identify the segment of the Kerala economy which has been the focus of the spending boom, itself identified as the second-round effect in the model of the Dutch disease. In Kerala the focus of the spending boom with the most immediate impact on the economy has been construction.

With reference to the decline of the agricultural sector in Kerala one role of heightened construction activity has been to alienate hitherto agricultural land, a type of resource movement effect that cannot be captured either by focussing on the effect of the boom on the labour market as I have here in Figure 1, or by focussing on producer equilibrium within the framework of the neo-classical theory of the firm as has been done by some researchers. Thus migration out of the state and the combined loss of land and labour to the non-agricultural sector have acted as a pincer movement on Kerala's agriculture, starving it of resources. Needless to say, of the two the latter movement has been far less important. Nevertheless, these two together explain sufficiently well the acreage and output trends with respect to paddy cultivation presented earlier on by me.

Having put forth my argument, I am encouraged to find myself in the respectable company of the President of the Janadipadhya Samrakshana Samiti. Speaking recently near Mavelikara, where she had stoutly defended the rights of Malayali farmers to grow exactly what they pleased, Gowriamma had also chosen to provide an explanation for why farmers did not grow paddy. She is reported[3] to have argued that this was due to the shortage of labour. We are here left with the puzzle of how farmers manage to find the labour for the other crops that they might grow. Clearly the lady has a model up her sleeve!

I now turn to the consequence for the Kerala economy of a declining production of rice. This is relatively easy to see. Obviously, the increasing shortfall in requirement is now being met by inflow into the state from the rest of India. As would be expected this has been from two sources, private suppliers and the so-called central pool of grain maintained by the Government of India. In a marked difference from the situation in most of the major states of the Union, a substantial part of the inflow into Kerala is made up by the latter source of supply.

What sort of figure may we reasonably place on the first source, supply by the national market? Above all, why do we need to know this? It has long been customary for the Government of India to publish the statistic 'public distribution as a proportion of total availability' for the economy as a whole. Availability is itself defined as production plus provision for seed plus net imports. A similar estimate of availability for each of India's states is more difficult to arrive at due to the difficulty of estimating inflow into the state from the rest of the country. However, I might state at the outset that for the argument I am set to make now such an estimate is not necessary. Nevertheless, to provide some perspective I draw attention to one of the relationships on which data may be had. This comprises the relative magnitudes for Kerala of rice production and the amount of grain distributed under the public distribution system in the state. For the most recent data points available, the figures are 8, 71, 000 tonnes and 16, 08, 000 tonnes, respectively. This implies that the grain distributed exceeds domestic production by close to one hundred percent.

The dependence of the state on grain distributed under the

public distribution system has several implications. Of these, however, one stands out and this is that the state now loses any control that it may reasonably have had over the supply price of grain. This immediately casts such policy as the state might wish to adopt in a purely reactive mould. Prior to arguing why this is inevitably so, however, I make two related observations on the public distribution system. The first is the relatively straightforward one, in my view overlooked, that the existence of any scheme of rationing ought not to be mistaken for a strong economy. It is a safety net and one of the many that all civilized societies must provide. However, the backbone of an economy it is not, and it cannot ever seriously be taken to be, for that position can be credibly occupied only by productive activity. Even if reference to the rice distributed under the public distribution system as 'unfit for human consumption' made[4] recently in Thiruvananthapuram by a former Malayali Minister of Civil Supplies at the centre presently out of office ought to be taken with a pinch of salt, the provision of fixed quantities of inferior quality grain, even though at less than current market prices, should be seen as a second-best supply-side arrangement. Obviously, the first best solution is that of expanding incomes via steady and widespread employment opportunities, ensuring adequate access to good quality grain. It is clear that the route to this is a vigorously productive agricultural sector combined with a dynamic non-agricultural sector. To appreciate the role of the public distribution system it helps to recall that it has its origins in the statutory rationing imposed by a panic - stricken British colonial administration in 1943. Recognizing the implications for rice supply by the fall of what was then Burma to the advancing Japanese Army and the determination to maintain at all costs defence production supplying the war effort in Europe, which in turn required the keeping of the peace, an embattled Government of India introduced compulsory rationing in the major urban centres of the country. This is also the origin of the so-called urban bias of the public distribution system even today. It prompts one to appreciate the comment by Daniel Thorner (1961: 12), albeit in another context, that '. . . the transition from British rule to independent India has been a fairly conservative process'. That such a bias is absent from Kerala is due to both the greater political awareness of its people and the pattern of settlement of its population. Be that as it may, I repeat, the existence of a widespread public distribution system is not by itself the sign of a strong economy, exactly as a widespread network of free markets *per se* can also never be.

I now turn to the second observation that may be made about a public distribution system. This is that a proper evaluation of food policy ought not to be whether the PDS price is less than the current open market price. This is, quite literally, a static exercise. Of course, in equilibrium under rationing this must be so for there to be any off-take. The comparison must be between the current price of food and the likely price in an alternative arrangement. In particular, the focus of our attention must be on whether policies cannot be devised to affect the market price itself. Otherwise, we should be content to live with an arrangement whereby the ration price is always lower than the market price, as under the Indian public distribution system, but these prices may themselves rise continuously. This can hardly be considered an arrangement conducive to food security. It leads me directly to the question of the determination of the open market price of grain in India and its implications for deficit states such as Kerala.

The government's role in the food economy of the country has entailed procurement and distribution. Over time, procurement has come almost entirely out of domestic production, ridding the economy of a dependence on imports. The last is an achievement of some significance given the not-so-distant experience of the drought of the mid-sixties when the country received American wheat by the discontinuous shipload, a strategy reportedly described by Lyndon Johnson as having been devised to 'keep India on a short leash'. Stung, the proud and patriotic Indira Gandhi had sprung a sleeping government machinery into action. The so-called green revolution that followed led to a phenomenal increase in production. To put this in perspective, the annual average rate of growth of wheat in the fifteen-year-period since the mid-sixties is comparable to that attained by the leading wheat-producing nations of today in their heyday. As has been noticed, the record with respect to the rice crop is less spectacular. However, the geographical base of the green revolution in India has ensured that the increase in the rate of growth of production has been accompanied by a concentration of the marketable surplus in the hands of farmers from the concerned regions. For this reason farmers from Punjab, Haryana and western Uttar Pradesh have come to exercise disproportionate power over the process of the determination of the procurement price.

Evidence of this is seen in the feature that while there may have been a much higher rate of growth of output since the mid-sixties, there has also been a much faster increase in foodgrain prices. Or, to put it in another way, we may say that it is no longer surprising that prices have increased so much even as output has grown so fast. The economist who most effectively popularized the idea that government intervention in India's grain markets is an entirely political affair is Ashok Mitra (1978). However, the germ of the idea is already contained in a paper by Dantwala (1967) which had appeared over a decade earlier, where he refers to the case of procurement price-setting as a reflection of what he terms the growing irrelevance of economics in planning. It is interesting that this paper was written barely two years after the practice of price intervention was launched. The point of my raising this here is to suggest that we need to probe a little the rationale of government intervention before accepting that it is well designed. Is the system geared towards the maximization of procurement or to the expansion of the access to food? The pattern of stock-holding by the Food Corporation of India suggests that the former might be the case. And in this effort to understand the workings of the system, little is to be gained by pointing out that since the mid-sixties the share of public distribution in total availability has increased. This is only to be expected, for as open market prices are driven up by the continuous raising of procurement prices, sections of the population whose incomes do not keep pace are poorer and need to take recourse to the safety net that is the PDS.

The concentration of the marketable surplus of grain among farmers of selected regions, and in this case contiguous ones too, of the country introduces a feature which has two dimensions. At the macroeconomic level, the implication of regional imbalances is that the Indian state has a disciplining problem on its hands. The origin of this is easily seen in terms of what is referred to as 'supplier power' in industrial economics. However, in the arrangements peculiar to India the farm lobby is twice blessed. The fact that the government stands by to purchase all grain offered to it means that the supplier power of the surplus farmers can never be checked by a countervailing buyer power as in a bilateral monopoly. Viewing from above, or to take a macro perspective, we are easily able to see that the proposal for the removal of regional imbalances should be seen as a move towards the strengthening of the hands of the centre. A regionally balanced growth enables the Indian state to be even-handed in a way that it is unable to be as of now, thus providing the preconditions for a nationally acceptable food policy.

Now to view the situation bottom-up, so to speak, or, to take a micro perspective. This shows us that for the deficit state such as Kerala the flip-side of supplier power is that the state government can have no control whatsoever over the supply price of grain. Note that here the existence of a public distribution system is of no consolation. From the beginning it has been made clear that the issue price, or the price at which the government releases grain to the states, will be a mark-up over the procurement price. Hence, while some temporary relief may be available, the central government's inability to deal effectively with the public finances has meant the periodic raising of issue prices. This means that the price at which the people of deficit states are to receive grain will be essentially determined by the influence of the surplus farmers elsewhere. This is one aspect of the question of food in today's Kerala, and it is inextricably linked to the decline of its own grain-producing capacity.

Any argument regarding the role of government intervention requires that we ought to be able to refer with some confidence to the nature of certain relationships, notable among them being the relationship between the procurement price and the open market price, and that between the issue price, the open market price and the off-take from the public distribution system. These are, adequately established, I believe, in my work with Bharat Ramaswami financed so generously by a grant from a research project coordinated by the late T.N. Krishnan.

In this lecture I have explored the idea that the decline of food-grain production in Kerala originated in the decline of agriculture following migration to the Gulf. I have also pointed out the implications of the consequent import dependence of food supply in the state. I desist, however, from embarking upon a discussion of a strategy for arresting the said decline. My objective in this lecture has been more to identify the reasons underlying the latter, which has proved to be a substantial task in itself. Nevertheless, attempting this task has left us with some clues as to what may be expected in the immediate future and it is to this that I turn even as I conclude.

While we might use models when they illuminate we ought to resist the temptation of seeing economies rather like certain mechanical devices that may be put to work in all directions. In the context, what may have held for the boom does not necessarily hold in reverse as the boom dies down, which it inevitably must do. Thus the presumption of 'homeostasis' or the replication of the original situation once the disturbance subsides, may not be warranted. Indeed that was the very concern with the Dutch Disease, that once the boom was over the manufacturing sector in the Netherlands would never really come back, that economies might permanently lose their competitive advantage in certain areas of production in return for temporary good fortune. The loss of competitive advantage in this context is itself best understood in terms of loss of potential productivity growth due to learning-by-doing, which leads to continuous shifts outward of the supply curve. A decline in output implies a lower level of accumulated experience and thus a permanently lower level of productivity. It is also worth noting that, when output has been kept down for a substantial period, recovery is hampered by the fact that history pins down the equilibrium. This feature has often gone by the name 'hysteresis' and has been used to highlight the problem of unemployment in the west of Europe and stagnation in its east. It has a direct bearing on what we might reasonably expect for Kerala agriculture in the near future.

Having started out discussing the theme of land reforms and the question of food in Kerala I have ended up devoting a substantial attention to the Gulf boom. This appears to be unavoidable given the extent to which this event has affected the economic land-scape and productive fabric of the state. Arguably, it is the event that has stood in the way of land reforms working themselves out completely, a process that may be expected to take time. An offshore boom from which one might nevertheless benefit ought not to be mistaken for prosperity on your shores. Any sustainable plan must have as its centre-piece domestic production within which agriculture must of course have a major part. To this is tied the question of food, for it is production that ensures both a continuous expansion of incomes and a steady increase in supplies. We are back to the objectives originally identified for, but not fully attained by, land reforms as implemented thus far in Kerala.

Postscript*

Why is the argument based on external stimuli, such as the boom in the Middle East, occurring to explain a phenomenon in Kerala? First of all, I must state that I find this approach smacking of a methodological dogmatism that I see as absurd even before it is authoritarian. In the case of Kerala it amounts to an unwillingness to recognize that it is a small open economy in the sense described in the lecture. More crucially, however, any explanation based on internal factors alone would be a non-starter here. It would be at a loss to explain the configuration of a steadily rising agricultural wage rate and an inexorable shrinkage in paddy production. At a wider remove, one would require a macroeconomic model, including remittances from migrant labour, to account for the gathering servitization of the economy contemporaneous with very slow growth of the commodity-producing sectors, a feature that has puzzled some.

On the question of the evidence required to validate the use of a model of the Dutch Disease, one of my observations in the lecture may have been a little off the mark. While I was right in pointing out, from the work of A.V. Jose, that the real wages of agricultural labour in Kerala had risen faster in the period 1956-71 when compared to the period 1971-85, it would not be correct to conclude from this, as I had done, that evidence on wages is irrelevant to the explanation that I had proposed. It is clear to me now that, based on the model I have used, a rise in the real wage would be a necessary condition for the argument to go through. However, while a higher wage must necessarily be observed for validating the use of the model of the Dutch Disease, the rise in the wage rate is not independent of migration, the 'resource movement effect' of the Corden and Neary model. It is in this sense that earlier studies which point to the growth of money wages outstripping the growth in the price of paddy are incomplete as explanations of the decline in paddy cultivation, for they cannot account for the extreme divergence of the trends in output and real wages, respectively. Openness is of the essence here and recognition of a labour market characterized by outmigration is central. Back to the question of evidence, in any case, it would have been premature to conclude from my observation of the rate of growth of wages before and after 1971 that evidence for an

*This brief note is in the nature of a response to questions that were raised on the occasion of the lecture.

explanation based on the Dutch Disease is thin. First, I now see that I had based my observation on the definition of the real wage as a measure of the standard of living, the money wage rate deflated by the consumer price index. Based on the Corden and Neary model, we should be looking at the product wage, or the wage in terms of the price of paddy. I am currently putting together a data set on the product wage and on the estimated annual outflow of labour from the Kerala economy. A tentative report is that there is a rapid acceleration of out-flow starting the mid-seventies, when rice acreage peaks, and a faster rate of increase in the product wage from about the same time.

On the other hand, contrary to the suggestions of some, I do not seek data on the relative price of paddy with respect to its major competitor crop, coconut. This is for three reasons. First, there is no clear trend in the relative price concerned. Second, the decision to plant coconut is an irreversible one with major implications and is likely to be mediated by factors other than prices alone. Third, and most crucially, there is a certain observational equivalence involved in trying to validate the hypothesis of acreage shifts in response to relative price shifts. Any observed acreage shift towards coconut is entirely consistent with a general shortage of labour in the agricultural economy post-migration. Indeed, that there may be a shift to coconut even in the absence of significant long-run price shifts in favour of the crop is very likely confirmation of the argument in terms of labour shortage. At an entirely different level, conversion of paddy land to coconut orchards in response to the unavailability of labour tends to defeat the very spirit of land reforms. For the cultivation of coconut is entirely suited to the practice of absentee landownership.

While the phenomenon of migration is widely recognized in discussions of the Kerala economy over the past quarter of a century, there is less than complete agreement on its role within the economy, at least in relation to production. In the model of the Dutch Disease, emigration reduces labour availability and, in the absence of compensating labour-augmenting technical progress, lowers output. In the context of the decline of agriculture it has been pointed out that migration from Kerala is actually the result of the decline rather than its cause. The argument is difficult to sustain in light of the very substantial increase in the product wage in paddy cultivation since 1975, the year in which paddy cultivation had peaked and from when there is the beginning of an intensification in migration. (For estimates of migration see

P.R. Gopinathan Nair's 'Asian Emigration to the Middle East: Emigration from India', Working Paper No. 180, Centre for Development Studies, Thiruvananthapuram, November 1983.) The widely reported labour shortage in the agricultural economy subsequently puts paid to the suggestion that migration of agricultural labour is the result of agricultural decline. The continuing increase in real terms in the wage since 1975 is inconsistent with the suggestion that labour was 'pushed' out of the agricultural economy due to a decline in production.

It has been averred, in response to the argument made in my lecture, that migration out of Kerala has been largely of the semi-professional kind, such as nurses, or when it comprises labour even it is skilled labour, such as carpenters and masons. While it is the case that migration from Kerala has contributed nurses, engineers and artisans, it has also contributed to the economies of the Middle East sheer labour power. Indeed, perhaps the best study of migration up to the early eighties states: 'A significant observation to make is that professionally qualified and highly educated persons migrating to the Gulf region was a rare phenomenon and concentrated in a specific area, which has sent personnel also to countries in the West and to Africa. Otherwise the migrants are all workers of unskilled and semi-skilled categories' (see Nair, 'Asian Emigration'). More importantly, some of the earliest surveys of migration to the Middle East from Kerala after 1975 record that the majority of the migrants are rural and explicitly cite 'agricultural labour' as among the original occupations of the members of this cohort. In any case, the argument here is not dependent on composition of the migrants. For agricultural cultivation to be labour-starved, labour must move out of agriculture without being replaced. It does require though that there is no disguised unemployment, but apparently this has perhaps been all too easily assumed to be the case in Indian agriculture by many.

Finally, the trajectory of paddy cultivation in Kerala during the last quarter century has an important bearing on the study of agriculture, an issue that had engaged Indian economists in the seventies. A stark reading of the central point debated would be whether institutions or incentives matter more in agrarian transitions. Kerala's experience with paddy cultivation is a crucial one for getting a handle on this debate. From the point of view of agricultural labour, land reforms may have contributed to their freedom by enabling a move out of agriculture since they were no longer bound to feudal arrangements of servitude.

Here, institutional change may have created opportunities that were hitherto unavailable. From the point of view of the beneficiary, ownership *per se* mattered less in the face of either greater returns from migration or from treating land as real estate or, most importantly, of an adverse wage-price shock. Here, the positive effects of institutional change—land reforms bestowing ownership to a beleaguered tenantry—were negated by a shift in the incentive structure.

In an evaluation of land reforms in Kerala, we cannot get rid of the obvious counterfactual which would proceed by querying the consequence for production of a programme that had succeeded in actually transferring land to the tiller. For, if the availability of hired labour is a factor that contributed to the decline in paddy cultivation, the land reforms culminating in 1970 may not have accomplished this crucial transfer.

For professional support and financial assistance in connection with the research underlying this paper, I thank my own institution, the Indian Institute of Management, Kozhikode. It was Dr. K. Saradamoni who proposed that I speak on this topic and who remained enthusiastic and encouraging. Professor Max Corden took me through his model of the 'Dutch Disease' over e-mail. My students Apurva Owalekar and M. Suresh Babu helped me prepare some of the material presented here. The Institute for Social and Economic Change at Bangalore granted me access to their library. For all of this I am grateful.

Notes

1 Data with the author.

2 *The Hindu*, Chennai. 22 January.

3 See report in *The Hindu*, Chennai, 16 February.

References

Balakrishnan, P. and B. Ramaswami (1999). 'Analysing Government Intervention in Foodgrain Markets', in N. Krishnaji (ed.), *Food Security in India*, forthcoming, Sage, New Delhi.

Corden, W.M. and J.P. Neary (1982). 'Booming Sector and De-industrialization in a Small Open Economy', *The Economic Journal*, December.

Dantwala, M.L. (1967). 'Growing Irrelevance of Economics in Planning', *Economic and Political Weekly*, 2, pp. 1945–47.

Ghose, A.K. (1983). 'Agrarian Reform in West Bengal: Objectives, Achievements and limitations', in Ghose (ed.) (1983).

Ghose, A.K. (ed.) (1983). *Agrarian Reform in Contemporary Developing Economies*, Sage, New Delhi.

Jose, A.V. (1988). 'Agricultural Wages in India', *Economic and Political Weekly*, June 25.
Mitra, A. (1978). *Terms of Trade and Class Relations*, Frank Cass and Company, London.
Raj, K.N. and M. Tharakan (1983). 'Agrarian Reform in Kerala and Its Impact on the Rural Economy: A Preliminary Assessment', in A.K. Ghose (ed.) (1983).
Thorner, A. (1982). 'Excerpts from an FBI file', *Economic and Political Weekly*, 22 May.
Thorner, D. (1961). 'The Agrarian Problem in India Today', in Daniel and Alice Thorner, *Land and Labour in India*, Asia Publishing House, Bombay.
Thorner, D. (1973). *Agrarian Prospect in India*, second edition, Allied Publishers, Delhi.

De-industrialization

Tirthankar Roy

In the context of India, 'de-industrialization' is a well-known argument about the historical roots of underdevelopment. It is an argument that British India, which started with a large and well-developed manufacturing tradition, saw a decline in its traditional industry during the colonial period, and that the modern industry that grew in its place did not compensate for the great loss in employment and income. This essay criticizes the argument and suggests an alternative perspective. According to this alternative perspective, traditional industry in colonial India changed due to two processes, and not one. The first process was a partial decline in textiles due to obsolescence. Outside these spheres, there was another dynamics at work, change in organization driven by increasing market-exchange. These latter changes, it is argued further, shaped the character of Indian industrialization in the long run.

The experience of the 'handicrafts' in colonial India has been a lively topic of debate, mainly because this case is used to illustrate the adverse impact of colonialism on India. Apart from that reason for choosing to discuss it, the subject has a special relevance for the present occasion. Daniel Thorner made a brief but influential contribution on this theme.[1] Thorner was a historian. One of his main interests was the expansion of western European capitalism in Asia. He wrote the first major study on the railways and steam shipping in India,[2] he is known for works done singly or with Alice Thorner on occupational structure, land reforms and rural development,[3] and on the peasantry.[4] Several of these works became famous for their unconventional but well-argued

This is the text of the Ninth Daniel Thorner Memorial Lecture, delivered at the Reserve Bank of India, Mumbai, on 11 February 2000.

views about the long-term trends in the Indian economy. It is one of those unconventional essays, reprinted in the celebrated collection *Land and Labour in India*, that I shall come back to later.

The rest of the essay will be divided into four stages: a statement of the de-industrialization thesis, criticism, proposal of an alternative thesis, and discussion of some wider relevance of that alternative.

The De-industrialization Thesis

At 1800, India had a significant presence in the world as a manufacturing country. Possibly about 15–20 per cent of its working population, or 15–20 million persons, were engaged in some form of manufacturing at that time. Important industries were spinning and weaving, manufacture of leather and leather goods, a range of metal work, carpets and rugs, and so on. These industries did not use machinery, were not organized in large-scale factories, and were not regulated by any law. In fact, most of the production units were family-labour oriented or 'households'. I call such activities 'traditional industry'. By contrast, any unit that used machinery and the large-scale factory, and was more or less regulated, can be called 'modern industry'. By this definition, modern industry was obviously a product of the Industrial Revolution, since machinery, regulation and the large factory were all relatively new inventions.

The Industrial Revolution in the nineteenth century deeply affected traditional industry in India. Trade between India and the world increased dramatically, and products of the mechanized textile industry in Britain began to compete with handmade yarn and cloth in the Indian market. What was the net effect of this 'globalization'? The de-industrialization thesis suggests that the net effect was negative. Traditional industry declined. Closer economic relationship with Britain did create some modern industries in India. But the creative role of globalization did not compensate for the destructive one. One of the reasons why modern industry did not grow enough is that it was a kind of implant rather than an extension or evolution of traditional industry. The term makes an explicit contrast between Britain, which experienced *industrialization*, and her major colony India, which experienced *de*-industrialization, at the same time and due to the same set of causes, namely, trade and technological change. Britain too experienced a decline in its traditional industry, but modern industry played a compensatory role there. In India, on the other hand, 'while foreign economic penetration intensified . . . ruin and pauperization of the artisans, . . . arrested industrial development put sharp limits to their . . . conversion into an industrial working class.'[5]

In what sense did traditional industry 'decline' in India? It is necessary to be careful about the definition of 'de-industrialization'. For, writings around the theme of an industrial decline are notoriously vague about points of detail. Four points specifically need to be clarified: whether the decline in question was a relative or an absolute one, why it happened, whether it was restricted to industry or part of a general economic regress, and when it happened.

A Relative or an Absolute Decline?

There are two senses in which there was a relative decline in Indian industry in the nineteenth century. First, India fell back in relation to the world. At 1750, India supplied nearly a quarter of the world's manufacturing output. By 1900, India supplied less than 2 per cent. Second, industry fell back in relation to agriculture. In fact, most authors now seem to use 'de-industrialization' to mean a rising share of agriculture in employment, or a ruralization of employment. The term can be used in these senses, but then it will not necessarily connote any kind of serious economic loss or retrogression. A *relative* decline in the world does not mean an *absolute* decline as well, for between 1750 and 1900 the total scale of world industrial output had grown enormously. Ruralization as such is no disaster in terms of incomes or welfare unless it is assumed that agricultural resources were already fully utilized when the shift occurred. Such an assumption cannot be made for the nineteenth century. The only sense in which 'de-industrialization' signifies a serious economic loss is that of a large *absolute* fall in the scale of industrial activity, however measured.

Why Did It Happen?

Why was there a decline, if there was one? In writings sympathetic to the idea of an industrial decay, two sets of causes are discussed. The first is political and the second economic. The political factor is colonialism. Nationalist writers sometimes alleged direct or indirect suppression of Indian enterprise by British policy. The economic factor is technological obsolescence, a result of competition between machinery and hand-tools. Now, all historically significant examples of industrial decline are examples of technological obsolescence and not of direct intervention. This essay, therefore, considers only the former cause of industrial decay. A case can be made that this competition was sustained by a commitment to free trade, but it will not be a strong case for a number of reasons.

Industrial or Economic Decline?

De-industrialization is not an argument about industrial transformation only. In different contexts, it has been suggested that the decline in traditional industry was part of an overall economic deterioration. The idea had two distinct roots. The first is an Indian nationalist tradition represented by R.C. Dutt, Dadabhai Naoroji and somewhat later by Jawaharlal Nehru.[6] The second root is the Marxist theories of imperialism.[7] In the post-war period, both these schools were revived in history, development studies and Indian historiography. In this last scholarship, de-industrialization became a part of what can be called the left-nationalist view of the impact of colonial rule on India.[8] It has not only been the most popular world-view among historians working in India but has also become a kind of unquestioned official ideology, and in that capacity, shaped the average Indian's sense of history in an overwhelmingly powerful way.

All these schools hold the perfectly acceptable view that economic and political changes from the eighteenth century led to decline in some activities and growth in some others. The left-nationalist view can be defined in terms of two propositions: that the decline outweighed the growth, and that both decline and growth derived substantially from colonial strategies.

In more detail the story is as follows. Pre-British rural India consisted of self-sustaining egalitarian 'village communities' that produced their own subsistence. British rule, by its revenue policy, forced production for the market and thus broke up these communities.[9] Production for the market was not profitable enough, leading to widespread rural indebtedness. Many peasants lost their land and turned into tenants or labourers. On the other hand, the moneyed people who came to control or own land were averse to productive investment. The net result was stagnation along with increasing poverty and inequality. De-industrialization added to rural poverty by pushing many former artisans into agriculture.[10]

In this essay, I shall ignore the thesis of a larger economic decay. My ground is that, there is so far no significant quantitative or qualitative data that support the thesis of an overall economic regression at any time in the nineteenth century. To be sure, there were regressive forces at work, especially in the early nineteenth century. But there were expansionary forces at work as well. The best available national income and export figures suggest that the latter outweighed the former for the period 1870s to 1914. We cannot measure the net effect for earlier periods. Furthermore, on points of detail the left-nationalist paradigm has been repeatedly questioned in recent historical scholarship.[11] Finally, in itself a decline of the crafts does not necessarily mean economic decline. When more efficient and more productive suppliers drive out less productive ones, there is usually not only a decline in employment but also an increase in welfare and purchasing power because of a fall in the price of the good or service in question. This point holds especially in the case of hand-spinning, an industry that probably lost several million workers, for machine-spun yarn was capable of reducing cloth prices by at least half.

The larger picture being at best ambiguous, I shall refer to 'de-industrialization' to mean strictly an industrial decay.

When Did It Happen?

When did de-industrialization take place? Underdevelopment theorists who cite India to illustrate the bad effects of colonialism make no fine distinction on timing. Their thesis should hold for British rule as such, which spanned most of the nineteenth century and half of the twentieth century. Indian nationalist writings, on the other hand, dealt with the nineteenth century.

It is only recently that scholars have become rather scrupulous about dating. There is a reason for this caution. As we shall see, available statistical data question the existence of a general industrial decay. But relevant statistical data start from the last quarter of the nineteenth century. Responding to this adverse evidence, some writers suggest that there was decay, but it occurred before the periods of these data-sets.[12] By implication, the process slowed down after 1880 so that the post-1880 data-sets are irrelevant to testing de-industrialization. Such an argument, however, is not acceptable either on empirical or on conceptual grounds.

Direct statistical data on the first half of the nineteenth century —either on industry or on overall economic performance—are not just thin, but non-existent. Indirect evidence is contradictory. There were undoubtedly regressive forces at work during the early part of the British rule. These arose from the loss of a world market for Indian textiles, decline of cotton spinning and weaving, early revenue policy in some regions, political instability, etc. But the early nineteenth century also saw strong expansionary forces at work. There was dynamism in north India, and export trends from the second quarter were significantly positive. These facts hint at some rise in demand for artisanal goods. Given that we cannot measure the net effect, the question of the experience of industry as a whole in the early nineteenth century can have only one answer: 'we do not know.'

In terms of logic, the suggestion that there was obsolescence in traditional industry as a whole until about 1880 and a revival thereafter raises a big problem. Scholars who hint at such a reversal have not been aware of that problem. It invites scholars to show how the crafts could resist obsolescence in the second period. How did the parameters influencing competition between machinery and tools change in such a way that the crafts suffered obsolescence in the first period and resisted obsolescence in the second? This question is not answered, not even asked, by those who believe in a more remote dating of de-industrialization. If the parameters of competition changed at all, they must change *adversely* for the crafts, for the pace of technological progress is always faster in the machinery-using industries compared with the tool-using ones. Technological obsolescence is an irreversible and advancing process. If the crafts survived, the very notion of pervasive competition and competitive decay is called into question.

Having said that, periods did matter. This essay will suggest further on that it mattered in the following way. First of all, the notion of pervasive competition is discarded. Second, there were two almost parallel processes at work in the colonial period—obsolescence in segments of the textile industry, and commercialization in a wide range of crafts that were *never* threatened by obsolescence. The former process dominated in the early nineteenth century, and the latter from the late nineteenth century.

On the basis of the above discussion, 'de-industrialization' in this essay is defined to include two basic propositions.

1. Traditional industry declined in India in absolute terms.
2. It declined mainly because of competition between Indian

hand-tools and British machinery, a competition that may have been partly sustained by politics.

Proposition 1 represents a stylized fact and proposition 2 suggests an explanation for it. To briefly state the critique that follows, the causation in proposition 2 needs to be qualified, devalued, and supplemented with another causation. These steps follow from re-examining the evidence, to which I now turn.

Evidence

Two types of evidence have been discussed most often in relation to proposition 1 above. These relate to the textile industry, and to employment statistics.

The Textile Industry

Foreign trade data, as well as estimates of employment, establish that a decline took place in cotton textile industry in the nineteenth century.[13] The major field of decline was cotton-spinning by hand. The employment loss in hand-spinning was unquestionably very large in scale (possibly several million), but the loss of income per head was very small. Spinning was so labour-intensive that if it were to employ specialized workers cloth prices would have been prohibitively high. Spinning, therefore, necessarily involved domestic workers. The opportunity cost of spinning labour was near-zero and the earnings, correspondingly, positive but trivial.

Spinning by hand, furthermore, is more or less the *only* significant example of traditional industry becoming extinct due to competition from British goods. Other examples exist, such as indigenous shipping and ship-building that declined in competition with steamships. But their scale is uncertain or small. Further, these cases were associated with significant gains in efficiency. If spinning and weaving are excluded, such obsolescence for the crafts was an exception than the rule.

Within textiles, handloom-weaving presents a curious case. Handlooms declined in the nineteenth century. In 1840 India imported about 100 million yards of British cloth. In 1912–15 India imported on average 2,600 million yards, which was the maximum scale that imports reached. Assuming constant market size, the latter figure and estimated mill output suggest a fall in handloom supply by about 3,300 million yards in 75 years. Assuming the maximum output of each loom was about 2,700 yards per year, this implies unemployment for well over a million looms. This figure will need to be adjusted marginally upward if we have reliable estimates of the size of cloth export from India in the earlier dates, and substantially downward if we can estimate the domestic market that seems to have grown rapidly in the pre-war period. Realistically, there was net loss of about 400,000 looms.[14]

The fact of a decline in weaving is neither disputable nor surprising. What is surprising is that after the 1880s, handloom cloth production was stable until World War I, and steadily rising in the inter-war period. Interestingly, this was precisely the period when mechanized weaving in the Indian mills expanded rapidly, from less than 400 million yards of cotton cloth to about 3 billion. The productivity per hour of a throw-shuttle type handloom was only about 10 per cent that of a power-driven loom. Why was *any* handloom cloth being sold alongside mill cloth despite such a wide gap in productivity?

In modern historical scholarship, Morris D. Morris first offered an explanation for the survival of handlooms. Morris suggests that the handlooms survived because total market for cloth expanded in nineteenth-century India.[15] This suggestion has been attacked, somewhat awkwardly, on the ground that total market for cloth did not expand during the colonial period, among other reasons because inequality increased.[16] Morris was probably right on the scale of demand. There is evidence that real national income grew significantly in the late nineteenth century.[17] Moreover, the empirical basis and theoretical relevance of rising inequality are questionable. However, without some reference to relative competitiveness, growth of markets by itself does not explain the survival of the handloom.

A.K. Bagchi suggests another answer. More accurately, other writers have seen an answer in Bagchi's discussion of the subject. The answer focuses on changes in relative costs of production, and attributes the survival to several new improved tools that became available to handloom weavers from about 1900.[18] This line of argument, again, is inadequate, because it can be shown that the new options did not anywhere near bridge the productivity gap assuming realistic wages.

A recent scholarship on the industry has explored a third possibility, market segmentation.[19] Hand- and power-weaving had comparative advantages in different types of cloth. There was continuing preference for the traditional garments that the handlooms were better able to make. It has also been suggested that these 'niche' markets experienced increasing commercialization or market transactions, in both product and labour. In turn, there was capital accumulation by merchants and master-weavers, the appearance of new organizations such as the factory in place of the family unit, and new investments. In this view, technological change in handlooms was an effect, and not the cause, of survival.

If we generalize from this example, handloom-weaving suggests that consumption and specific skills not easily reproducible in machinery ensured the survival of many traditional industries. The competition between British machinery and Indian crafts did occur, but in special cases (spinning and a segment of weaving). Outside these, there was no general obsolescence.

Trends in Employment

Census data on aggregate employment have been used as the major and clinching evidence supporting de-industrialization. The censuses tell us that industrial employment declined steadily and sharply between 1881 and 1931. It declined from about 20 million to 13–15 million, while at the same time employment in agriculture increased from 71 to 100 million. The percentage of workers in agriculture increased from 62 to 71, and that in industry declined from 18 to 9. A.K. Bagchi finds a similar trend for Gangetic Bihar.[20] Does this suggest a big decline in traditional industry and a ruralization of employment? There are two sets of critique suggesting that it does not. The first questions the statistics, and the second questions the interpretation to be drawn from it.

Detailed work by Daniel and Alice Thorner shows that these shifts in occupational structure were probably spurious and arose from several problems with the census definitions.[21] In their reconstruction, occupational structure hardly changed between 1881 and 1951. This basic finding has not been seriously questioned in subsequent work.

However, this finding rests, among others, on a disputable argument about women's employment. Women's presence in industrial work-force declined dramatically in the census period. If women's data are excluded, occupational structure shows rather little change. If women's data are included, the share of industry in work-force shows a fall. The Thorners suggest that the trends in women's industrial work arose from a reporting problem, and therefore, they should not be given too much credence. Women who were mainly engaged in household duties and marginally in commercial production tended to be classified as workers. In other words, there was a possible overestimation of women workers in the earlier censuses.[22]

Now, the point that declining presence of women in industry is mainly a reporting problem is disputable, among other reasons, because the decline has been a very long-lasting one. It occurred over nearly a century. It is difficult to accept that a reporting bias carried on that long. In my view, there *was* a real decline in employment here, which involved mainly women. Further, the decline derived from a retreat of household industry in competition with units using mainly wage labour. To this point I shall return.

Let us now consider the second critique of employment data, which does not dispute a decline in employment but questions what it means. Does decline in employment mean technological obsolescence? Not entirely, because employment declined in a number of industries where no serious competition with machinery was in existence (such as dress and toilet, wood, ceramics, construction). Does decline in employment mean technological obsolescence of Indian goods in competition with foreign goods? Not necessarily, for as noted by J. Krishnamurty in 1967, a fall in industrial employment could have resulted from modern industry replacing traditional industry *within India.*[23] How do we test this? If incomes in industry increased even as employment fell, that could mean rising capital intensity within Indian industry.

National income data suggest that total and per worker real income in industry grew at significant rates (in the range 1.5–2 per cent per year) between 1901 and 1947.[24] Several authors explain this by rising capital intensity. In this view, what we see in census and income statistics is the beginning of a large-scale substitution of craft labour by machinery within India.[25] Such an inference, however, is counter-intuitive and unrealistic because modern industry engaged a tiny percentage of industrial employment (4–6 per cent) in the early twentieth century. With such marginal weight in employment, it is not credible that it could compensate for the decline in traditional industry even in income. Part of this increase in productivity, in fact, derived from the emergence of a semi-mechanized small-scale industry segment in

India, engaged in processing basic materials. These new firms used slightly improved tools and slightly higher capital per worker compared to their artisan counterparts.[26]

But when we look at national income data more closely we see signs that in fact real incomes increased within traditional industry as well. More surprisingly, income per worker probably increased at a faster rate in this sector than in modern industry.[27] Evidence of productivity increase is strong also in specific industries like handloom textiles, tanning and metal work. In textiles, real value-added unquestionably increased, and in all of them, output indicators show growth whereas employment indicators show stagnation or fall.[28]

To sum up, traditional industry probably experienced a fall in employment in the period after 1881, though not as large a fall as it may seem. But since there was no fall in incomes, the employment trend cannot mean a general decline in demand. Proposition 2 (see the last section) must be discarded, for the later periods at least. Fall in employment in the census period derived from not only technological unemployment but also a drive to replace low-productivity workers, or a drive to improve efficiency. Where did that drive originate from? We need an alternative perspective on traditional industry that can answer this question.

The alternative I propose starts from two premises. First, British machinery and Indian tools were not competitive, with the important exception of cotton yarn and some cloths. By and large, Indian artisans made labour-intensive consumer goods for which there were no imported mechanized substitutes available. Or such substitutes were not profitable because capital was relatively costly in India. Second, traditional industry changed not due to external competition but due to internal competition. From these premises, we can suggest an alternative story, which I shall call 'commercialization'.

In the next part of this essay I shall discuss commercialization in more detail. The raw material comes from recent research on traditional industry, of which my own research forms a part. [29] I shall not describe this raw material but only state the major conclusions.

The Commercialization Thesis

The 60 years spanned by the opening of the Suez Canal (1869) and the Great Depression (1929) were a period of rapid commercialization in India. Long-distance trade expanded and regional markets integrated on an unprecedented scale due to, mainly, three factors: foreign trade, modern transport and communication, and the definition of contract law and private property rights. The effects, which were quite dramatic, are well-researched for agriculture. It is not so well-recognized that traditional industry was also transformed by commercialization. Production for subsistence, production under various types of non-market and barter distribution arrangements such as *jajmani*, and production for local, rural, periodic and other spot markets declined in favour of production on contract for distant markets. Such a process had begun before the 1860s and it certainly continued beyond 1930, but the intervening period saw its full impact unfolding. This rise in long-distance trade had two types of effects: increased competition, and changes in industrial organization.

Industrial organization changed in two ways. First, long-distance trade had made information and working capital essential resources. But these were scarce resources. The small number of entrepreneurs who had access to these resources expanded scale of business, could take closer control of the manufacturing process, and sometimes make technological experiments and improvements. Capitalists and labourers became more clearly distinguishable. So did employer–employee relationships. Second, competition among manufacturers led to increased specialization and division of labour. There are two major examples of specialization. Formerly, many rural artisans performed agricultural labour on the side, such as tanners and coarse cotton weavers in most regions. Such part-time industrial activity generally declined, whereas specialized artisans survived to a greater extent. A second example is the decline of household industry in favour of small factories employing wage labour. The family as a production unit had certain advantages. But it also had serious disadvantages. It could not specialize enough and could not be supervised closely enough. *It is this competitive decline of the family that explains the long downward trend in women's presence in the industrial work force.* Women formerly worked in industry mainly as members of the household. The preference for the home as a work-site still remains strong among women workers in South Asia. When the household declined as a unit of production women workers exited industry, and were replaced by male hired labour. Women are returning now to the factory, not because the household is coming back, but for other factors that influence women's participation in the factory.

Conclusion: Summary and Wider Relevance

I set out to test two propositions with which the thesis of 'de-industrialization' has been defined here: (1) there was an absolute industrial decay in colonial India, and (2) it derived from competition between machinery and crafts. I restated a well-known critique of the data-base, owing to the seminal work by the Thorners, which qualifies proposition 1. My critique here deals with proposition 2 specifically. The 'de-industrialization' thesis explains trends in employment solely by competition between nations of unequal technological capability. This significance of competitive decay in the crafts is questioned by citing two facts: (a) productivity and income growth in the crafts, and (b) insufficient examples of industries where external competition occurred.

The alternative 'commercialization' thesis proposes that there were *two* almost parallel processes at work in the colonial period—obsolescence in segments of the textile industry, and commercialization in the other crafts not threatened by obsolescence. The former process dominated in the early nineteenth century, and the latter from the late nineteenth century. Traditional industry in the latter period changed in organization due to increasing market exchange. The decline in employment, at least in the census period, was a symptom of *internal* competition. Equally, as a result of internal competition, there emerged segments of growth and capital accumulation. The commercialization story, thus, explains not a one-dimensional decay, but a *duality* in the experience of traditional industry. There was decline as well as growth, external as well as internal competition. The net result was a positive one for as long as we can measure.

I shall end this essay by suggesting three ways in which this alternative story matters to our views about development and industrialization.

First, at the level of theories of history, there is a difference. We are looking at British India more from Adam Smith's point of view, rather than the Marxian viewpoint that has ruled post-independence Indian historiography. Marx and the Marxists were too preoccupied with technological change. Smith, by contrast, was concerned with markets, competition and efficiency. In this sense there is a shift in accent.

Second, the commercialization story suggests several areas of continuity between the past and the present. The processes I just described have not finished happening. Let me mention three points of continuity. The first is the overwhelming importance of labour-intensive industry in employment. The majority of manufacturing workers even now work in small unregulated factories, use simple general-purpose tools and a great deal of manual skills. In that respect the past and the present are not different. And they are not different because India's factor endowment has changed relatively little in the long run. A second example of continuity is that many small-scale labour-intensive industries today have traditional roots. For example, many owners of small powerloom factories today are handloom weavers by ancestral occupation. If we investigate the background of today's powerloom capitalists, we find that some of their great-grandfathers made money in long-distance trade in handloom cloth or raw material in the inter-war period. De-industrialization cannot explain how this happened. The commercialization thesis can. To repeat a point mentioned already, commercialization created segments of decline and segments of growth. It is these segments of growth that form the major link between the past and the present of Indian small-scale industry. A third example of continuity is organizational change. Post-independence censuses suggest a continuous decline in household industry, and shift of employment out of families into tiny factories. The rate of employment growth in industry since 1961 has been rather small, only about 1.2 per cent per year. But, as with British India, this small growth is an illusion, being the average of a negative growth of employment in family enterprises, and a very high growth rate of employment in unregistered factories. Our story shows that the long-lasting and ongoing shift from families to small factories did not somehow begin at 1947. It began long ago. It began within traditional industry. And it began because of increasing internal competition in traditional industry.

Finally, the alternative story matters to views about industrialization as a global process. De-industrialization suggests that the nineteenth-century globalization that industrialized Europe destroyed industry in Asia. Our story suggests that there was no essential difference in the beginning of industrialization between Europe and

Asia. At different times and places—eighteenth-century Europe, early twentieth-century Japan and British India—a similar form of industrialization began that was based on utilizing labour more productively, rather than on replacing labour by machinery. The key process was commercialization and modernization of traditional industry. Such a process was stimulated by long-distance trade, and resulted in capital accumulation. In the course of this transition, there was a persistence of traditional organizations in the short run, and a movement towards the labour market in the long run. These messages are now well-known to historians of early-modern Europe and East Asia. We suggest that South Asia is an example of the same thing. If, however, such common roots gave rise to different levels of prosperity, that difference needs to be explained not by such global factors as trade or colonialism, but by local variables and also by what happened *after* the British rule ended.[30]

I am grateful to Alice Thorner for her comments on the text of the lecture, especially for pointing out an error in it. I wish to thank members of the audience for their comments and questions, which led to revision and elaboration of some of the arguments.

Notes and References

1 '"De-industrialization" in India, 1881–1931', in Daniel and Alice Thorner, *Land and Labour in India,* New York, 1962.

2 *Investment in Empire: British Railway and Steam Shipping Enterprise in India 1825–1849,* Philadelphia, 1950.

3 Essays in *Land and Labour in India* (see note 1 above), and Daniel Thorner, *The Agrarian Prospect in India,* Bombay, 1976; first published 1956.

4 'Chayanov's Concept of Peasant Economy', in T. Shanin (ed.), *The Theory of Peasant Economy* (Delhi, 1987).

5 P.C. Joshi, 'The Decline of Indigenous Handicrafts in Uttar Pradesh', *Indian Economic and Social History Review* (*IESHR* hereafter), I, 1963.

6 Bipan Chandra, *The Rise and Growth of Economic Nationalism in India,* Chs. II and III, New Delhi, 1966.

7 Karl Marx saw England fulfilling a 'double mission' in India, one destructive and the other creative. The destruction of industry was an example of the former role. The railways built with foreign capital were an example of the latter. Lenin and other early theorists of imperialism explored the latter role, which they felt would become stronger as export of capital from rich to poor countries became inevitable for the survival of capitalism in the west. A post-war scholarship, led by Andre Gunder Frank, argued that such forms of globalization further retarded the poorer countries.

8 Some recent generalizations include S. Sarkar, *Modern India: 1885–1947,* Delhi, 1983, the section 'The Colonial Economy'; I. Habib, 'Colonialization

of the Indian Economy, 1757–1900', *Social Scientist*, III, 1975; and A.K. Bagchi, *The Political Economy of Underdevelopment*, sections 4.3–4.5, Cambridge, 1982.

[9] This view of precolonial rural India, articulated in the 1950s, later changed. The notion of self-sufficient rural communities has been more or less discarded in favour of a view that admits of a great deal of inequality and commerce in rural India.

[10] For different versions of this story of increasing misery, see S.J. Patel, *Agricultural Labourers in Modern India and Pakistan*, Bombay, 1952, and the references cited in note 8 above.

[11] See T. Roy, *The Economic History of India: 1857–1947*, Chs. 1–4, College and University Level Textbooks series of the Oxford University Press, Delhi, forthcoming, .

[12] See, for example, R.K. Ray, 'The Spinning Wheel is My Husband . ..', review of T. Roy, *Traditional Industry in the Economy of Colonial India*, Cambridge, 1999, in *The Book Review*, XXIV, 2000.

[13] See M.J. Twomey, 'Employment in Nineteenth Century Indian Textiles', *Explorations in Economic History*, XX, 1983.

[14] Domestic market for cotton cloth increased by almost 50 per cent between 1900 and 1914. That order of growth was rare. But even with very modest growth rates between 1840 and 1900, the handlooms probably lost about 1000–1200 million yards overall, or about 3–400,000 looms between 1860 and 1914. Cloth exports probably never exceeded a few hundred million yards.

[15] Morris et al, *Indian Economy in the Nineteenth Century: A Symposium*, Delhi, 1969.

[16] Habib, 'Colonialization', p. 38, and Bipan Chandra in Morris et al, *Indian Economy*, pp. 47–52.

[17] M. Mukherjee, *National Income of India*, Calcutta, 1935, Table 2.6, p. 65.

[18] A.K. Bagchi, *Private Investment in India 1900–1939*, section 7.2, Cambridge, 1972. See also the section 'De-industrialization' in I. Habib, 'Studying a Colonial Economy without Perceiving Colonialism', *Modern Asian Studies*, XIX, 1985.

[19] See T. Roy, *Traditional Industry*, Ch. 3, for a discussion.

[20] Based on the statistics collected by Buchanan-Hamilton in the early nineteenth century, which did not adjust for the presence of non-specialized and underemployed labour among the work force. See Bagchi, 'Deindustrialization in India in the Nineteenth Century: Some Theoretical Implications', *Journal of Development Studies*, XXII, 1978; Marika Vicziany, 'The De-industrialization of India in the Nineteenth Century: A Methodological Critique of Amiya Kumar Bagchi', *IESHR*, XVI, 1979; J. Krishnamurty, 'Deindustrialization in Gangetic Bihar during the Nineteenth Cnetury: Another Look at the Evidence', *IESHR*, XXII, 1985.

[21] Daniel Thorner, '"De-industrialization"', and Alice Thorner, 'The Secular Trend in the Indian Economy, 1881–1951', *Economic Weekly*, XIV, Special Number, July 1962. A detailed discussion of the critique of census data will

take us too far away from the main theme of this essay. A discussion appears in Roy, *Economic History of India*, Ch. 9.

22 In a more recent essay, Alice Thorner takes the position that women's participation rate may not reflect purely a reporting problem. See 'Women's Work in Colonial India, 1881–1931', School of Oriental and African Studies, London, 1984. The essay comparing regions and occupations is perhaps the only detailed investigation into the long-term trend now available.

23 'Changes in the Composition of the Working Force in Manufacturing, 1901–51: A Theoretical and Empirical Analysis', *IESHR*, IV, 1967.

24 The national income data used here come from S. Sivasubramonian, 'National Income of India, 1900–01 to 1946–7', Ph.D. Dissertation, Delhi School of Economics, Delhi, 1965; and his 'Revised Estimates of the National Income of India, 1900–1901 to 1946–47', *IESHR*, XXXIV, 1997.

25 See, for example, Deepak Lal, *The Hindu Equilibrium. I. Cultural Stability and Economic Stagnation: India 1500 BC–1980,* Delhi, 1988, p. 186. W.J. Macpherson seems to have been the first author to make the capital intensity critique about de-industrialization.

26 For example, old manual processes of grain-milling by women inside peasant families changed to mechanized processing inside small and seasonal factories; wooden mortars for crushing sugar changed to iron rollers; old ways of warping threads for handlooms by members of the weavers' families gave way to warp-beams prepared in small factories; or old ways of cleaning cotton gave way to new ones.

27 S. Sivasubramonian, 'Revised Estimates'. Total income calculations for traditional industry in this paper, and in Sivasubramonian's earlier work done in 1965, rest on two sets of data. The first is census employment in industry (also includes construction) outside official factories. The second is an average wage index for small-scale industry, derived from a large number of wage and earning estimates for different occupations, time-points, and types of worker. When we say that total income increased despite a fall in employment, it means the income estimates show increase in real terms. This income series has problems, but the problems are not so bad as to call into serious question the conclusion of a rise in income per worker in traditional industry. The finding that traditional industry experienced productivity growth of the order that Sivasubramonian finds it did, has surprised other commentators on Indian national income, such as Alan Heston and Angus Maddison. But no alternative method or estimate has been used that can upset this result. In the essay cited, Sivasubramonian has defended the finding with additional qualitative evidence.

28 For evidence, see the discussion in Sivasubramonian, 'Revised Estimates', pp. 127–29; T. Roy, *Traditional Industry*, Ch. 2.

29 See Roy, *Traditional Industry.*

30 How did local contexts matter? Population growth is an example. A labour-intensive industrialization can transform itself into a capital-intensive industrialization only when rates of growth in supply of labour begin to fall below those in demand for labour. In India, that turning point has been delayed

by sustained high rates of population growth. How did post-independence policies matter? India after independence had the option—which Japan had exercised until a decade or two previously—of selecting a growth path based on export of labour-intensive manufactures. India's deliberate withdrawal from export-led growth deprived the traditional industry from external markets. And the Gandhian bias for protecting traditional industry deprived them of healthy competition. When India returned to globalization in the 1990s, predictably the industries that benefited the most from export opportunities were labour-intensive small-scale industries. But by then, what India had to offer the world was a small-scale manufacturing sector that had serious problems of accumulated inefficiency.

Lost Visions?

Imagining a National Culture in the 1950s

Dilip M. Menon

At the end of a millennium, and more than half a century into independent India, when we look back from a time of despair, of religious fundamentalism and a fraying of our social and political order, inevitably the 1950s appear different. In different moods the first decade of the new nation appears either more open—an India engaging with hope—or as the beginning of a kind of closure—*raison d'etat* prevailing over the will of the people. This was also the time when scholars like Daniel Thorner, among others, came to India to chart the construction of a new nation as work in progress. I am currently engaged in working on an idiosyncratic, personal look at socialism in India, and this lecture provides me with the opportunity to present an initial and hesitant foray. It is intended as an exercise in intellectual history in which I shall look at attempts within cultural forms to imagine equality and a good society and, to anticipate, suggest that the process of nation-building compromised any radical initiative. Indeed the imagining of the nation was done by the few for the many; the 'people' were to be mute witnesses to the drama of development being staged for them. But how does this connect with the life and textured work of Daniel Thorner? It is a tangential approach: an interest in the larger history of socialism and radical cultural practice in our times, and an attempt to understand the first decade of independence in whose dawn, presumably, it was bliss to be alive. Why the fifties, why this nostalgia for a decade I neither inhabited nor witnessed? The first canto of Dante's *Inferno* gives me a point from which to reflect:

This is the text of the Tenth Daniel Thorner Memorial Lecture, delivered at the Centre for Economic and Social Studies, Hyderabad, on 29 January 2001.

Midway on our life's journey, I found myself
In dark woods, the right road lost

... How I came to enter
I cannot well say, being so full of sleep
Whatever moment it was, I began to blunder

Off the true path. But when I came to stop,
Below a hill that marked one end of the valley
That had pierced my heart with terror, I looked up

Toward the crest, and saw its shoulders already
Mantled in rays of that bright planet that shows
The road to everyone, whatever our journey.

Was the right road lost as early as the inception of the nation? The idea of modernity, cast within the paradigm of development and modernization, was the keyword as India embarked on its post-colonial journey. Debates on development and political economy inevitably framed the imagining of a national culture—the project of 'achieving our country', to borrow a phrase from the American philosopher Richard Rorty.[1] To speak of ideas of 'modernity' and 'national culture' in the 1950s may seem anachronistic. While it may have been words like development or being progressive that were being bandied about, the desire to become modern was the penumbral presence within all of these articulations. I believe that the visualizing of the modern—through art, film and the theatre—characterized the 1950s and was a parallel and integral project alongside the building of modernity through dams, scientific establishments and the acquisition of nuclear capability. The question to be asked is whether these cultural imaginings managed to create a vision that we have only now lost. Or is it our present nostalgia that does not let us recognize that it was an already compromised vision of the future that was set in place after independence? In my mind the decade comes to be framed by Faiz's poem on the 'leprous daybreak' of 15 August 1947 (*Yeh daag daag ujaala, yeh shab gazida sehar*), and Sahir Ludhianvi's poignant verse of disillusionment suffusing Guru Dutt's *Pyaasa* (1956), in which men, trust and friendship were as nothing.

The fifties increasingly appear as a decade of closure—in questions of politics as much as aesthetics. And it is these two themes—of the visualizing of modernity and of closure—that this essay deals with, albeit in a provisional and tentative formulation. This closure was reflected in three arenas. First, in the process of state-led development that came to be determined by the parameters of a passive revolution. Second, in a notion of modernity that envisaged a landscape of a techno-future studded with dams, nuclear establishments and steel mills but devoid of people and a past to which they would be mere witnesses, leaving a contemporary practice of the present suspended in an ahistorical space. Third, in a rendering of the very idea of the 'people' as a romantic abstraction, their pre-modern 'encrustations' being rendered as popular culture rather than awaiting radical historical transformation. In the political arena, there had already been intimations of an emphasis on disciplining the people over mobilizing them. The reaction of the nationalist leadership, particularly Nehru, to the RIN Mutiny of 1946, had already shown up the Congress as a government-in-waiting impatient of popular unruliness. The horrors of partition were followed by a war of diplo-macy between India and Pakistan over the repatriation of abducted women—where the body of women was proxy to territory. And, in 1948, the Indian state deployed its military and police power against its own people in Telengana.

I

When thinking about the question of aesthetic representation it is important to remember that it cannot be separated from the discourse of the reconstruction of independent India along the axes of modernity, development and equity. Both aesthetics and development had to reckon with the persistence of 'tradition' and a 'people' for whom modernity was to be staged since the nationalist movement had never envisaged a revolution of the Indian masses. Two framing arguments could be borne in mind: one of the Gramscian idea of 'passive revolution', and the other of an emerging consensus across ideologies. On the question of development, Sukhamoy Chakravarti has observed that the central problem was one of reconciling accumulation with legitimation. This meant evolving both ways of avoiding the unnecessary rigours of an industrial transition as well as attempting to resolve conflict through change—but not radical change. Thus far and no further.[2] The post-colonial project concerned itself with the means by which the condition of modernity could paradoxically be brought about but as an already existing, indigenized and naturalized state of being. Nationalist political activity had largely left precapitalist sites, structure and classes intact, even in the process of mass mobilization. And, as in most ex-colonies, what Gramsci has termed a passive revolution became the characteristic mode of transition. The establishment of a nation-state was the priority and a process of reform from above would follow this. The institutional structures of 'rational' authority set up by colonial rule—of law or administration—were neither broken up nor transformed. Nor was there a full-scale attack on precapitalist dominant classes. Partha Chatterjee has argued that what came to be incorporated within the framework of rule was not a representative mechanism operated by individual agents, but entire structures of precapitalist community. In the political field this was manifest in the idea of vote banks. In the economic field, the notion of community development presumed already existing and harmonious communities.[3] This timorousness on the part of the state led to a suspicion towards its rhetoric in popular consciousness. While the post-colonial state claimed to lead from the front, it was clear as to who was pushing it.

There was also emerging a broad consensus on issues relating to industrialization and the village. Nehru, the left and Gandhi are conventionally seen as exemplifying distinct positions on a scale running from outright and rampant industrialization at one end to a valorization of the village on the other. By the 1950s, arguably, the vocabularies had become quite indistinguishable and the differences were more rhetorical than substantive. Nehru's *Discovery of India* concluded with a critique of modern industrial society that could have been penned by Gandhi. He wrote of 'excessive individualism', the prevalence of 'competitive and acquisitive characteristics', and the avid enthronement of wealth above everything else.[4] Gandhi plumped for an ethical socialism premised on the immoral character of capitalist economic institutions. He denounced both private property and production for profit as fundamental causes of exploitation. When he writes in *India of My Dreams* (1947) that 'land and all property is his who will work for it',[5] or in *Towards Non-violent Socialism* that the capitalist was committing theft when appropriating 'surplus value' as profit,[6] he sounds no different from the Kerala communist theoretician, K. Damodaran, writing his ten popular Malayalam primers on Marxism in the 1950s. Marxism and socialism in India were heavily influenced as much by the experience of Gandhism as by participation in the Nehruvian dream of modernity and development. To rephrase the American philosopher Richard Rorty, perhaps for us Indians it is important not to let Marxism influence too much the story we tell about our own left.[7] We need to reflect seriously on what this consensus and confluence of ideas mean: the consequences of running Gandhi, Nehru and the left together as it were.

II

The political orientation of the Indian intelligentsia was significantly affected by the refashioning, even reinvention, of the past and tradition by Gandhi, which came to be exemplified either in the evidence of 'ancient moral glory' or in a certain romanticization of the idea of the people. The consequences for an elaboration of an uncompromisingly radical modernity—of freeing the people from the shackles of the past—were at best profoundly ambivalent. Not only was the relation to the idea of a past that was to be transcended rendered suspect, the conception of the people as a historical force for change came to be recast by seeing them as the repositories of a timeless wisdom. In art this ambivalence towards tradition expressed itself in more complex ways. Geeta Kapur, in a series of insightful essays, argues that the idea of modernism has no firm canonical position in India. Being progressive (or modern) is sometimes staged as a deployment of tradition, and at other times as a subversion of it. The modern therefore acquires an emblematic or, as she puts it, 'heraldic' value; newness comes into the world in the name of the modern. However, modernism, arising as it does out of the chronological tryst between nationhood and modernity, becomes embroiled in the demand for the revealing of an authentic national self. And, modernization becomes both desired and abhorred as the self oscillates between what Kapur calls the modern and the authentic. This conflation of modernization (the process), modernity (the desired state of being) and modernism (the aesthetic form of the modern) is characteristic of developing post-colonial societies, adding a further dimension to the 'heraldic' modern. As Kapur astutely puts it, it is a euphemistic modernism that finally emerges which keeps in tow notions of a people's culture, or folk/tribal art, as a legitimating genealogy.[8] What indeed are the consequences for a cultural practice or politics of this sentimentalizing of the people as a sign of authenticity? We shall return to this question again when looking at both film and political theatre.

The idea of the modern necessarily involves the invoking of a national culture that breaks free of the distortions of a colonial modernity. It requires a sense of history as well as a sense of past, present and future imagined along a continuum, each in dialogue with the other and bearing an organic relation. However, the compromise of the passive revolution rendered both the past as well as the future ambivalent, even suspect, categories. To imagine too radical a future raised the spectrum of social upheaval on a large scale. Moreover, it posed the question of authenticity yet again: would India's civilizational values be undermined? The past, for the progressive thinking with socialism, lay too close at hand, coiled around the present and manifested in structures and attitudes as well as in the all-embracing metaphor of feudalism. Visualizations of modernity—the imagining of national culture—reflected this central tension. The present, rendered as contemporaneity, was suspended between a past that stretched into the dark backward and abysm of time imbued with the aura of ancientness, and a future that was hyper-modern, an imaginary space disconnected from the immediate social and historical space. The contemporary, thus, lay between an over-theorized past rendered as embodying civilization and a hyper-modern, beyond-history future.

Let us take a dominant visualization of the future structured around the fetish of science and technology. While Nehru's famous 'scientific temper' was harder to inculcate in a country oscillating between reverence for the past and genuflection to the idea of a future, what became easier was the representation of science through artefacts. Itty Abraham calls it a socialist realist style of monumentality—represented through the photographs and publicity material of the Directorate of Audio-Visual Publicity and the Films Division documentaries. Dams such as the Bhakra Nangal, the Durgapur Steel Mills (built with British collaboration), the hyper-modern city of Chandigarh where grids ordered human irrationality, and, above all, the gleaming domes of the Bhabha Atomic Research Centre, indicated an oxymoronic already present yet distant future.[9] These visual representations were accompanied by the fetishized litany of numbers—of tons of steel, miles of road—and invocations to the ineffable power of the atom. The very size and awesomeness of these monuments seemed to locate them in a disconnected future inhabited not by the ordinary Indian, but by categories like the engineer and expert. It was a landscape *sans* the human, a hyper-modern geography of catwalks, girders and gleaming shapes. The eighteenth-century colonial picturesque of the Daniells had created a sense of the sublime and awe through a depiction of India's landscape and ancient monuments dwarfing the loincloth-clad native. This was a high modern picturesque in which the factory and reactor loomed over the Indian people. Mitter Bedi's photographs (albeit from the decade of the sixties)—classic black-and-white projections of a future—are a case in point. They feature the smokestacks of the Dhuwaran power station, the coolant towers of the NOCIL plant—a landscape of the future without people.[10] One can put alongside this the classic documentary, 'The Story of Steel', directed by Harisadhan Dasgupta in 1956, with music by Ravi Shankar and scripted by Satyajit Ray. Here again it is the product (the emblem of India's striving to be a modern industrial nation) rather than labour that is visually glorified.

III

Let us get back to ideas of art and culture and the grid of development discourse within which they functioned. The process of institution-building of the 1950s—the National Museum (established in 1948), the National Gallery of Modern Art (1954) and the FTII, Pune (1959)—was possibly an attempt to modernize through a centralized mandate. It has been suggested that centralized action by the nation-state was a way of disentangling the modern from earlier nationalist polemic (which had to speak in the name of tradition). There are several consequences that follow, the least being the idea of a state that stands outside and above while shaping what is within. Indian modernism, observes Kapur, developed without an avant-garde.[11] State patronage for the arts absolved progressive elements from adopting confrontational initiatives.

To return to our argument about the disconnectedness of past, present and future in India's visualization of modernity, let us look at the museum and the idea of the past. Nehru was convinced of the power of the museum—the visual representation of the past—in an illiterate country. The peasants would discover their India through sight alone, even as Nehru had done through reading and reflection in the uncertain comfort of colonial jails. In 1948, an exhibition of sculpture and miniature paintings that was held in the halls of the Government House, Delhi, presaged the formation of the National Museum. What was clearly excluded was any reference to the modern; modern Indian painting had been included when the exhibition had travelled to England earlier. As an aside here, it is significant that when the

National Gallery of Modern Art opened in Delhi, the core representative collection was the paintings of Amrita Sher-Gil—the part-Hungarian painter who had honed her images in Paris. The National Museum, Guha-Thakurta has argued, objectified and memorialized the past in sharp dissociation from the present—the 'masterpieces' of Indian art were very clearly associated with achievements in early Indian sculpture.[12] Moreover, the collection embodied Nehru's delightfully vague characterization of what was central to Indian civilization— 'that worthwhile something', as he put it. The pastness of Indian art came to be expressed in that reified, static opposition between western realism and Indian idealism—the spiritual, transcendental, civilizational spirit. If E.B. Havell and A.K. Coomaraswamy had looked back to early Buddhist art to escape from the anxiety of Greek influence, now an all-embracing notion of what was Hindu was jerry-built as the master tradition of Indian art, engulfing Buddhist genres in the idea of a great Indian synthesis.[13]

While the past came to be rendered as both distinct from the present, indeed excised from it, and was also given a religious, civilizational intent, there was another problem—one of silencing. If the hyper-modern future lay under the sign of the factory and reactor, with the people absent or at an awed distance, the reified past similarly was rendered as an object of wonder. The organic connection with the people was severed. Nowhere is this more evident than in the ironic story of the 'museumization' of the Didarganj Yakshi.[14] The Yakshi was the object of intermittent popular worship, and dispensed her aura under a makeshift shrine. Once identified as an object of art and an icon of India's civilizational depth, she was plucked away and planted in Patna Museum, the first station of the cross in a journey that was to end in the National Museum, Delhi. Over the next few decades icons were to be recovered from 'inappropriate' uses and locations and 'rescued' from popular village worship. The past was excised from the present and from the people, who were rendered as the inappropriate guardians of value. Moreover, in the spectacle that was to be India's art heritage, the 'modern' was to be conspicuously absent. This reluctance, even refusal, to incorporate the idea of the people as a historical changing entity towards an idea of the modern was to be the failure in the imagining of a national culture. Modernity came to be visualized against a static body of the people: they were to be witnesses rather than actors in the drama of the post-colonial nation. With a future devoid of people and a past to which they were only to be witnesses, what of the present?

This romanticization of what would remain an abstraction received a classic enunciation in Gandhi's *The India of My Dreams*: 'the moment you talk to (the Indian peasants) and they begin to speak . . . wisdom drops from their lips. . . . Take away the encrustations, remove his chronic poverty and his illiteracy and you have the finest specimen of what a cultured, cultivated free citizen should be.'[15] The cultural expressions of this narodnik miasma reflected the irony that when thinkers start associating popular forms with the 'common people' it reflects also an elite dissociation from a culture in which they had earlier participated.

IV

The search for the authentic in the visualization of national culture was an attempt also to straddle the debate on tradition vs. modernity. In the case of Satyajit Ray representation in the realist genre becomes a way out of the dilemma.[16] A painstaking attention to the lucent, even historical, representation of the grain of traditional, popular life is only one end of Ray's conviction regarding the inexorable autonomy of the individual that modernity brings. In one sense when the American critic Stanley Kauffmann, speaking of Ray, drew the parallel with Joyce's Stephen Dedalus forging in the 'smithy of his soul the uncreated conscience of his race', he was not far wrong. The *Pather Panchali* trilogy was in a significant sense the Portrait of the Artist as a young nation, linking modernization with individual autonomy. The anecdote goes that when Ray ran out of money while shooting *Pather Panchali* he approached Dr B.C. Roy, the then Chief Minister of West Bengal. Some money was allotted out of the road-building programme of the Public Works Department, both because of the English title 'The Song of the Road' as well as its documentary appearance. The twinning of the ideas of modernization and modernity are also evident in the fact that the train sequence in *Pather Panchali* was the first to be shot, though it appears late in the film. Apu and Durga running across the field encounter a train for the first time in one of the most poignant moments in the film. This encounter with the modern is a watershed, followed by a series of deaths, including that of Apu's beloved sister Durga, which inexorably propel his departure from the village towards a sovereign identity. The final shot of *Apur Sansar* (1959) with his son perched on Apu's shoulder looks beyond to an unsentimental modernity. Ray was different, indeed unique, in his commitment to modernity, stemming both from his cosmopolitan Brahmo background as well as his location within an international film aesthetic. Reconstruction of folk tradition, middle-class urban life and intellectual existential angst could be kept separate and distinct: the rural fairy-tale world of *Gupi Gyne Bagha Byne* and the urban alienation of *Pratidwandi* have little in common.

The Hindi film industry was another entity: Salman Rushdie calls it a love song to India's mongrel self. While there were attempts at an authentic neo-realism as in films like *Do Beegha Zamin* and *Dharti Ke Lal* (the latter with its authentic footage incorporating peasant union marches), we must be clear as to the nature of this realism. The call for realism arose from the need to project images of India as she should be rather than as she was (hence the controversy over the starkness of *Pather Panchali*). Ideas of realism came to be conflated both with a social conscience as well as with a desire for modernity which would retain the special, idealistic nature of an Indian essence. The same issues that characterized the debate on development as of heritage, surface here. Material affluence and the very idea of money came to be tainted, as was the idea of excessive accumulation: the irascible hero was always pitted against industrialists, moneylenders and the feudal rich, or the smuggler. Poverty was to be embraced, but in a sentimental formulation: it was the act of becoming poor, not the state of being poor that attracted the filmic imagination. Whether in Raj Kapoor's *Shri 420* (1955) and *Jagte Raho* (1956), or Guru Dutt's *Pyaasa* (1957), poverty came to be detached from the poor and was conflated with the civilizational idea of renunciation (the taking up of a life of poverty as it were). This was a closure of any further debate on the question of the conjoined fates of poverty and modernity.

Even in the overtly 'social film' of the 1950s the people are abstractions.[17] Urban streets, shot as metaphors of India's diversity, teem with newspaper vendors, hawkers, construction workers, pimps and layabouts, but the people are only the backdrop against which the moral vicissitudes of the hero are played out. For instance, a famous precursor to the social films of the fifties, *Neecha Nagar* (1946), directed by Chetan Anand, went on to win the Grand Prix at Cannes. It is the story, allegorical in conception, of a town where the industrialist and the rich occupy Ooncha Nagar while Neecha Nagar holds honest, working folk. The conflict is staged as hindrances in the love between Balraj from Neecha Nagar and the daughter of the industrialist. There is an epidemic caused by leakage of dirty water. Balraj leads the protest, the industrialist dies, the lovers are united, and presumably the hero will now run the industry with a social conscience.[18] The representation of the people is romantic—the happy, singing poor who provide an honest diversion from the protagonists' travails. The rendering of social hierarchies and the possibility of transformation in the form of love requited stemmed from the passive revolution that India had undergone. It was an affective solution rather than a political one that was offered, akin to the Gandhian formula of change of heart, whether of the upper caste or the capitalist.

Recent film criticism has suggested that the Hindi film is best apprehended as melodrama with its stereotypical, morally bipolar characters, and the narration itself being driven through the awareness of a single character.[19] Within the genre of melodrama the class structure remains resolutely feudal: the distinction between the hero and the other characters are as between king and peasants. The film critic Madhava Prasad has argued that within a narodnik rhetoric of 'the people', what ensues is an aristocratic self-legitimation—where the hero/noble is in an organic relationship with his subjects. He becomes their metaphor and subsumes them. In a typically modern manoeuvre, it is an egalitarian feudalism, all are presumably equal, but the hero is nearly always well-born. Love opens up the possibility of crossing over, of opening up a space, but within a peculiarly modern rendering in which the only difference can be one of class. Inter-caste, inter-religious or even taboo love, such as that of desiring widows, is inconceivable. In a modernity premised on a passive revolution and driven by it, the pre-modern lurks beneath the rhetoric of the modern, as that which dare not speak its name.

There are two other issues to be considered here. Films such as Raj Kapoor's *Aawara* (1951), Chetan Anand's *Taxi Driver* (1954) and Guru Dutt's *Aar Paar* (1954) present the street—the space of the people—as the space also of a possibility of the dissolution of the hero's social identity. But within that the hope of social renewal or redemption for the hero alone is never closed off.[20] Becoming one of the people, and one among them, remains a liminal activity. Moreover, the narratives of films remained rooted in the present, and while the narrative may reflect a troubled engagement with the past—either literally a personal secret or trauma, or figurative peasant selves of the modern hero—the future remains outside the space of the narrative. The future is deferred to a non-existent space outside the film. This may not be surprising, indeed is to be expected, within a mainstream cinema concerned with representation rather than utopias.

V

In the final part of this essay, we turn to Kerala and the visualization of a modern, radical culture in the plays of Thoppil Bhasi (1924–1992), who became synonymous with the cultural productions of the KPAC (Kerala People's Arts Club). Bhasi's plays were avowedly about social transformation and reflected an attempt to create a new radical cultural practice founded on the lives of the 'people'. Bhasi's turn to the theatre also reflected his faith in an immediacy which, he felt, could not be translated on to the screen. The KPAC was founded in 1950 in Ernakulam by a group of committed student activists at the Law College. In 1951 they staged a play, *Ente Makananu Sheri* (My Son is Right), that caused only a minor ripple. It was with Bhasi's *Ningal Enne Kammyunistu Aaki* (You Made me a Communist) of 1952 that KPAC became a force to reckon with both regionally as well as nationally, through its association with the IPTA (Indian Peoples Theatre Association) based in Bengal. The decade of the fifties saw six major productions, starting with *Ningal Enne. Sarveykallu* (Survey Stone) 1954; *Visakunna Karinkali* (The Hungry Scab) 1955; *Mudiyanaya Puthran* (The Prodigal Son) 1956; *Muladhanam* (Capital) 1958; and *Puthiya Maanam Puthiya Bhumi* (New Sky, New Earth) 1959 followed in quick succession. Bhasi, who himself had been accused in a conspiracy case and had spent four years between 1948 and 1952 both in jail and in hiding, wove his own experiences into the plays. The plays appeared with dedications to heroes and heroines among the common people who had provided him refuge.

Before we look at the plays themselves, a brief excursus into the history of communist politics in Kerala becomes necessary. In northern Kerala (Malabar), the formation of peasant unions from the 1930s had led to a whole-scale questioning of feudal modes of landholding as much as that of imposed caste behaviour. A live culture of reading rooms, processions and performances of plays, particularly K. Damodaran's *Pattabakki* (*Rent Arrears*, 1938) and *Raktapanam* (*Draught of Blood*, 1939), had led to the crystallization of an incipient, alternative proletarian aesthetic. In southern Kerala, in the princely states of Cochin and Travancore, the struggle had been directed more against the intransigent monarchy than against the colonial state. The communist movement here had to contend primarily with the politics of caste and community associations more than the feudal landholding system, as in Malabar. While the People's War Line of 1942 had put the brakes on radicalism and precipitated the moves towards an agrarian consensus, the post-independence period saw the outbreak of radical activity yet again. Alongside the *tebhaga* agitation in Bengal and the insurrection in Telengana, the Malayali region witnessed the first working-class revolt in India in 1946 at Punnapra Vayalar and militant agrarian radicalism in Malabar. The calling off of the Calcutta thesis of 1948 was brought about as much by state repression as revolutionary fatigue.[21]

The decade of the 1950s was to be different. If the earlier decade had been one of militant popular activity, with the people as agents, the discourse on the people now assumed different overtones. The fifties began with the acceptance by the Communist Party of participation in the electoral process: the move towards 'parliamentary cretinism', as K. Damodaran put it in Marxist argot.[22] Debates had begun and were reaching a head aroundthe issue of the linguistic reorganization of states. On 1 November 1956, the Malayalam-speaking areas of the southwest coast were brought together as the state of Kerala. And, in 1957, the first communist ministry to be elected to power anywhere in the world assumed office in Kerala. These three conjunctures, of parliamentary communism, linguistic statehood and the communist ministry, were also to transform communist cultural expression towards a more conservative practice centred on the state rather than the people.

One of the most important expressions of a growing closure had been E.M.S. Namboodiripad's book of 1948, *Keralam Malayalikalude Mathrubhumi* (Kerala, the Motherland of the Malayalis). This was primarily concerned with the linguistic and cultural region of Keralam and sought to find the unities underlying differences and inequalities. One of EMS's fundamental concerns was to posit an intellectual challenge to the Dravidian position that the brahmins, who were foreign to the Dravida space, had historically wrought inequality in South India. The issue of caste hierarchy had come up within the party in 1944, when the senior Tiyya labour organizer C.H. Kanaran had been removed from the district committee. There had been accusations of casteism and a lot of soul-searching in the party, almost precipitating the resignation of Krishna Pillai, one of the founders of the movement itself. EMS in his text looked forward to linguistic statehood and put forward two simple and telling propositions: first, that caste had been a rational form of economic organization in its day, allowing for the creation of a class responsible for cultural production, i.e. the Nambudiri brahmins; and second, that it was brahmin cultural production, i.e. a high culture, which could form the organic basis of the new state. This moment of manoeuvre was not unique. In Tamil Nadu the Dravidian movement put the lid on the caste question and the challenge from untouchable groups by an exaltation of the glorious Tamil culture and the personification of the Tamil language as mother. Linguistic statehood, I would argue, represented the closure of the caste question and lower-caste radicalism much more than Gandhi's intervention in the 1930s.[23]

When Bhasi put pen to paper these transformations were already in place. One way into looking at the conditions for his writing is to compare his plays with those put up by IPTA in the early 1940s, particularly Bijon Bhattacharya's *Nabanna* (1944), dealing with the Bengal famine. They were largely performed by peasant and working-class squads, much as K. Damodaran's plays of the 1930s had been. It was a localized people's art merging folk traditions with the exigencies of a contemporary politics. The concern was less with the aesthetic form of the play and more with the political present and its transformation. While Bhasi's plays too are concerned with the transformation of the present—the evolution of the protagonists is always towards a political ideal and an association with everyman (within limits which we shall discuss later)—there is an anxiety regarding form. *Ningal Enne Kammyunistu Aaki* appeared with a preface by the theoretician of the CPI, C. Unniraja, remarking on how Bhasi had freed Malayalam drama from the song-and-dance tradition of Tamil theatre. His second play, *Sarveykallu*, carried a glowing introduction by Joseph Mundassery, a powerful literary critic of his time, signifying that Bhasi had enlivened a moribund tradition. Alongside these were brief notes recording Bhasi's own indebtedness to the lives and words of ordinary people made heroic by circumstances. These opening pages reflect the contrary pulls on Bhasi's own aesthetic—were the plays to be well-wrought and conforming to the canon, or were they a form of political practice?

I have argued that the decade of the fifties represented a moment of closure after the opening up and culmination of the national movement in the tryst with destiny. If during the national movement the masses had been held in thrall by the disciplined *satyagrahi*, the post-colonial discourse of development offered the engineer and the scientist as objects of devotion. If earlier they were to be disciplined and mobilized, now they were to be mute witnesses to the drama of development being staged for them. I shall take up three themes within Bhasi's plays to show how even a radical regional cultural practice came to share in the discourse of modernization envisaged by the post-colonial state.

The first theme is Bhasi's construction of the idea of the people, particularly the untouchable Cherumas and Pulayas. In *Ningal Enne Kammyunistu Aaki*, Karamban, the Cheruman, is shown as part of the moral community of the Nair household. He is characteristically obedient and hesitant about involving himself in political activity. The one moment in the play when he shakes off his trepidation is when Gopalan, the upper-caste Nair peasant union organizer and Karamban's patron, is beaten up. Karamban and the other Cherumans impulsively reach for their implements and sticks, and wish to seek revenge for their master. They have to be disciplined and reminded of political norms. Karamban's character—obedient, impulsive and emotional—undergoes little transformation during the play. He remains someone who will witness the political activity of the upper-caste protagonists who lead him into controlled political participation. In *Mudiyanaya Puthran*, Chathan, the Pulayan, is a stereotype—largely ineffectual and impulsive, emotional and given to belief in black magic. His one desire is to get his daughter Chellamma married to a lecherous ex-MLA, Sastri. Chathan constantly reiterates dependence as a matter of honour: that Pulayas work for the master's house rather than a wage. Again, in *Visakunna Karinkali*, Kittu is a tubercular opium addict given to long-winded anecdote and a constant harking back to a dismal past when he lost his wife and child. These are static, ethnographic sketches of an idea of the people—the vestiges of a past in the present, which the central characters have to leave behind. There is no redemption, progress or transformation for them.

At the same time we have to look at another dramatic device. One of the reasons for the phenomenon called the KPAC were the songs written by O.N.V. Kurup and Vayalar Rama Varma. While a number of them were exhortatory political songs speaking of a redemptive future, the majority were based on folk tunes and rhythms, and represented a veritable invention of a tradition of *naadan pattu,* or folk songs. Here again we see a romantic recovery of the folk with female characters like Chellamma the Pulayi and Thankamma the coir factory worker of *Visakunna Karinkali,* who break into song as a matter of habit expressing a range of moods. While upper-caste women like Sumam in *Ningal Enne,* Vasanthi in *Sarveykallu* and Radha in *Mudiyanaya Puthran* sing because they have been trained in music, the lower-class/caste women sing in the spirit of the indomitably happy poor. The plays are suffused by nostalgia for a rural idyll of the happy peasant. The problem here is of carrying the peasant into modernity while retaining the structures of deference as well as a culture structured around the lost routines of work in the fields. There is a sentimental rendition of labour as the site for production of folk culture rather than depicting it as demeaning or back-breaking.

While these are in a sense political plays, they are structured around love fulfilled, thwarted or betrayed. Why is the question of politics rendered as one of affect? Social stasis, decay and inequality are captured and represented in the impossibility of love within a space as yet to become modern. In *Ningal Enne,* the love of Mala, the untouchable Cherumi, for Gopalan, the Nair political organizer, is thwarted by the barriers of caste. In one scene Gopalan contemplates marrying Mala by giving up Sumam, the woman who loves him. At the end of the play we are left with the assumption that he will indeed marry Sumam, though Gopalan has said nothing to revise his altered position. In *Sarveykallu,* Kesavan and Vasanthi's love is destroyed by the incessant feudal litigation over land between their families. In *Visakunna Karinkali,* Thankamma refuses to countenance Sankaran's love for her after he becomes a blackleg to feed his family. His refusal to aspire towards class-consciousness away from an attachment to family marks him as less than modern. And, in *Muladhanam,* the family of Ravi is scattered and his wife commits suicide, presumably, because of the functioning of capital itself. The refrain is that when our *sarkar,* the government of the people, is established there shall be no incomplete families, or indeed, unfulfilled loves. The structuring of the idea of political transformation around the idea of the possibility of love is a distinctly melodramatic mode that brings Bhasi's plays in line with popular cinema. This may indeed explain why former members of the KPAC then found their way into mainstream cinema, draining the KPAC of its talent and force. And where the plays fall in line with the closure effected in popular cinema is evident in the loves that are *not* countenanced. In *Mudiyanaya Puthran*, the protagonist Rajan Nair loves Chellamma the Pulaya woman, but his own martyrdom at the end prevents the consummation of a love that dare not speak its name. Similarly Sankaran the Hindu and Thankamma the Christian in *Visakunna Karinkali,* and Gopalan and Mala in *Ningal Enne.*

The world of the Nairs is what Bhasi is most comfortable with and there are brilliant portrayals of crumbling households, litigious families, shady land deals and a critique of Nair nostalgia. Paramu Pillai, the small landlord of *Ningal Enne* and one of Bhasi's most memorable characters, moves from being mired in the past to holding up the red flag in the last scene. The Nairs as anchors of the plays undergo transformation towards a universal consciousness, while the others remain trapped within their stereotypical renditions. Thus the future remains vague and located in a space outside the text: the metaphor of the red flag has to serve. The plays, in keeping with the national imagination, work with the notion of a hypostatized past, a present in flux witnessed by a passive 'people' and a future indeterminate and unimagined. Whether it is Paramu Pillai finding redemption from his feudal past through holding the red flag, or Sankaran the scab finding expiation in a planting of the red flag, it has become merely a politics of gesture.

Bhasi's plays reflect at the regional level the contradictions within the cultural practice of the 1950s. His plays are remarkable in terms of the trajectory that they chart away from a radical politics of peasant mobilization (albeit controlled) to a participation in the national rhetoric of development to which the people shall be witness. If his first play dealt with the progressive radicalization of a small landlord towards an acceptance of 'communism', the play with which he ended the fifties, *Puthiya Manam, Puthiya Bhumi,* is a paean to the development project, and the peasant organizer has been displaced by the engineer as hero. Ironically, the play itself is dedicated to the first 'martyr' (*raktasakshi*) in the cause of progress: the British engineer Alexander

Minchin, who contracted malaria while building the Pechipara dam. Sukumaran, the engineer protagonist of the play who is in charge of building a dam, constantly refers not only to the litany of numbers characteristic of development (kilowatts of power, acres to be irrigated and so on) but also to his sense of duty towards the nation and its people. Bhasi in this play moves beyond regional concerns to participate in the task of building the nation. The people of the village for whom the dam is being built are represented as unquestioning, obedient, and emotional, and Sukumaran's relation to them is one of patient patronage (or of ineffable condescension!). In a revealing moment Sukumaran tells Ponnamma the village girl: 'My relation to all of you has got entangled in my emotions. My relation to my job too has become emotional. Was the relation of your father to his ox only that of a man towards an animal on which he had spent sixty or seventy rupees?' And this from the most radical playwright of his time in Kerala!

I would like to end with a few lines from Archibald McLeish's 'The Metaphor'. They capture the poignancy of the closure of the national imagination in the first decade of independence, struggling to find a passion now lost and striving towards images yet to be wrought.

> *A world ends when its metaphor has died*
> *An age becomes an age, all else beside*
> *When sensuous poets in their pride invent*
> *Emblems for the souls consent*
> *That speak the meanings men will never know*
> *But man-imagined images can show:*
> *It perishes when those images, though seen*
> *No longer mean.*

I have retained the text of the lecture very much as it was when it was delivered. A number of the themes dealt with here require elaboration of an order I am unable to undertake at present since they form part of a larger project on socialism in India. I thank Alice Thorner for allowing me the opportunity to present the kernel of a project that I am engaged in and for her close, sympathetic and critical reading of the first version. I also thank G. Arunima for her insightful comments.

Notes and References

1 Richard Rorty, *Achieving our Country: Leftist Thought in 20th Century America*, Harvard, 1999.

[2] Sukhamoy Chakravarty, *Development Planning: The Indian Experience*, Oxford, 1987.

[3] Partha Chatterjee, 'Development Planning and the Indian state', in T.J. Byres (ed.), *The State, Development Planning and Liberalization in India*, New Delhi, 1998.

[4] Jawaharlal Nehru, *The Discovery of India*, New York, 1946, p. 567.

[5] M.K. Gandhi, *The India of My Dreams*, Bombay, 1947, p. 96.

[6] M.K. Gandhi, *Towards Non-violent Socialism*, Ahmedabad, 1951.

[7] Rorty, *Achieving our Country*, p. 41.

[8] Geeta Kapur, 'When was Modernism in Indian Art?', *Journal of Arts & Ideas*, Nos 27–28, 1995–96, p.108. See also, 'Place of the Modern in Indian Cultural Practice', *Economic and Political Weekly*, 7 December 1991; and 'Contemporary Cultural Practice: Some Categories', *Social Scientist*, 18 (3), 1990.

[9] Itty Abraham, *Making of the Indian Atomic Bomb: Science, Secrecy and the Post Colonial State*, London, 1998.

[10] See the report by Ranjit Hoskote on the exhibition of Mitter Bedi's photographs, Photography as an Art Form, Piramal Centre, Mumbai, October 2000: 'In black and white', *Hindu Magazine*, 22 October 2000.

[11] Kapur, 'Place of the Modern', p. 2804.

[12] Guha-Thakurta, 'Marking Independence: The Ritual of a National Art Exhibition', *Journal of Arts & Ideas*, Nos 30–31, 1998.

[13] Ibid., pp. 96–97.

[14] Ibid., p. 105.

[15] Gandhi, *The India of My Dreams*, p. 44.

[16] See Geeta Kapur's insightful essay, 'Sovereign Subject: Ray's Apu', in Neera Chandhoke (ed.), *Mapping Histories: Essays presented to Ravinder Kumar*, New Delhi, 2000.

[17] See Ravi Vasudevan, 'Shifting Codes, Dissolving Identities: The Hindi Social Film of the 1950s as Popular Culture', *Journal of Arts & Ideas*, Nos 23–24, 1993; and 'Film Studies, the New Cultural History and the Experience of Modernity', Research in Progress Paper, Second Series, No. CV, Nehru Memorial Museum and Library, 1995.

[18] See the discussion of the film in Sumita Chakravarty, *National Identity in Indian Popular Cinema 1947–1987*, Delhi, 1996.

[19] See Madhava Prasad, *The Ideology of the Hindi Film: A Historical Construction*, Delhi, 1998.

[20] See Vasudevan, 'Shifting Codes, Dissolving Identities'.

[21] See Dilip Menon, *Caste Nationalism and Communism in South India: Malabar, 1900–1950*, Cambridge, 1994.

[22] K. Damodaran, 'The Tragedy of Indian Communism', in Tariq Ali (ed.), *The Stalinist Legacy*, Harmondsworth, 1984.

[23] For a discussion of these issues see Dilip Menon, 'Being a Brahmin the Marxist way: EMS Nambudiripad and the pasts of Kerala', in Daud Ali (ed.), *Invoking the Past: The Uses of History in South Asia*, New Delhi, 1998.

Thorner Memorial Lecturers

BINA AGARWAL Economist, ecologist, feminist, Professor at Institute of Economic Growth, Delhi.

PULAPRE BALAKRISHNAN Professor of Economics at Institute of Management, Kozhikode, Kerala.

NANDITA HAKSAR Lawyer, human rights activist, Goa.

N. KRISHNAJI Economist, statistician, demographer, Achuta Menon Institute, Thiruvananthapuram.

DILIP MENON Reader in History, University of Delhi.

UTSA PATNAIK Professor of Economics, Jawaharlal Nehru University, New Delhi.

JACQUES POUCHEPADASS Historian, Directeur de Recherche, Centre National des Recherches Scientifiques, France.

TIRTHANKAR ROY Economic Historian, Indira Gandhi Institute of Development Research, Mumbai.

ATUL M. SETALVAD Lawyer, Mumbai.

ELIZABETH WHITCOMBE Neurologist, historian, climatologist, London.

Index